Digital, Political, Radical

For my gorgeous Dad, who would never have read it but would have understood why I wrote it.

Digital, Political, Radical

Natalie Fenton

polity

First published in 2016 by Polity Press

Polity Press
65 Bridge Street
Cambridge CB2 1UR, UK

Polity Press
350 Main Street
Malden, MA 02148, USA

ISBN-13: 978-0-7456-5086-9
ISBN-13: 978-0-7456-5087-6 (pb)

A catalogue record for this book is available from the British Library.

Library of Congress Cataloging-in-Publication Data

Names: Fenton, Natalie, author.
Title: Digital, political, radical / Natalie Fenton.
Description: Malden, MA : Polity Press, 2016. | Includes bibliographical references and index.
Identifiers: LCCN 2016005344 (print) | LCCN 2016018009 (ebook) | ISBN 9780745650869 (hardback) | ISBN 9780745650876 (pbk.) | ISBN 9781509511693 (Mobi) | ISBN 9781509511709 (Epub)
Subjects: LCSH: Political participation–Technological innovations. | Communication in politics–Technological innovations. | Democracy. | Radicalism. | Critical theory.
Classification: LCC JA85 .F46 2016 (print) | LCC JA85 (ebook) | DDC 323/.042–dc23
LC record available at https://lccn.loc.gov/2016005344

Typeset in 10.5 on 12 pt Sabon
by Toppan Best-set Premedia Limited
Printed and bound in Great Britain by Clays Ltd, St. Ives PLC

For further information on Polity, visit our website: politybooks.com

Contents

Acknowledgements

This book has been made from good conversation, a lot of politics and the best of friendships. During its gestation I was co-head of the Department of Media and Communications at Goldsmiths, University of London; working in two campaign groups for media reform (Hacked Off and the Media Reform Coalition – work that is ongoing); engaged in long-standing negotiations on behalf of my trade union; and suffered the death of my dear Dad. Fittingly, maybe, it has been a political journey as well as an emotional and an intellectual one. Along the way very many friends have accompanied me and provided sustenance – some talking incessantly (they will know who they are), others making me laugh (thank goodness), feeding me (when I forgot), dancing with me (when I needed to forget), crying with me (when it mattered most). Many have carried my baggage as I have laboured through bureaucratic times and administrative overload and directed me down roads that led to new discoveries and fresh adventures reminding me of my original purpose. I am deeply grateful to each and every one of you – there are too many to mention individually but you know who you are.

Politics always brings passions to the fore, and for those who share this passion it is a constant delight to indulge in their company. I have benefited hugely from sharing these passions and sharpening my arguments with many in seminars, lectures, conferences, cafes, bars and pubs, on beaches, on buses, in swimming pools, rivers and seas; with students on the MA Political Communications, my doctoral students, colleagues, friends, family and a fair few strangers! Some even provided precious feedback on earlier drafts despite the pressures of their own working lives. An extra-special thank you goes to Veronica Barassi, Lisa Blackman, Andrew Calabrese, Jacqui Cheal, James Curran, Mariam Fraser-Motamedi, Deborah Grayson, Dave Hesmondhalgh, Sarah Kember, Ben Levitas, Angela McRobbie, Graham Murdock, Angela Phillips, Joanna Redden, Jorge Saveedra, Justin Schlosberg, Mila Steele, Bev Skeggs, Gavan Titley, Hilary Wainwright and Joanna Zylinska and all of the activists who gave of their time to be interviewed and talk all things political in the course of this research.

The Department of Media and Communications at Goldsmiths is a special place. It is one of the few university departments that exist where transformative politics are actively discussed as a seminal part of what we do. The department has provided the structure, the freedom and the inspiration to get this book written. Amid the ever-increasing pressures constantly to neoliberalize our working practices, it is still a place where ideas can breathe, where creativity is embraced and shared learning is relished. To all of my colleagues I owe an almighty thank you. I cannot imagine a more challenging, more collegiate, or more supportive department or a better place to think, theorize and practise politics. Each and every one of you – from faculty to technicians to office staff – has enabled me in ways many of you will be completely unaware of – such is your generosity, such is my good fortune. A particular and heartfelt mention goes to my two co-heads of department – Nick Couldry and Julian Henriques – whose encouragement and friendship not only helped me finish but also made the institutional politics along the way that much more doable.

The research centres of which I am part and the people I work alongside have provided intellectual breathing spaces in which to linger, explore and interrogate ideas and data. As spaces for critical thought (see chapter 1) they have energized and enthused me – thank you to the many people who have given of their time to contribute to the Centre for Global Media and Democracy (with special thanks to Kate Nash); the Goldsmiths Leverhulme Media Research Centre (with special thanks to James Curran) and the Centre for Feminist Research (with special thanks to Sara Ahmed). Long may they last.

Of course, there are always certain people that you rely upon more heavily than others. Friends whose ability to politically inspire, intellectually challenge, emotionally support and above all, when things get tough, to tell me incredibly bad jokes (in the most inappropriate of places) is truly a gift that I cherish. So to the original goody-two shoes Des Freedman, the poet Gholam Khiabany and Milly-the-seal-Williamson – thank you for oh so very much. Life is simply better when you are around.

Finally, to the wonderful Justin, Isaac and Jude – the source of all my passions, political and otherwise – for enduring all the politics all of the time and understanding why it matters. When all the talk has died down, I am ever more amazed and so very thankful that you simply 'get it'.

1

Introduction: Sowing the Seeds of Dissent

In 2007 global capitalism cracked. A financial crash exposed the abuses of the banks and financial agencies, which had worked economic systems to their advantage until those systems fractured under the weight of debt they had created. A chink of light shone through that crack. This was the moment when the brutal and aggressive form of deregulated financial capitalism, which, vampire-like, had been sucking the blood from the body politic, saw sunrise and was rendered momentarily blind. And for a brief period the optimists among us thought that this economic crisis was a moment for radical change. Nine years on, the increased power of corporations and transnational financial agencies over public priorities continues unabated. The glorious promises of liberal democracy continue to morph into the torturous agonies of neoliberalism, where free markets and human freedom are pretty much interchangeable. Inequality has increased. The poor have become ever poorer. The rich continue to prosper. Ecological disaster looms large on the horizon. As the poor get poorer, so they also have less and less influence over policies and politicians and vote less. And democracy is undone.

But the last decade has also been marked by public manifestations of dissent, with uprisings in the Arab world and North Africa against vicious dictatorships; mass protests in Spain, Greece, Italy and Portugal against an austerity politics that prioritized banks and financial agencies over people and publics; the Occupy Wall Street movement in the US, heralding the rights of the 99 percent, which spread to many parts of the globe; the demonstrations in Istanbul against the urban development plans for a public park; the protests against racist police discrimination in Ferguson (Missouri), to name but a few. Yet, as if believing it were possible to deter vampires merely with the odours of garlic, dissent was met with pepper spray, batons and, in some cases, tanks and gunfire. Still, new parties on the left have begun to emerge with the electoral victory of Syriza in Greece and the rise of Podemos in Spain (see chapter 6). Other emergent publics are tussling with new forms of progressive collectivism that pitch the idea of the demos from a different vantage point, challenging many of the assumptions of liberal democracy. All the while the digital age continues to get under our skin and into our bloodstreams, as being online and ever more connected is ingrained into the rhythms and rituals of our daily lives – at once seducing us with consumer delights, capturing and selling our digital footprints, and enabling and empowering oppositional mobilization to spread far and wide.

A mediated radical politics that often circulates in online networks through social media can be understood only in relation to its non-radical counterparts – mainstream politics as well as legacy media. Mainstream politics has not escaped unscathed. With a few notable exceptions, we have seen a decline in the support of establishment political parties and in voting publics. In many places around the globe, social democratic parties have shifted their policies ever rightwards. In general, in Western democracies, party politics has shifted to a 'consumer' style of representation: this can be seen in terms of political parties, which in order to win elections must engage in persuasion, and impression management – what Louw (2005: 25) refers to as 'image making, myth making and hype' on behalf of elite political actors; in terms of the media, which, hungry for news fodder, routinely access and privilege these elite definitions of reality and are claimed to serve ruling hegemonic interests, legitimize social inequality and thwart participatory democracy; and also in terms of the citizenry, where being political now includes a vast range of social behaviours (not just campaigning, organizing, and argument, but lifestyles, consumer ethics, diet and musical taste).

As participation in parliamentary democratic elections declines (Sloam, 2014), we face a critical disjuncture in a deep and multifaceted crisis of our representative democratic systems, of our political systems – systems long regarded as weakened by the competitive imperatives of economic globalization and the declining counterpower of organized labour in the deliberate diminishment of the trade union movement through anti-union legislation; through the criminalization of protest and the ever-increasing attempts to de-public everything; and through the monetization of ourselves, as our citizenry becomes consumer-channelled and our common humanity is replaced with individualism and me-politics. Media institutions have been implicated in this pattern of erosion as subject and object of economic restructuring that favours elites, both through sustained messages that legitimate the upward transfer and concentration of property and wealth and through the deregulation and privatization of the media, thereby arguably placing media out of reach of democratically organized political will-formation (Calabrese and Fenton, 2015).

In this maelstrom of contradictions, how can we begin to make sense of what radical progressive politics might mean? How does a politics of emancipation form and materialize? How are the progressive political values of politics in common forged, moderated and channelled into concrete practices in the digital age? How do we work towards what E. P. Thompson (2014: 109) described as 'the dignity of actors in the making of their own history' – our history, our dignity – in systems where, as Brown (2015: 18) states, democracy is not only overthrown or stymied by anti-democrats but also 'hollowed out from within'.

This book is an attempt to consider the above questions in the deep context of actually existing politics while also taking into account the pragmatic possibilities of our progressive political futures. So many scholars, who link the forms of communication, the means of organizing protest and demonstration and disseminating our political passions and desires, to claims of a revival of a counter-politics of the twenty-first century, leave the practical problem of doing politics and the dream of democracy untouched. How do we do democracy better? What are the conditions required to live together well? By focusing on the transformative potential of new technology, the concrete goals of liberatory action in all spheres (material, legal, state) are too often left out. Protest is easy to identify; how to bring about political change, less so. Too often we are left asking: What is the politics? Where is the democracy? In other words, by concentrating our gaze on the mediation of politics, we are seduced by the thrills and excitement of revolutionary prowess on offer and neglect, at our progressive peril, both the constraints that must be overcome and the concrete feasible politics that must be developed to take their place. Surely, what matters is how protest turns into the practice of politics that can redress imbalances of power. Yet too frequently we map a range of responses, we track the mobilizations, we may even spot the contradictions, but rarely do we critique the move to political power or even try to imagine what it might look like. So, we are left with political absences and political emptiness.

This book, then, starts from the simple position that we need to understand 'the political' if we are going to critique politics (and the mediation thereof). And, in order to do critique, we need to tackle both power and politics as *concepts* and as *practices* if a progressive politics is to move forward. The rest of this introduction sets out this foundational premise, situating the arguments in the chapters that follow within a framework that is critical, political, radical and contextual. Below, I explain the necessity of each as ballast to my thoughts.

Critical

This book takes its inspiration from the school of critical theory. As director of the Institute for Social Research (the so-called Frankfurt School) Horkheimer (1982: 244) said that a critical theory is distinguishable from traditional theory because it has a specific practical purpose: to seek human emancipation, 'to liberate human beings from the circumstances that enslave them'. Just as there are many circumstances in this regard, so there are many theories, but all share a desire to provide the basis on which we can seek to understand forms of domination and oppression and thereby seek to increase forms of liberation and freedom.

Horkheimer also said that critical theory is adequate only if it meets three criteria: it must be *explanatory*, *practical* and *normative*. Critical analysis must be empirical social inquiry and be framed by normative philosophical argument – such that it can explain what is wrong with current social reality, so it can evaluate society, identify the actors to change it, and provide both clear norms for criticism and achievable practical goals for social and political transformation. In order to do this, critical theory directs its attention to empirical analyses of the contemporary world and of those social and political movements which attempt to transform society in progressive ways (Kellner, 1990). As it is concerned with changing the conditions of suffering, a critical theory takes a materialist approach because it wishes to transform material conditions that produce suffering. Critical theory, then, must combine social theory, empirical research and radical politics in theory and in practice.

Critical theory is also multidisciplinary – it draws from political economy, cultural theory, sociology, philosophy, anthropology and history – and for good reason. Our mediated lives are not disconnected from the economy, from politics, from the social or from the philosophical. So surely it is a rather mundane point that we should seek to study them in all their (in)glorious context. Yet so often this is where we find our scholarship – trapped in disciplinary ghettoes fiercely protective of their boundaries. A critical theory should be able to reach outside of disciplinary borders and connect with the external world, including social movements and political organizations that are trying to transform society in progressive ways. When it comes to radical politics, this means understanding the individual and notions of identity that emerge from social psychology, understanding the organizational in relation to sociology and social movement studies, and the institutional in relation to political economic accounts alongside the cultural and the technological – acknowledging the complexity of the mesh that connects culture and economy, state and citizens, consciousness and society.

Crucially, a critical theory is dialectical. In other words, no one factor is determinate by virtue of being unchanging. Thus, as Horkheimer (1982: 28) states:

> the development of human character...is conditioned both by the economic situation and by the individual powers of the person in question. But both these elements determine each other continuously, so that in the total development neither of them is to be presented as an effective factor without giving the other its role.

Economic determinism is shunned. Rather, the socio-material world is seen in historical context in which objective conditions (material factors) contribute towards the constitution of the subject (the human agent) and the subject, in turn, helps constitute those objective conditions. Insisting on a dialectics insists on the possibility of change. But in taking a materialist stance it also recognizes that 'the fundamental historical role of economic relations is characteristic of the materialist position...Understanding of the present becomes more idealist, the more it avoids the economic causes of material need' (Horkheimer, 1972: 25).

Approaching the debates in this book from a critical theory stance is a deliberate attempt to refocus our critical lenses on a politics of transformation in the field of media and communication studies. Of course, there is a rich and diverse tradition of critical research in the field, stemming from the Frankfurt School to the UK's Birmingham Centre for Cultural Studies, to those situated more within critical political economy. Such approaches have long embraced a historical, material, interdisciplinary critique of the political with a view to social and political transformation. But in a digital age that has left us floundering to describe what on earth it now means to talk about 'the media' and at a loss to explain the most basic of questions – who is saying what to whom and why it matters – where too much of our scholarship is left fumbling around in a fog of description, it seems appropriate to restate a purpose to our practice.

As we marvel at the abundance and multiplicity of platforms and communicative realms online, as we struggle to keep pace with the latest apps and the best technical widgets, as we are enthralled by the interactive capabilities and creative affordances of the latest software, too frequently we get swept along in doing no more than describing their uses and mapping their existence. Mapping and describing undoubtedly have their place. We need to know what we are dealing with. As networks proliferate and become more complex, mapping and describing their presence is necessary but will only ever take us to first base. The problem is that, as mediated spaces expand and multiply in endless reiterations, the mapping and describing take over and threaten to forever blunt our analyses, rendering them bland to the point of pointlessness. As Rod Benson (2014) puts it, with this 'new descriptivism...the moment for explanation so often never seems to arrive.' Being critical means moving beyond description; it means having a point. This book is at pains to be explanatory, normative and pragmatic. I am sure it fails on all three. But it is an attempt to be reconstructive as well as deconstructive.

Political

Being based in critical theory, this book also seeks to understand 'the political'. By being normative and evaluative, it is also, itself, political in its endeavour.

There is an enormous debate on what constitutes 'the political', and various elements of this debate are addressed at different points throughout the book. I have approached 'politics' both as ordinary and as extraordinary. On a daily basis, in our ordinary lives, politics has to do with how we as individuals view our own positions in the world and how we relate to others both far and near. In dealing with our differences, it has to do with the difficulties of living together locally, nationally and on this planet. As such, politics will always involve passion, desire, antagonism, contestation and conflict. Recognizing dissymmetry and agonism (Mouffe, 2005) as crucial to political life is about recognizing that politics is about everyone. Identifying the particular needs of individual and group differences in radical politics acknowledges the political subjectivity of each person. As Foucault says (2004: 39), 'The subject that speaks is a warring – I won't even say a polemical – subject.'

Dissymmetry and disagreement do not preclude collective political subjectivity; rather, they are fundamental to it. There is no whole without acknowledgement of the parts. There is no politics without contention. There is no contention without feelings of injustice, unfairness, sadness, anger and hope. The passion that drives politics I refer to as the *'politics of being'* (see chapter 6). An often visceral response to the symptoms of problems of the prevailing social system – I am cold, my family is hungry, I cannot find work, I am discriminated against – that stirs us to protest (it does not, of course, have to relate to the self; it can be felt on behalf of others, and resistance can take place in private as well as in public realms). The politics of being includes the affective response to oppression that Holloway (2002: 6) calls 'the scream of rage'. The scream is a negative anti-something impulse, but, in its reaction against, it also opens up the possibility of otherness, that things could be different.

This runs contrary to what is considered political by others. Indeed, it would fall under the ambit of what Gramsci calls apoliticism (1991: 147). Gramsci recognizes that 'the scream' is in response to political events and possibly even structural relationships but argues that, until these are actively construed as political interventions aimed at transforming relationships of power, they are not truly political. To be political in Gramsci's view is not merely to hold or express political opinions that are informed by or in reaction to a political situation but to seek to alter the terrain of power. In this book I draw a similar distinction between 'being political' (referred to below as extraordinary politics) and the 'politics of being' (referred to above as ordinary politics) but, rather than refer to the latter as apolitical, I see it as a vital part of understanding how radical politics emerges at any one time.

Politics is extra-ordinary when it is transformative and can radically change the balance of forces. In a Gramscian (1991) sense, this is the political as engagement with power relations and structures. And so it relates directly to the unequal distribution of resources at all levels (within the home, at work, within our communities, the nation-state, the globe) and the consequences of the allocation of these resources. Politics is about the organizational practices that seek to play a part in these processes of distribution and allotment – who gets what, why, how and where. We are *'being political'* when we address these questions and translate them into organizational and institutional practices. It is in this act of translation, the identification of a concrete end point, which generates so much hostility in radical

political movements. How can one singular ending adequately interpret the needs and requirements of so many different subjects? So
politics necessitates negotiation, compromise, reconciliation, bargaining, settlement and, occasionally, even consensus. This then begs
questions such as: What forms of organization are likely to be enduring and to develop a programme for social change that can be translated into everyday practice? Does state power always have to be the
means of social change? Politics is both philosophy and strategy;
structure and tactics; protest and project. In seeking to interpret a
radical progressive politics (see below), I have, then, considered the
individual as political subject, the organizational as political endeavour and the institutional as political translation.

How 'the political' gains meaning is deeply embedded in social
context. In developed democracies, the horizons of 'the political' are
ever widening, not merely in terms of global range but also in conceptual scope, to include a vast range of social behaviours. Being political
now refers not just to the traditional activities of voting, campaigning,
organizing and argument but also to lifestyles – Are we ecological or
not? – to consumer ethics – Do you buy fair trade or not? – to diet –
Do you care about how your food is farmed or not? – and to musical
taste – Do you prefer to buy mass-produced formulaic pop supporting
the likes of *The X Factor*[1] or not? The ways in which we communicate
this to one another are changing dramatically in a digital world. For
many, both inside and outside the formal organizations of national
politics, how to express politics or a sense of political ethos actually
has extraordinarily little to do with the government, political parties
or other constitutions of the state. The UK is now looking at one of
the lowest party membership rates in Europe: fifty years ago, one in
eleven people joined parties; now it is only one in eighty-eight. In
2005, only 1.3 per cent of the electorate was a member of one of the
main political parties (the Labour Party, the Conservative Party and
the Liberal Democratic Party), having fallen from nearly 4 per cent in
1983 (Marshall, 2009). In 2015, less than 1 per cent of the British
population belonged to one of the three main political parties (Keen,
2015), and more people were members of the charity the Royal
Society for the Protection of Birds (RSPB), which has over 1 million
members, than all the political parties put together. However, according to the British Social Attitudes Survey, interest in politics and individual political activity has risen since the 1980s (Park et al., 2013).
And it is interesting to note that, although membership of trade unions
is now lower than at any other time in UK post-war history, it remains
substantially larger than that of political parties, with 6.449 million
members recorded in 2013 (TUC, 2015).

During the global financial crisis, the decline in establishment parties has generally been accompanied by a shift to the right of social democratic parties and a rise in popularity of far-right xenophobic and neo-fascist political organizations, such as the English Defence League in the UK, the Golden Dawn in Greece, the People's Party – Our Slovakia, the Swedish Resistance Movement, the Nationalist Party of Bulgaria, Jobbik in Hungary, the Danish People's Party, Austria's Freedom Party, Belgium's Flemish Interest, the American Freedom Party and the Front National in France. In 2014, nine neo-Nazi parties sat in the European Parliament. The eurozone crisis also led to a succession of unelected technocratic governments in Bulgaria, Italy and Greece, as mainstream parties admitted failure to carry out the core business of government. Acting as caretaker governments, these administrations were variously criticized as handing power to the bureaucrats and usurping democracy (Skelton, 2011). But we have also witnessed the rise of new left parties such Podemos in Spain, Syriza in Greece and the Green Party in the UK, as well as the election of the leftist candidate Jeremy Corbyn as the new leader of the UK's Labour Party. All of these political shifts and turns are fragile and may well struggle to survive and thrive, but within these emergent left parties there is an increasing attempt to respond to the wave of protest and demonstration in the face of austerity. Being political is deeply connected to these shifts and turns and the particular histories on which they are based.

Radical

While I am fully aware that the term 'radical' has been applied to a range of right-wing conservative politics (such as that espoused by Margaret Thatcher), that is not what I am concerned with throughout this book (as relevant as it is). When I use the term 'radical politics', I am referring to the radical progressive politics mostly construed as 'of the left'. I use 'radical' to refer to democratic gains over global capitalism, which has been part of the historic ambition of the left. I am also using 'radical' in relation to the Latin origins of the term in 'roots'. A radical politics is of the 'grassroots'; it emerges from below and nourishes what happens above. It is a politics that is of the people – the roots of a politics feed from the earth around them. The depth of the roots signals the strength of the plant – this is not superficial politics or a politics of posturing. Roots also nurture and sustain an ecosystem – this is a politics that is more than momentary; it establishes a way of being and is a support system for all forms of life. Roots can spread far and wide. A radical politics is far-reaching and seeks to look beyond the parameters of a dominant rationality. For example, if neoliberalism is a clustering of economic policies that cohere around the principle of asserting free markets (Brown, 2015), such as deregulation of industries, the reduction of the welfare state, privatization and the outsourcing of public goods, regressive tax schemes that are anti-wealth redistribution, the commodification of all human needs and desires into profitable enterprise, along with the financialization of everything, with financial agencies providing the dominant rationales for economic, cultural, social, political and eco-logical national systems and structures, then a radical progressive politics would be expected not only to object to these approaches but also to suggest long-term alternatives to them. In doing so, it need not be revolutionary in order to be radical. Where authoritarian and repressive regimes are concerned, overthrowing the system and start-ing again is often the only possible radical response. But, in other contexts, it is perfectly possible to have a politics of radical reform according to the circumstances and histories involved as long as the reform undertaken alters substantively the system in question. This may well mean a break from tradition, a creative approach that aims for far-reaching change. So the feminist movement that brought about voting for women and a raft of equalities legislation (among many other things) had a radical impact, as did the introduction of welfare systems and universal health care – both essentially reformist but nonetheless radical.

To counter what Brown (2015: 1) calls 'neoliberalism's stealth revolution' requires a radical politics that can also root out the core problems of the current system in order to suggest long-term progres-sive alternatives. In this book I offer evidence to support the argument that, in order to work towards far-reaching change, a radical politics must address imbalances of power and social, economic and cultural inequalities (all of which are linked). As much contemporary radical political activism is located around single issues, then a radical politics also requires the coming together of these disparate but connected concerns in order to address wholesale the politics of inequality in neoliberal political and economic configurations. This will in turn require the positive relinquishing of a politics based on debt and limitless credit in the relentless pursuit of economic growth and capital enhancement. To do so will entail reworking a politics that is not at the beck and call of global capital and financial agencies. Since this runs so staunchly counter to the neoliberal rationality of our times, it will further require a radical politics that is risk-taking. We have seen the beginnings of such a radical politics of coalescence with the emergence of Podemos in Spain and Syriza in Greece. But they represent only the beginnings and have often struggled to keep the fragile raft of an anti-austerity politics afloat in the face of the juggernaut of financial capital and the hostility of all those who crew its decks.

It should be clear from the above that the approach to radical politics I am taking in this book is concerned with political efficacy. Informed by critical theory, as outlined in the preceding section, I adopt a position of political pragmatism. How can a radical politics effect progressive change? And what are the conditions required, including the communicative conditions, to bring about radical progressive change? It is a mark of the perversity of academia that so many books can be written on social movements and new technology, online activism and Twitter revolutions, all of which deal ostensibly with radical left politics, yet so very few ever deign to broach what is at stake in the actual politics on offer. Without putting this question at the heart of our research and scholarship, we end up not dealing with politics at all and are too frequently seduced into technological theses.

A political pragmatism must also grapple with the issue of power. While I recognize that micro-power can be claimed from the individual to the organizational in minor victories in both the public and private realms, a politics that transcends neoliberalism must also tackle power at the macro-level of the state and the economy. This raises the long-standing concern regarding the corruption of power and how, once power is claimed, 'power over' is abused to the detriment of the 'power to' effect progressive change. Littler and Gilbert discuss the issue of power in relation to the rejection of overarching strategic aims connected to a radical politics and suggestive of grand narratives and political closure and argue in favour of a tactical politics that embraces difference and dissonance:

> A particular tendency in 'radical' thought...tends to assume that true radicalism can operate on a purely 'tactical' level, and that 'strategy' must always be the property of authoritarian organizations and projects.... Such a position inevitably ends up endorsing a range of 'tactical' manoeuvres which give expression to a 'radical' identity but have no apparent impact on power relationships at any level: examples of such ineffectual gestures include 'subvertisements', short-term squatting, conceptual art shows, or spectacular political 'actions' involving large numbers of arrests and no change whatsoever to the policies being protested. (Littler and Gilbert, 2009: 128)

To be radical, they argue, necessitates impacting on power relationships. Proposing alternatives to dominant relations of power is 'visionary' to a certain extent (it is not only pragmatic) but it is not determinate. In accord with the notion that a radical progressive politics is a politics of coalescence of a variety of causes and campaigns, a radical politics is *not* more than the sum of its parts; it is its parts. As these parts are ever shifting and fluid, so a radical politics is open and unending, as it takes account of diverse and plural sources of knowledge and resistance. Risk-taking demands that it is so. A constant dynamic process of inclusiveness, engagement, debate and struggle to realize alternatives is what politics *is*. When this is no longer, then radical politics stops. In this manner, democracy can never be finished.

Contextual

There is no politics without context, since it is the context in which a politics comes into being and against which a counter-politics struggles. I cannot hope to cover all the critical contextual aspects of radical politics, but two areas require particular consideration: economics and the role of the state. I should say from the outset that, while I have separated economics and the state conceptually to draw attention to their particular dimensions in the complex dynamics of neoliberalism, I do not see the state and market as operating in distinction. One of the successes of neoliberalism is that it has managed to sell itself as a straightforward economic endeavour, a simple response to market needs. This has concealed the politics within, denying the manifold ways in which political decisions push certain economic agendas over others. With this in mind, but recognizing that it is impossible to do justice to the importance of either, the following section is indicative of the broader argument that forms the basis of this book.

Economics – The Injuries of Neoliberalism

As neoliberal democracy has failed, so economic inequalities have increased. As inequality has increased, so social mobility has fallen. Thomas Piketty's (2014) analysis lays bare the extent to which neoliberalism has steered a resolute path to wealth concentration, inequality and impoverishment unrivalled since the late nineteenth century. The gap between the rich and the poor is currently larger than it has been in the majority of OECD countries in the last thirty years (OECD, 2014). In 2012, the richest 1 per cent in the world saw their share of global assets increase to 46 per cent, while the bottom half of the world's population own barely less than 1 per cent. In 2014, Oxfam reported that the five richest families in the UK were wealthier than the bottom 20 per cent of the entire population. Just five households had more money than 12.6 million people – almost the same as the number of people living below the poverty line in the UK. In the same year, Credit Suisse (2014) produced a *Global Wealth Report*, in which they noted that, in 2013, the richest 70 million people held 41 per cent of the wealth of the planet; by 2014 this had increased such that the richest 70 million held 48 per cent of global wealth. If a 7 per cent increase in the wealth of the richest in a single year were to continue, within five years the richest 1 per cent of the planet would have everything and the poor would have nothing. We are faced with astounding and increasing inequality; we are almost becoming used to hearing about it. All around us we have analyses of how inequality damages our societies, our economies and our democratic systems (Piketty, 2014; Dorling, 2014; Oxfam, 2015; Wilkinson and Pickett, 2009). Research shows (Bartels, 2008) how the poor have no influence over policies and politicians and vote less (McChesney, 2012). Voter participation increases with income simply because the wealthier are more likely to be listened to. Inequality is not a condition conducive to a sustainable democratic politics. Inequality makes certain political subjects less visible. Inequality bleeds democracy dry.

It is not only the poorest in society who are feeling the consequences of rampant inequality. The middle classes must also deal with precarious employment, shrinking pension schemes and less pay, often as a result of the diminishment of the trade union movement. Because inequality damages our democratic systems (the rest of this book outlines how), it should come as no surprise that more inequality reaps more protest, and yet the less things change for the better.

Our representative democratic systems also rely on the adequacy of processes, institutions and organizations of knowledge production and meaning-making of which media and communications are vital parts. The use of information and communication technologies is also marked by inequalities (Fenton, 2008b). Rich nations enjoy far more internet usage in general than poorer nations. In Afghanistan, only 6 per cent of the population use the internet; in Iraq it is 9 per cent, in Pakistan this figure rises to 15 per cent, in China to 47 per cent, and in Egypt to 53 per cent. Compare this to the wealthier nations, and we find 95 per cent of the population using the internet in Norway and Sweden, 94 per cent in Australia, 90 per cent in the UK and 88 per cent in North America (Internet World Stats, 2015a) – and the economic disparities are abundantly clear.

Capitalizing on communications falls not only to rich countries but to rich individuals, who enjoy far greater access to technology. In the UK, almost all of the wealthiest people use the internet, while this falls to 58 per cent among the lowest income group (those earning less than £12,500) (Dutton et al., 2013). The picture is similar in the US, with 93 per cent of those in the income bracket of $100,000 plus using the internet compared with only 48 per cent of those earning less than $25,000 (File and Ryan, 2014). Just as patterns of economic inequality are replicated in access to health care and educational attainment (Wilkinson and Pickett, 2009), so they map onto access to technology (Pew Research Center, 2015). There is a 'digital divide' between the haves and the have-nots: internet users are younger, more highly educated and richer than non-users, are more likely to be men than women, and are more likely to live in cities.

These concerns do not just refer to access to the internet and the huge gaps prevalent between the global North and South; they also refer to online activity (and hence to political activity online) within developed nations and to traditional divides between those who dominate public discourse and those who are on the peripheries or excluded altogether (Hindman, 2008). When we are assessing the impact of communication technology on radical politics and protest movements, these numbers are critical. Cammaerts (2008) notes that leading bloggers around the world most often come from elite backgrounds. In a survey on digital activism by Brodock et al. (2009), digital activists, particularly in developing countries, were much more likely than the population at large to pay a monthly subscription fee to have access to the internet at home, to be able to afford a high-speed connection, and to work in a white-collar job where the internet is also available. In short, digital activists are likely to be prosperous. The authors also found that intensity of use, rather than simple access, is critical to whether or not a person is a digital activist. High use is only possible for people with the ability to pay for it. From a very basic political starting point, it is clear that the ability to form groups is crucial to the ability to mobilize: social power depends upon a coalition of interests. Some groups (particularly those lacking in resources) are vulnerable to the difficulties of undertaking collective action and are less likely to form. While the latest smart phones have enabled many (particularly the young) to engage in political dissent and action, these phones are more expensive than most and not available to all. Also, particularly for the young, knowing how to harness the power of the internet for political action requires not just technological know-how but political proficiency. Where one is present, the other may be absent. If political mobilization is dominated by social media tools, it will likely be restricted to a certain stratum of society that will in turn influence the nature of the politics that develops. The conclusion is simple. The internet may be democratizing but, more often than not, its effects are felt most strongly in the global middle class.

With only 42 per cent of the world's population using the internet (Internet World Stats, 2015a) and this usage being concentrated in the richest nations among the richest people, the political consequences are more likely to be quite the opposite of progressive. As the wealthier and more developed nations have been able to use modern communications technology to conduct business and represent their economic interests and cultural values worldwide, so we are faced with a global hegemony of corporate ideology, speech and activity that accords with the pre-eminence of the transnational corporation and global corporate capital. Curran (2016) also points out that the dominance of the English language online, as a result of Britain's imperial legacy and the international soft power of the US, excludes great swathes of the world's population. Those who can communicate in English have access to a vast network, while those speaking Arabic communicate with only 5 per cent of users (Internet World Stats, 2015b). The English-speaking world has more wealth and more power, and this is reproduced online.

Ortiz and Cummins (2013) examined the impact of the financial crisis from 2007 through to the forecasts for 2013–15. Using data from the International Monetary Fund (IMF) on 181 countries, they found that a quarter of the countries are experiencing excessive contraction (defined as a cut in government expenditure as a percentage of GDP). This fiscal contraction is most severe in developing nations that are experiencing acute austerity. Sixty-eight developing countries were projected to cut public spending by 3.7 per cent of GDP on average between 2013 and 2015, compared with 2.2 per cent in twenty-six high-income countries. Sassen (2014: 25) points out that one of the main processes feeding inequality is the 'ascendance and transformation of finance, particularly through securitization, globalization and the development of new telecommunications and computer-networking technologies'. Technologies make possible the hypermobility of capital on a global scale. Market deregulation then enables the maximum performance of this hypermobility as financial inventions, such as securitization (which liquefies illiquid capital and allows it to circulate faster), generate additional profits (or indeed losses).

To understand contemporary manifestations of radical politics and digital media, we must appreciate how such structuring forces impinge on both the practice and the realization of radical political imaginaries. If progress is associated with growth and growth is attributed to the unstoppable dynamic of global economic competition, then we must consider what is required to counter this narrative. If our systems of knowledge production, which include systems of media and communications, perpetuate a neoliberal logic in various ways, then we need to understand what is required to change them. Understanding radical politics in the context of the broader social order is part of what defines a critical approach. In contemporary neoliberal times, this means understanding how this social order imposes certain constraints on political change taking place.

Economic Dislocation

The main space for political struggles to win practical political ground remains at the national level. But currently, in many places around the world, when it comes to the economy, the sovereignty of the state has been transferred from national institutions to supranational authorities such as the European Central Bank, the IMF and the World Trade Organization (WTO). This was made painfully clear in the aftermath of the global financial crisis in 2008, when these organizations instructed national governments how to order their economies so that banks and financial agencies could recoup the finance they had lent to governments, in order to resolve the problems the banks had brought about in the first place by recklessly encouraging economic growth through individual debt (i.e., advancing credit to people who could not afford to pay the money back). We saw financial capital flex its muscles again in 2015, when Greece was unable to repay its loans following the bailout packages it had received on the back of the financial crash, despite severe austerity policies that had seen public-sector wages plummet. The Greek government, run by the populist left-wing Syriza party, was then told by the unelected and unaccountable financial creditors of the eurozone what its next budget (and, indeed, the shape of its government) should look like[2] (see chapters 3 and 6), in complete disregard of the wishes of the Greek populace and without any pretence of democracy.

Meanwhile, the likes of the WTO seek to maximize the free flow of international trade, uninhibited by 'interference' from national policies that seek to protect the public and national interest and to the advantage of mega global corporations, which threaten to remove their business from national shores if individual countries do not comply with their demands. In a corporate neoliberal pact, democratic institutions become economic ones captured by the requirements of transnational traders and at once remove any sense of politics, and therefore of the public, from some of the most crucial decisions that govern our lives (see chapter 6).

As supranational organizations such as the IMF and the WTO are not accountable to the public, it is hardly surprising that successive and global protests against the WTO have met with a deafening silence. This political disjuncture, the way in which the global flow of capital has been *dis*located from a politics of the state, puts acute constraints on the possibilities of being political to effect radical and progressive social change. If the ability to effect political change to systems of governance remains state-bound, yet states have lost the power to do much about it because they no longer have control over their economic means, then the revolutionary potential of the internet starts to look somewhat limited.

The State and The Market

The state, having forfeited control over the broader economic dynamics that operate outside and above its territory, is forced into a relationship of intimacy with corporate and finance capital on account of the destabilizing effects of the dramatic fluctuations of financial markets. Sassen (2014) points out that the 2000s saw a relentless rise in corporate profits and a reduction in corporate taxes. This in turn has led to widespread growth of central government debt as a percentage of GDP across a range of state systems: Germany's central government debt rose from 13 per cent of GDP in 1980 to 44 per cent in 2010; the US government debt went from 25.7 per cent to 61 per cent in the same period, and China's rose from 1 percent in 1984 to 33.5 per cent in 2010. Government deficits have been exacerbated by an increase in tax evasion as well as the bypassing of tax residence payments by global corporations (such as Google, Apple, IBM and Twitter). In 2012, Google's chairman, Eric Schmidt, was quoted as saying he was 'proud' of the way his company avoids paying taxes: 'It's called capitalism. We are proudly capitalistic...I am very proud of the structure that we set up. We did it based on the incentives that the governments offered us to operate' (*Huffington Post*, 13 December 2012). Politics and market combine under the economic logic that taxation of global corporations is anti-competition for nation-states – an increase in corporate taxation simply means global corporations take their business elsewhere.

As central government debt rises, so there are fewer and fewer resources to distribute to counter the effects of unemployment, lower wages and increased inequality. Having lost economic power, the state has increased its powers in other ways largely through its disciplinary and policing roles. This analysis offers no solace – the state, having lost control, is left to attempt to sort out the problems this leaves behind. Wacquant contends that, as it has privatized its social welfare provisions (in the interests of corporate capital), so the state has also strengthened its 'penal fist' (2009: 289) as it seeks to contain those who can't work and discipline those who can, thereby weakening the capacity of subordinate groups for political action. These policies exist alongside an enormous increase in others designed to pre-empt dissent, including surveillance, anti-union legislation, criminalization of protest and incarceration. For example, in Spain, where the Indignados movement has been actively campaigning against austerity since 2011, a new law dubbed the 'gag law' has been brought in to make public protest in front of Parliament and other government buildings illegal and punishable by a fine of €30,000. People who join in spontaneous protests near utilities, transportation hubs, nuclear power plants or similar facilities would risk a jaw-dropping fine of €600,000. The 'unauthorized use' of images of law-enforcement authorities or police (often taken on mobile phones by protesters as a means of protection) would also draw a €30,000 fine, making it hard to document abuses.

This presents a double whammy for radical political organizations and movements – influencing those supranational financial agencies and corporations that now control our economies in ways that are often hidden from view and are fiercely undemocratic is incredibly hard. At the same time, the increasing criminalization of dissent makes it ever more difficult to launch protests and carry out demonstrations within the law at a national level. And just as digital media are used for liberatory ends, so they are also used to suppress dissent through state censorship, internet filtering and surveillance, as noted in chapter 2 (Calingaert, 2012; Diamond, 2012). Deibert and Rohozinski (2012) reveal how both authoritarian and democratic governments engage wilfully in a range of activities, among them restricting and intimidating certain forms of online content, putting pressure on internet service providers to monitor and remove certain types of content and organizations deemed troublesome, and employing 'just-in-time' blocking through distributed denial-of-service (DDoS) attacks with the purpose of freezing oppositional organizations at vital political moments, as well as targeted and blanket surveillance. During the uprising in Tunisia, a number of Facebook users inside the country discovered that their accounts were being phished by the government. Elkin (2011) notes how the Tunisian Internet Agency was modifying web pages by injecting them with JavaScript to steal usernames and passwords on sites such as Google, Yahoo and Facebook. People logging onto the sites unknowingly had their sensitive log-in information stolen. The government then quickly moved to delete Facebook accounts and groups. Social media companies are far from innocent bystanders when it comes to censoring and restricting forms of dissent (Hintz, 2015) through the sharing of citizen data with state authorities and intelligence agencies. Corporate platform owners also hold the power to switch off users from the networks or to switch off entire networks. This may be rare, but it can be used to good effect. Such practices are well known in authoritarian regimes, where the disabling of instant-messaging services during periods of unrest and tracking, arresting and torturing protesters active online are commonplace (Morozov, 2011; Mackinnon, 2012; Deibert, 2012). But Elmer (2015) shows how predictive policing is also prevalent in Canada, where social media data is relied upon to plan how to limit the size, length and impact of protests. Canada is not unusual in this regard.

These types of constraints illustrate the broader context in which a radical politics, albeit facilitated by global online networks of resistance, must play out. A radical politics adequate to counter the material inequalities and structural grievances of global financial capitalism requires access to and redistribution of wealth. It necessitates the protection of democracy from the footloose logic of the market or, at the very least, democratically harnessing the dynamics of the international capitalist market to the needs and interests of the majority of citizens in any given political community. Until we address these issues and concerns in our analyses and evaluations of radical politics and digital media, our understanding of a politics of transformation in the digital age will be severely lacking.

Chapter Outlines

Claims for the extension and reinvention of activism through digital media need to be considered in the context of the material social and political world of inequality, injustice, corporate dominance and the financialization of everything. This means taking account of neoliberal formations of the subject, the state, the social and the economic. If it is true that a global civil society is developing on the web, it is one that is segmented by interest and structured by inequality. The

pre-eminent users of global communication networks remain corporations and governments attempting to strengthen the dominant
economic order. The online world is firmly anchored in the offline
world in terms of the social constraints to which all participants are
subject. Issues of cultural and economic capital are ever prevalent.
So, while growing socio-economic divides, continued pressure on
global resources and the financial crash have all contributed to people's questioning of global capitalism, and the wisdom and sustainability of neoliberalism has found voice online and on the streets, this
is occurring amid a culture of the neoliberal state wedded to further
marketization and deregulation of media that also impacts on the
formation of political identities. Both contribute to the felt experience
and contradictions of being political in contemporary neoliberalism.
Through a critical, holistic approach that reflects upon structure and
agency, political economy and cultural theory, the rest of this book
will attempt to interrogate the complexity of the relations among the
state, the individual, collective shared purposes and the role of the
media therein.

Chapter 2 begins by discussing some of the key technological
characteristics that have been claimed to mark out the internet as
particularly suited to contemporary transnational political activism.
Assessing a range of literature, the chapter organizes approaches to
online activism and radical politics into three dual and interconnected
themes – speed and space; connectivity and participation; diversity
and horizontality – that, it is argued, correspond to an integral affinity between the global, interactive technology of the internet and the
development of the more internationalist, decentred and participatory form of radical politics seen in the likes of the Occupy movement, which is said to lead to a new *means of* and a new *meaning
of* being political. A critical appraisal of these themes requires an
approach that can take account of structural questions of power,
oppression, inclusion and exclusion while also appreciating and
accounting for aesthetics and performance and the affective dimensions of radical politics. Such a holistic and critically contextual
perspective is rare, often leading to a misunderstanding of the nature
and impact of the internet on the political contours of contemporary
life and, consequently, of the nature of the political and the complexity of power therein.

Any debates that draw on ideas relating to political engagement,
citizenship and the media inevitably fall back on criteria proffered by
Habermas in relation to the role of the media in a fully functioning
public sphere. In recent years, with the explosion of space online and
the interactive possibilities that the internet opens up, these debates

have seen a resurgence. But the use of all conceptual frameworks must deal with the difference in time, space and politics from their origin to their contemporary application. It is all too easy to claim increased pluralism with the abundance of information online and communicative freedom with the usability of social media in the digital age and then to move somewhat seamlessly to claim that this leads to political gain through enhanced participation. Chapter 3 discusses the difficulties with this approach and how a certain Habermasian perspective that is dependent on the notion of liberal democracy may be inappropriate for the various forms of radical politics of the contemporary digital age.

From the critical theory of Habermas situated in the political economic tradition, I cross over to the cultural ramifications of politics through a consideration of the subjective experience of radical politics and its theorization in terms of political passion and the desire for democracy (chapters 4 and 5). A consideration of the subject in politics forces the theorist to address the political. If new political subjects are emerging in the digital age, what defines their politics? If there is a new politics emerging in new media, it is a politics of non-representation, a politics of affect and antagonism. It includes a multiplicity of experiences that are contradictory and contingent. It is this embrace of difference and a refusal to accept that one view can encompass all – a rejection of the basis of representative politics – that distinguishes much of the likes of Occupy's activity. Politics is passionate. There is no politics without feelings of injustice, anger, unfairness and hope. It is what I refer to as 'the politics of being' (chapter 6). Theoretical frameworks that refuse to account for the passion in politics simply cannot understand what radical politics is. But just as the political subject expresses their activism affectively, so we are also subjected to the mechanics of neoliberalism. Chapter 4 argues that the macro-pessimism of much political economy can and should be combined with the micro-optimism of much cultural theory. Both are vital to understand new media and radical politics, yet frequently one dominates and blocks out the other, and often this is why we find ourselves stuck with binary oppositions of the good, bad or downright ugly consequences of new technology.

Chapter 5 moves on to discuss what it means to enact our political passions with others. It deals with the notion of the organization of politics and debates that surround the notions of the multitude and the parallel notion of individual creative autonomy. This chapter begins to broach the notion of a feasible politics, the possibilities of achieving a new hegemony and of transforming the existing political order. It asks what forms of organization are likely to be enduring and to develop a programme for social change that can be translated into everyday practice. What are the conditions required (including the communicative conditions) for political organizations to endure and build capacity? Has the understandable desire for leaderless (dis) organization fetishized multiplicity and difference to the point of political hindrance? How can we 'be radically political'?

Through a discussion of 'being political and the politics of being', chapter 6 then attempts to bring together a politics that springs forth and is sustained by passion with the daily grind of being political and organizing for change. These two polarized debates, which suffer from the centrifugal tendencies of approaches that deal with either structure or agency, are viewed through the lens of a radical mediated politics that argues for a broader and deeper understanding of what 'the political' means and the context required for an adequate assessment of the terms of its mediation. The chapter ends with a bold argument for the need to repoliticize the economy and resocialize the political in order for a radical politics to take hold. This argument is developed further in the conclusion, where the consequences for media studies more generally are explored.

Thus, through a review and critical appraisal of key empirical research and theory from politics and sociology, as well as media and cultural studies, the book builds an argument concerning the problems with conceptualizing radical politics in the digital age and the ways in which we talk about its mediation and practice that may ultimately act to restrain both our theoretical ruminations and our political imaginations. The chapters work iteratively, developing an argument as they go along and attempting to weave together debates on structure and agency, political economy, cultural studies, and social and political theory to strengthen our understanding of contemporary radical politics. The difficulty is how to map these theoretical debates onto such complexity and contradiction in a contemporary mediated world. This is where this book takes its leave. I hope it will contribute to political debate on contemporary (re)configurations of radical progressive politics through a consideration of how we experience politics in the digital age and how this may influence our being political.

Conclusion: Left Out? Bringing Radical Politics in from The Cold

Della Porta, writing about the relationship between social movements and the media, makes the important point that both media studies and social movement theory 'consider both political institutions and mass media as given structures' (2013: 28) when, in reality, they have been moulded by powerful interests to appear as 'desirable' and 'immutable'. In doing so, she rightly identified a major problem with much research and analysis concerned with digital media and activism, protest, and mobilization – it cannot address adequately issues of social change when issues of social change are often the very point of these activities in the first place. Such studies can only ever hope to be superficial. This problem has arisen partly through the evasion of the political.[3]

I hope, then, that this book will act as a direct challenge to scholars in this area to engage more candidly with the political. How can we begin to tackle the challenges posed to democratic politics if we do not talk about actual politics as part of our research? This problem is both conceptual and practical. A politics requires a practice. We cannot understand the nature of the practice without understanding its politics; we cannot understand the politics without appreciating its processes and organization. Yet so many studies do just this. A fugitive politics will always limit our abilities to take progressive thought and action forward. And, worse, by ignoring the actual politics we end up depoliticizing counter-politics because we offer precious few suggestions as to how we can do democratic politics better (on both a small and a large scale). Without an understanding of how progressive politics can develop, then the politics itself will remain nebulous and ill-defined. What might it mean, then, to put the development of a radical politics at the heart of our analyses? What are the conditions required (including the communicative conditions) for radical political organizations and collectives to endure, build capacity and effect social change in various places at particular moments in time? What are the circumstances in which politics are rendered open to contestation and revision today?

This book hopes to challenge political silences and contest political complacencies in our field to urge a rediscovery of a critical politics of transformation adequate to the materiality of how increasing inequalities in societies lead to vastly impoverished democracies. There is no time like the present.

2

Digital Activism: A New Means of and a New Meaning of Being Political

Introduction: Online and Oppositional

Digital media have undoubtedly changed the way radical politics is communicated across the globe, but it is also claimed, in turn, that they have changed the nature of radical politics itself (Klein, 2000; Salter, 2003; Castells, 2009, 2015). This chapter considers the debates that surround the relationship between the form of media, in particular in relation to the internet, and the nature of political activism.

The forms of mediation, the means of organizing protest and demonstration and communicating one's political passions and desires, are connected to the claims of a revival of radical politics of the twenty-first century (e.g., Roberts, 2014; Hands, 2011; Alexander, 2011; Juris, 2008; Gerbaudo, 2012; Castells, 2015). This is partly to do with the straightforward yet dramatic increase in speed and ease of communication brought about through online mobilization. But claims go beyond a simple premise of enhanced communication linking new technology to shifts in political ontology – a transformation in the very nature and practice of politics. So, there are those that argue that we are entering an era of post-foundational politics (Marchart, 2007) that corresponds to the hybridity, reflexivity, mobility and performativity characteristic of networked society (Dean et al., 2006; Terranova, 2004). From such perspectives, digital media are seen as the perfect means for a more fluid, issue-based and institution-less politics that crosses boundaries of both identity and territory. Such approaches criticize those who view the field of political practices as separate from culture and the economy and argue instead that networked technologies accelerate, intensify and hybridize political, cultural and economic practices to (re)configure and produce new political spaces, fronts and opportunities, producing assemblages of power that coalesce in often unpredictable ways (Terranova, 2004). Others have even gone so far as to claim that the nature of the internet as a technological system offers a semantic and social web composed of networked people and technologies that could bring forth a new economy of contribution (Benkler, 2006) with the potential for a new public and a new commons (Hardt and Negri 2004; Castells, 2009).

This chapter begins by discussing some of the key technological characteristics that have been claimed to mark out the internet as particularly suited to contemporary transnational radical political activism. Assessing a range of literature, it organizes approaches to online activism and radical politics into three dual and interconnected themes:

- *speed and space* – the internet is claimed to facilitate international communication among political activists, non-governmental organizations (NGOs), grassroots organizations and other political groups, allowing protesters to respond rapidly on an international level to local events while requiring minimal resources and bureaucracy;
- *connectivity and participation* – the internet is described as a mediated activity that seeks to raise people's awareness, give a voice to those who do not have one, offer social empowerment through participation, allow disparate people and causes to organize themselves and form alliances on a transnational level and, ultimately, be used as a tool for social change; and
- *diversity and horizontality* – where the internet is also claimed to be more than an organizing tool. It is an organizing model for a new form of political protest that is not only international but decentralized, with diverse interests but common targets, although the targets may be perpetually contested.

These three dual themes point to a heady mix of ingredients that is argued to correspond to an integral affinity between the global, interactive technology of the internet and the development of the more internationalist, decentred and participatory form of radical politics seen in the likes of the Occupy movement, which is said to lead to a new *means of* and a new *meaning of* being political. Radical politics of the moment are also connected indelibly to the political history of any one place or context. Technology is embedded in deep-rooted normative, social, political and economic forces. Thus, the chapter ends by putting radical politics in a radical context and asking not just: What is the relationship between digital media and radical politics?, but also, as the end of chapter 1 signals: What are the circumstances in which politics are rendered open to contestation and revision today?

Increasing the Speed and Expanding the Space of Political Activism

There seems little doubt that spaces for political engagement have expanded in a digital mediascape and that the internet is now central to an understanding of the mediation of political identities and enactments of political belief. Klein (2000) was one of the first to argue that the internet facilitates international communication among NGOs and allows protesters to respond on an international level to local events while requiring minimal resources and bureaucracy. This occurs through the sharing of experience and tactics on a transnational basis to inform and increase the capacity of local campaigns. According to Klein, the internet is not simply a technical aid to political mobilization. It is much more than that. Klein argues that the internet has enabled a whole new type of politics to emerge based on forms of protest which travel easily across geographic borders – a politics that is organizationally dispersed and embraces a diverse range of interests while also retaining a sense of commonality in the things that are being protested against (see the section on diversity and horizontality below). Since Klein's description, similar claims have been made for the Indignado movement in Spain (Castells, 2015). This was a movement that developed out of the neoliberal politics of austerity enforced in the aftermath of the financial crisis in 2008. It led to an array of protests across the country which were communicated via the internet to the rest of the world. These protests were said to have inspired the Occupy movement, which began on Wall Street in the heart of New York City's financial district to protest against social and economic inequality and then, via the internet, spread to many parts of the globe. The internet was also instilled with the revolutionary prowess that gave rise to the falling dominoes of revolts across the Arab and North African world in 2011 (Mason, 2012) – all linking new media to radical political possibilities in a manner termed by Diamond (2012: xi–xii) as 'liberation technology', which can 'empower individuals, facilitate independent communication and mobilization and strengthen an emergent civil society'.

The use of the internet for such radical oppositional purposes is said to alert people to issues they would not otherwise know about; to give a means of expression to those who previously had no way of making their dissent known; then to enable this diverse array of dissenting voices to come together in a connective form of politics, facilitated by the internet, that will ultimately, it is claimed, lead to social change. It is the ability to form networks and build alliances at the click of a mouse that is felt to be conducive to the building of radical political movements which can spread across national borders and merge a variety of topics under broadly common themes, though the themes may be subject to frequent change. Sometimes, such radical politics take the form of new social movements that are themselves often hybrid, contradictory and contingent and include a huge variety of voices and experiences. At other times, the radical politics on display is better described as an alliance of groups, organizations and individuals with a political affinity that coalesces at a particular moment in time.

The internet has another characteristic that is well suited to radical politics – it is a medium that is more readily associated with young people (e.g., Ester and Vinken 2003; Livingstone and Bovill, 2002; Loader 2007); and young people, in particular, are increasingly associated with disengagement from mainstream politics (e.g., Park 2004; Wilkinson and Mulgan 1995; Sloam, 2014) and engagement with the internet (Livingstone et al., 2005; Ofcom, 2010). The extensive literature that discusses young people and politics falls largely into two camps: one that talks of a disaffected youth and the other of citizen displacement (Loader, 2007). In the former, studies speak of the decline of young people voting in conventional national party political elections as indicative of their extensive alienation from society's central institutions and warn of the long-term dangers this may have. In the latter, an engagement with traditional politics based on a sovereign nation-state is displaced: 'Young people are not necessarily any less interested in politics than previous generations, but...traditional political activity no longer appears appropriate to address the concerns associated with contemporary youth cultures' (ibid.: 1).

Rather, civil society, or certain parts of it, comes to the fore as an alternative arena of public engagement (Sloam, 2014). It is argued that politically motivated young people tend to look to non-mainstream political arenas often populated by non-governmental organizations and new social movements – alternative forms of political activism that work at the margins of the dominant public sphere

(Roberts, 2014; Sloam, 2013; Kahn and Kellner, 2004, 2007; Bennett, 2005; Hill and Hughes, 1998), now more easily discovered in an online world. As these spaces open up, so they also allow for an increased diversity of views to find expression. It is further claimed that these forms of political engagement better fit the experience of social fragmentation and individualization felt by citizens (Loader, 2007), as well as being directly compatible with the structure and nature of communications via the internet – a medium with which young people are commonly well acquainted. This also relates to the internet as, first and foremost, an expressive medium that allows the felt experience of politics to be relayed without intermediaries, editing or distortion by media elites (Fenton, 2012b). The space given is largely (and often naively) perceived to be open and free from state or corporate control. This appeals to young people, and particularly to black and minority ethnic young people, who feel excluded and misrepresented by the mainstream news but more in control of their identity and their politics online (Wayne et al., 2010; Ofcom, 2007).

The combined elements of the speed and space of technology with youth and counter-traditional politics – each conducive to the others – mark out the internet as particularly suited to contemporary (transnational) political activism. The expanded space and increased speed communicates protest to a far wider geographic spread of people than has ever been previously possible, opening the potential for greater national and international solidarity to form, for building alliances, for organizing protest and for co-ordinating action over time and in real time. This may add to a heightened political atmosphere at key moments of protest, as events unfold and digital media (including digital phones) enable a broader public to bear witness to the experience through footage and reports relayed instantaneously from those actively involved in protest on the streets. In this manner, contemporary radical politics, often mediated through transnational social movements, are a combination of collective action and individual response.

To some extent this is nothing new. Radical politics have always been at the forefront of mobilizing protest and demonstration. A willingness and desire to participate in such political activism is one of the defining features of 'being radical'. What is unprecedented is that this is now happening on a transnational basis and at high speed, resulting in ever more complex networks of intensely expressive and often highly personalized forms of oppositional activism (Bennett and Segerberg, 2013) that are also public and deliberative, fuelled and sustained through the communicative capacity of social media that can also spread solidarity and hope (Fenton, 2008a).

Surveillance and The Suppression of Dissent

But this is only one small part of the stories that form the age of new media and radical politics. The flip side to speed and space is that those in political office, and other elites holding power through economic dominance, can also capitalize on these dimensions, and with more resources they can do so more forcefully. Just as new media is used for liberatory ends, so they are used to suppress dissent through state censorship, internet filtering and surveillance. A 2011 report by Freedom House, *Freedom on the Net*, documents the increase in extent and diversity of internet restrictions around the world. Calingaert (2012: 159) reports that these include 'bans on social media applications, denial of internet access, intermediary liability for service providers, online surveillance and digital attacks'. Deibert and Rohozinski (2012) note that 'malware' (malicious software that can gain control of an unsuspecting user's computer for the purposes of crime, surveillance or sabotage) is now estimated to exceed legitimate software (Diamond, 2012). They describe a raft of surveillance and censorship activities carried out by both authoritarian and democratic governments designed to manage and control dissent – from capturing gargantuan amounts of personal information of ordinary citizens in programmes of mass digital surveillance to targeted surveillance of particular individuals (on a huge scale), and from restricting certain types of online content to freezing online activity of oppositional organizations at crucial political moments. Mackinnon (2012: 78) describes a situation akin to 'networked authoritarianism' in China, with an estimated 50,000 internet police, where a wide range of repressive tactics are in play, from military-grade cyber-attacks on the Gmail accounts of human-rights activists to device and network controls, domain name controls, localized disconnection and restriction, and the employment of hundreds of thousands of people to work as pro-government online commentators.

For the most part, many of us in 'democratic' states remain blissfully unaware of the dark underbelly of the internet, but in 2013 Edward Snowden revealed a number of mass-surveillance programmes undertaken by the National Security Agency (NSA) – the phone and internet interception specialist of the US – and the Government Communications Headquarters (GCHQ) in the UK. Snowden revealed the extent to which private companies such as Google, Apple, Microsoft and Facebook are co-operating with intelligence agencies (Deibert, 2012) and collecting vast swathes of personal information and metadata in a wholesale spying operation. Such actions are claimed to be justifiable on protective grounds of anti-terrorism and the defeat of cybercrime, but it is easy to see just how such massive powers of unfreedom can be exploited for non-progressive ends that will undermine liberal democratic norms relating to individual rights and constitutionalism. The push towards the securitization of cyberspace appears to be mainly defensive, but Deibert and Rohozinski (2012) also outline the pursuit of offensive capabilities, enabling governments of all persuasions to wage cyber-attacks for political ends, that they say are increasingly commonplace.

In the UK, controversial legislation is in the process of going through Parliament (April 2016) that will expand the legality of data collection under the Data Retention and Investigatory Powers Act of 2014 (DRIPA). Under DRIPA, otherwise known as the 'Snoopers' Charter', almost every digital action would legitimately be able to be logged, intercepted by intelligence agencies and subject to scrutiny. It proposes to make government hacking legal, enabling bulk datasets to be collected and mined and encrypted services to be subject to state restrictions. It has been criticized by human rights organizations as using terrorist attacks as an excuse to override civil liberties.

Communicative Nirvana or Political Naivety?

It would be a mistake to frame the above debate as either repression or liberation. In mediated practices it is highly likely that both exist, and they do so in differential contexts and emerge from varying social and political histories. Castells (2009) developed the debates put forward by the likes of Klein (2000) by linking the acts of protest more directly to the process of social change. Castells (2009: 300) argued that social movements that engage in oppositional politics – 'the process aiming at political change (institutional change) in discontinuity with the logic embedded in political institutions' – now have the chance to enter the public space from multiple sources and bring about change. The question then arises as to precisely how they will do this. It is not enough simply to state that the *potential* of a new communicative nirvana offered by the internet *will* bring about political transformation without considering the ways in which this protest actually translates into political reality. The mobilization of protest is easy to identify, political change, less so.

In Castells's argument, the multiple prospects for intervention and manipulation coming from a myriad of social nodes combine to create a new symbolic counter-force that can shift dominant forms of representation. The counter-political response swells to such a size online that it simply cannot be ignored offline and is, in turn, taken up by the mass media. By using both horizontal communication networks and mainstream media to convey their images and messages, they increase substantively their chances of enacting social and political change – 'even if they start from a subordinate position in institutional power, financial resources, or symbolic legitimacy' (Castells, 2009: 302). Even as Castells moderates his thinking somewhat to take account of 'cultural and institutional specificity' (2015: 309), as well as 'actual practices of the movement and of the political actors' to effect political change, he continues to state 'confidently... that significant political change will result, in due time, from the actions of networked social movements... Minds that are being opened up by the winds of free communication and inspire practices of empowerment enacted by fearless youth' (ibid.: 312).

So the argument goes, technological ease of communication leads to an abundance of information which automatically results in political gain. But such accounts depend on an implicit assumption about the consequential relations between networked communication and political demands and then the institutional translation of those demands into practical, deliverable politics. This leap of faith is hard to reconcile with the enduring realities of poverty and inequality mapped out in the first chapter. Leaving change to chance alone predicated on the means of communication is a risky business that refuses a deep and broad interrogation of the conditions required for people power to overtake corporate and state power and bring about social and political change wherein democracy flourishes, leading instead to an over-emphasis on technology as the solution, to the detriment of the social, political and economic context. If the context – the conditions which provoke a radical political response and under which a progressive politics can emerge and gain credence – dissolves into the background, then we are left with a conception of radical politics without base or substance. Such accounts often manage to avoid the broader framing of a dominant politics and thereby neglect the crucial issue of what is considered to be possible in terms of alternative social and political formations and under what circumstances.

Furthermore, the sheer abundance of space and information available to us has been argued to breed misinformation and lack of understanding (Patterson, 2010) because the daily habits and rituals of news seeking have changed. People are no longer required to sit in front of the television for a set period of time each day or to read the newspaper over breakfast. Instead we do news snacking. But there are so many other more tempting treats on offer that 'healthy' news snacking is rapidly replaced by the more immediately gratifying tasty tit-bits of entertainment. Even more worryingly, Patterson identifies a pattern whereby in a high-choice media environment the less well informed are more inclined to opt for entertainment while the better informed include the news junkies, leading to increasing inequality of knowledge between the more informed and the less informed. Patterson (2010: 20) also argues that speed 'increases sensation but decreases learning', noting that about 60 per cent of those who regularly read a daily newspaper spend at least half an hour doing so compared with only 40 per cent of those who read an online daily newspaper.

So the likes of Castells's argument may focus on the means of radical political communication in the digital age as being liberatory, but it offers little understanding of how general communicative use develops into everyday political culture. As accounts such as those of Castells (2009, 2015) offer little analysis of actual media use and how this may translate into changes in political culture, so they also fail to address the question of *context*. In particular, they manage to avoid the broader framing of a dominant politics and, thereby, what is considered to fall within the domain of what is possible as forms of radical politics and under what circumstances. Whereas the economic dominance of multinational corporations is usefully discussed in depth in Castells's work, there is little critique of how such dominance may sustain the wider myths of social 'order' (Wrong, 1994). Identifying economic dominance, yet at the same time sidestepping the importance of interrogating neoliberal discourse as a powerful and largely successful attempt to reshape the ways in which the political is interpreted and remains powerfully in force in the individualistic values that saturate much life and action online, including the ways in which protest itself has become highly personalized (Bennett and Segerberg, 2013; Papacharissi, 2010b), leaves a theory of social change somewhat bereft.

Diversity and Horizontality

The nature of many contemporary radical political struggles resides in the political embodiment of the diversity of social relations they embrace. The horizontality and diversity of the internet are also claimed to enhance the liberatory potential of the oppositional political movements found online. These forms of radical politics, which circulate via a network of networks, embrace a politics of non-representation, where no one person speaks for another and differences are openly welcomed. They are based on more fluid and informal networks of action than the class and party politics of old. The nature of such struggles resides in the political embodiment of the diversity of social relations they embrace – an explicit contention to resist the perceived dogma of political narratives within traditional leftist politics believed by some activists to be the harbinger of outmoded understandings and values.

In this vein, the forms of radical politics online often profess to be leaderless, non-hierarchical, with open protocols, open communication and self-generating information and identities. Mobilizations facilitated online are said to reflect this fluidity and informality: frequently they display a rainbow alliance of NGOs, new social movements, trade unions, church groups, and a range of political activists from different backgrounds. The differences within and between the various approaches to the politics under contention and the decisions as to a unified collective response to a particular cause or concern often raise political dilemmas for activists. They are, however, intrinsic to understanding the vibrancy of a form of politics that prefers to operate with a variety of positions and perspectives and often from a highly personalized approach, as opposed to a traditional class politics of old, which may rely on established political doctrines. These networks are often staunchly anti-bureaucratic and anti-centralist, suspicious of large organized, formal and institutional politics, and want to resist repeating what they see as the mistakes of those models in the politics that they practise. These acclaimed characteristics also speak to the nature of politics online, which has been associated with protest rather than a long-term fixed political project (Fenton, 2006) – a bid for involvement and voice, along with a refusal to determine or even presume a singular approach or direct political outcome or end point that may signal exclusion and/or hierarchy within any grouping or alliance. And the architecture of the internet is claimed to have enabled such diverse, leaderless and horizontal politics to emerge and thrive.

One dated but much quoted example is the anti-globalization (also referred to as the alter-globalization or social justice) movement, which gained public recognition at what is now commonly referred to as 'the Battle of Seattle' – a protest that is commonly understood to have kick-started global internet activism. On 30 November 1999, an alliance of labour and environmental activists congregated in Seattle in an attempt to make it impossible for delegates to the WTO conference to meet. They were joined by consumer advocates, anti-capitalists and a variety of other grassroots movements. Simultaneously, it is claimed that nearly 1,200 NGOs in eighty-seven countries called for the wholesale reform of the WTO, many staging their own protests in their own countries (*The*

Guardian, 25 November 1999, p. 4). Groups integrated the internet into their strategies. The International Civil Society website provided hourly updates about the major demonstrations in Seattle to a network of almost 700 NGOs in some eighty countries (Norris, 2002). The Independent Media Center (www.indymedia.org), established by various independent and alternative media organizations and activists for the purpose of providing grassroots coverage, acted as a clearing house for information for journalists and provided up-to-the-minute reports, photos, audio, and video footage. It also produced its own newspaper, distributed throughout Seattle and to other cities via the internet, as well as hundreds of audio segments, transmitted through the web and internet radio station based in Seattle. During the demonstration, the site, which uses an open-publishing system, logged more than 2 million hits and was featured on America Online, Yahoo, CNN and BBC Online, among others. The Seattle demonstration was one of the first indications of how radical politics could mobilize participants in the era of the internet and was heralded as a success for transnational internet activism. Consequently, hundreds of media activists set up independent media centres (IMCs) in London, Canada, Mexico City, Prague, Belgium, France and Italy over the following year. Since then, IMCs have been established on every continent with variable success. A decade and a half later, many of these centres have closed, but they have done so amid a flourishing of other online alternative news sites or sites oriented more towards the organization and mobilization of radical politics. The IMCs also provided a template for the media activities of the Occupy movement that followed over a decade later (Costanza-Chock, 2012)

Diversity or More of The Same?

However, as enticing as horizontality and diversity may be to notions of future radical politics, we don't have to dig very deep to realize that the limitless diversity apparently on offer online is not quite so wide-ranging as many assume. Research on the digital divide notes that internet users are younger, more highly educated and richer than non-users, more likely to be men than women, and more likely to live in cities (Norris, 2001; Warschauer, 2003; Haight, Quan-Haase and Corbett, 2014). As chapter 1 outlines, these concerns map on to massive disparities between the global North and South as well as online activity within developed nations. The internet does not surpass established inequalities between the well-educated middle class who dominate public discourse and those on the peripheries or who are excluded altogether (Hindman, 2008) – far from it. Horizontality, it would seem, is reserved for the privileged.

Patterns of privilege are repeated in digital activism. Brodock et al. (2009) show how digital activists, particularly in developing countries, are well resourced and often have the advantages of high-speed internet access at home and work in white-collar jobs where the internet is readily available. Digital activism has a price. Respondents with more features on their mobile phone – such as internet, video and GPS – are more likely to use their phones for political activism. This is another indicator of the importance of financial resources for the politically engaged, both quantitatively, in terms of greater technology access, and qualitatively, in terms of better (mobile) hardware. The conclusion is simple. The internet may be democratizing, but more often than not its effects are felt most strongly in the global middle class.

Nonetheless, the claimed diversity of communication is argued to be connected to an emergent sense of the political that resides in multiple belongings (people with overlapping memberships linked through polycentric networks) and flexible identities (characterized by inclusiveness and a positive emphasis on diversity and cross-fertilization) (Tarrow and della Porta, 2005) that is only just beginning to be appreciated (see chapter 3). Following on from the Battle of Seattle and the raft of transnational protests it inspired, the work of Hardt and Negri (2004) took the notion of the 'network' and gave it heightened significance as an ever-open space of politics. From this perspective, the network is not simply the expression of networked individuals but the manifestation of self-constituted, unhierarchical and affinity-based relationships, which extend beyond state borders and have at their core the combined notions of 'autonomy' (everyone's right to express their own political identity) and 'solidarity' (to overcome power/neoliberalism) (Graeber, 2002: 68). In such accounts the internet is claimed not only to herald the dawn of a different type of communication but also to have contributed to the emergence of a different form of left radical politics premised on horizontality and diversity. Here, the space of new media enables a broader range of voices and types of material to be communicated to a wider audience without the constraints of needing to comply with or follow a particular political creed or direction other than the expression of an affinity with a particular cause. It is a form of politics that cannot be identified by a party name or definitive ideology and is often liable to rapid change in form, approach and mission – it is pulsating with energy, erratic and uncontrollable by design. Many extend this argument to claim that the meta-narratives of a politics of old, organized around unifying ideologies such as socialism and communism, are being replaced with a type of post-foundational politics (Marchart, 2007).[1]

Perspectives that advocate contemporary radical politics as post-foundational not only talk about the materialization of new political subjects that operate within different types of political spaces but also claim that that the material 'stuff' of politics is changed in the process, as politics morphs from formal participation in traditional representative systems to networked action, as exemplified in the critical sociology of Castells (2015). These are grand arguments trying to make sense of the political zeitgeist of a particular moment in the context of rapid technological change. What they tend to overlook is that dissent, demonstrations and actions for democratic social change are rarely, if ever, the products of the internet but emanate from people's material existence rooted in concrete histories of oppression and struggle. It is helpful to turn to another type of post-foundational political thought – post-Marxist discourse theory – to elaborate upon this point.

Post-Marxist Theories

Post-Marxist discourse theory is central to an understanding of the connection between radical politics and diversity. In particular, the anti-essentialism made popular by *Hegemony and Socialist Strategy* (Laclau and Mouffe, 1985) challenged the notion that there was any such thing as an absolute, objective reality to social and political identities. Rather, the authors argued that these identities were always contingent upon the outcome of political struggles. Unitary identities such as 'the worker' or 'woman' came to be viewed as positions within discourse that were provisional and based upon ever-shifting relationships with other identities. In this manner, they were seen to provide a framework for understanding the faltering development of traditional political identities post-1968 and the experience of the emergence of new social movements (NSMs) in the decades that followed, alongside the decline of organized labour and the forms of socialism associated with it (Nash, 2000). It is a history that is important to appreciate and helps us to understand many contemporary configurations of radical politics.

NSMs exhibit a politics that has grown out of a fragmentation of political culture fuelled by the rise of an identity politics that recognizes diversity and allows for differentiated notions of citizenship among diverse counter-publics. It is a politics defined by the multiple, shifting and overlapping meanings attributed to certain identities and the various struggles to define them rather than the particular characteristics of the technology they may use to mediate their causes. NSMs can arguably be seen as the closest realization we have seen to date of Laclau and Mouffe's (1985) formulation of politics and political identities. Just as post-Marxist discourse theorists proposed that no single identity and no social situation endures forever, therefore we no longer need be beholden to a traditional Marxist revolutionary politics of the past, so we see this reflected in the radical politics of the digital age where many types of political activity are readily embraced, including coalitions of diverse groups and individuals. The notion of diversity in relation to radical politics and its online manifestations refers, then, to the content and the cast of politics and not simply to its forms of mediation. The space of new media may enable a broader range of voices and types of material to be communicated to a wider audience without the constraints of needing to comply with or follow a particular political creed or direction other than the expression of an affinity with a particular cause. But radical politics also has a political history that predates the internet.

Building on the poststructuralist philosophy of, most particularly, Derrida and Lacan, Laclau and Mouffe (1985) seek to reject the authoritarianism, centralism and homogeneity of more traditional forms of left politics based on essentialist conceptions of class and to put forward a response to the psychological issues that relate to identity politics which Marxism largely ignores. But they also seek to differentiate themselves from the more distinctly postmodern perspectives of difference and dispersion through an emphasis on hegemony developed from Gramsci. In their post-Marxist formulation, a new radical form of hegemony is considered necessary to unite all the disparate struggles of new social movements and workers. Laclau and Mouffe recognized that politics is not concerned solely with the struggle between social classes. Rather, it is concerned with a struggle between complexes of meaningful social practice or discourses. However, discourse here is not simply ideas or words but social *practice* based partly upon material conditions and partly on identity and intersubjectivity. As such, it is a politics that resists essentialist politics and embraces difference, since there are no natural, inherent connections between various forms of identity (race, sex, gender, class, etc.) and different sets of political demands.

Although Laclau and Mouffe (1985) rid Gramsci's formulation of hegemony of its rootedness in class structures, they embrace the notion of identities as subject to change through the hegemonic process itself that creates a collective will. Their stress on contingency, the multiplicity of identities, the complex psychological nature of human desire, and the depth of human antagonism ensures that openness to new forms of struggle can be maintained within their formulation of a radical and plural democratic framework.

However, the horizontality and politics of NSMs can also be seen as the realization of other post-Marxist theories, particularly Deleuzian-inspired 'post-hegemony' theory (including that of autonomist Marxists – see chapter 5), which is expressive of a very different type of politics to that proposed by Laclau and Mouffe (1985). The politics envisaged in post-hegemony theory (Day, 2005; Graeber, 2002), and also seen as practised in new social movements, is highly porous and more organic than the radical politics of old and operates horizontally rather than vertically (Tormey, 2006), creating networks of resistance. This is a politics characterized by phases of visibility and phases of relative invisibility, with people moving frequently within and between different manifestations as they come in and out of focus, with a persistent refusal to subsume the diversity at their core into one overarching political identity and, thereby, allowing potential differences in political ideologies to be sidelined in favour of the inclusivity of the importance of protest and struggle. Tormey refers to this, drawing on Deleuze, as a rhizomatic form of politics that has no single centre and can spread indefinitely:

> Horizontality is from this point of view not a question of joining a party, but of dissolving the axiomatic of parties in the quest for combinations that fully express the availability of autonomy and authentic modes of univocal engagement with and alongside others.... Horizontalist strategies...self-consciously eschew the capturing of power in favour of alternative strategies that maintain the integrity and autonomy of all constituent singularities. (Tormey, 2006: 221–2)

Laclau and Mouffe did not 'eschew the capturing of power'; rather, counter to Deleuzians/autonomist Marxists, and through the concept of hegemony, they emphasize the necessity for vertical relations of identity and representation as well as horizontal forms of political participation in a search for the *articulation* of terms and demands. Here, articulation means the joining together of common terms of reference to create a united front. By insisting on the need for a unified front, a universalism of sorts, they accept that groups with separate sets of different demands will undertake a process of partial transformation as all those who partake in the coalition adjust to each other's concerns in order to occupy and lay claim to common ground. This form of hegemony creates 'a nodal point' of 'radical and plural democracy' based upon 'the struggle for a maximization of spheres on the basis of the generalization of the equivalential-egalitarian logic' (Laclau and Mouffe, 1985: 167). The creation and maintenance of this common ground is also seen as partly dependent on 'empty signifiers' – symbols or terms shared by a political community that mean very little but signify the coalition as a community. Mouffe (2000) argues that what distinguishes a radical democratic community is the ability to acknowledge publicly the emptiness of such signifiers while also recognizing that their meanings are shaped by sedimented understandings and historical articulations and thereby enter into open contestation about how that community should be defined. In this formulation, the worst-case scenario would be for an ideal vision of the community and its political future to become fixed and naturalized, excluding the possibility of contestation that is considered to be at the heart of democracy itself. Rather, each grouping would be equally valid and reciprocally free to enable a new utopianism to develop. In this manner, diversity, equivalence and individual autonomy combine to reveal a space for the hegemonic 'logics' of complete identity and difference to be renegotiated (Laclau and Mouffe, 1985: 188).

What, then, are the implications of such hegemonic politics for democracy and the question of diversity? Radical democracy of the sort proposed by Laclau and Mouffe (1985) seeks persistently to contest the dominion of the majority, which is the logical conclusion for liberal deliberative democrats, through the constant struggle to maximize difference of identity and struggles. On another level, the way in which liberal democracy is to be radicalized is through hegemonic struggle that involves, at some point, a transcendence of the particular struggle of any one grouping into a form of universalism expressed as the collective will, even if this is recognized as strategically and discursively constituted. Thus, there is a tension for discourse theory between the practices of diversity and the concept of hegemony. This tension continues to the present day and is evident in the debates within the new left political parties of Podemos in Spain and Syriza in Greece (see chapter 6), which have largely rejected the post-hegemony politics of autonomist Marxists (see chapter 5) in favour of an approach that resonates much more easily with the ideas proposed by Laclau and Mouffe (1985).

The Forgotten Political

Claims for a radical politics that embraces horizontality and diverse identities in the post-hegemony frame are also subject to counter-arguments by those who interpret such horizontality and diversity not as political pluralism but as political dissipation and fragmentation (Habermas, 1998). As Diamond (2012: 14) notes, 'there are fine lines between pluralism and cacophony, between advocacy and intolerance and between the expansion of the public sphere and its hopeless fragmentation.' Those who contest the political efficacy of online oppositional politics refer to the network society as producing localized, disaggregated, fragmented, diversified and divided political identities (earlier work by Castells (1996) also fell into this frame). Taking Castells's earlier view, the fragmented nature of new media limits the capacity of new social movements to create coherent strategies as a result of the increasing individualization of labour. Problems of quantity and chaos of information challenge the way analysis and action are integrated in decision-making processes. Hence, how political change can be realized becomes difficult to imagine let alone achieve. Writing in relation to the use of social media in the Green Revolution in Iran, Yahyanejad and Gheytanchi (2012: 151) support this view, stating that, '[t]hough social media can widen the grassroots base of social movements, such media (with their open, horizontal nature) can also breed confusion when there is a need to deal with complex issues and tactics that require discipline, strategy and a degree of central leadership.'

Furthermore, in his analysis of the Purple Movement (Popolo Viola) in Italy and its extensive use of Facebook, Coretti (2014) demonstrates that, while the myth of the network as open and inclusive persists, it acts as a disguise for the communication protocols of commercial social networking platforms that may well enable large-scale mobilization but ultimately, through their very functionality, encourage organizational centralization and fragmentation in social movements. Popola Viola was planned and organised on Facebook in 2009 in opposition to the politics of Silvio Berlusconi's government. Along with 460,000 members on its home page, thousands of other pages and groups within Italy and beyond were established on Facebook in support of the principal aim of the resignation of Italy's then prime minister. Facebook both galvanized and damaged the movement. Although it is a social networking platform, Facebook is designed on the basis of individual self-promotion (see chapter 5) and engineered to maximize consumer spend (Leistert, 2015). The algorithms at work operate within a business model devised on the basis of extracting value from individuals through selling commodities and data. The inability to manage Facebook pages and groups according to commonly agreed values promoted vertical power structures within the Purple Movement that led to internal divisions and the demise of solidarity. Such fragmentation cannot be attributed solely to the technology and reflects the values and interests of the political actors themselves, but the technology did not help. Leadership and hierarchy are not dispensed with online if other controlling (structural) forces are at play. Of course, if the political organization has a tendency towards non-dialogic politics, then it is highly unlikely that any network capability is going to change that. Politics and political organization emerge from histories that do not evaporate in the face of technology. In fact, the technology itself is thoroughly steeped in a politics that operates in direct opposition to the emancipatory ideals of many social movements.

Habermas forewarned us of this when he registered his ambivalence towards new information and communication technologies as a potential source of equal and inclusive communication, arguing that the internet might contribute to the fragmentation of civil society, as well as political mobilization and participation:

> Whereas the growth of systems and networks multiplies possible contacts and exchanges of information, it does not lead per se to the expansion of an intersubjectively shared world and to the discursive interweaving of conceptions of relevance, themes, and contradictions from which political public spheres arise. The consciousness of planning, communicating and acting subjects seems to have simultaneously expanded and fragmented. The publics produced by the Internet remain closed off from one another like global villages. For the present it remains unclear whether an expanding public consciousness, though centered in the lifeworld, nevertheless has the ability to span systematically differentiated contexts, or whether the systemic processes, having become independent, have long since severed their ties with all contexts produced by political communication. (Habermas, 1998: 120–1)

Greater pluralism is regarded by Habermas as a risk for deliberative democracy rather than its saviour. This concern is echoed by Sunstein, who argues that the internet has spawned large numbers of radical websites and discussion groups allowing the public to bypass more moderate and balanced expressions of opinion in the mass media (which are also, he argues, subject to fragmentation for essentially technological reasons). Moreover, these sites tend to link only to sites that have similar views (Sunstein, 2001: 59). Such findings are supported by other empirical work, such as that by Hill and Hughes (1998). Sunstein argues that a consequence of this is that we witness group polarization (2001: 65), and this is likely to become more extreme with time. As such, Sunstein contends that two preconditions for a well-functioning, deliberative democracy are threatened by the growth of the internet and the advent of multi-channel broadcasting. First, people should be exposed to materials that they have not chosen in advance. This results in a reconsideration of the issues and often recognition of the partial validity of opposing points of view. Second, people should have a range of common experiences in order that they may come to an understanding with respect to particular issues (Downey and Fenton, 2003). In sharp contrast to analyses by Bohman (2004) and Benkler (2006), these arguments are framed by a particular understanding of democracy that accepts the institutional structures of representational politics and applies a liberal pluralism model of democratic practice inherent in Habermasian thought. Arguments such as these are based on an understanding of participative democracy that functions through collective consensus and political projects that are problematic for a contemporary politics of the multitude. It is to this debate that we turn in more detail in chapters 3 and 5.

As stated in chapter 1, the theoretical premise of any discussion on digital media and radical politics requires an understanding of what 'the political' means – a simple point, too often forgotten. The political refers both to institutional and to non-institutional forms of political practice – to a civil society throbbing with non-governmental organizations, pressure groups and activists; it refers to the conscious and carefully planned political projects as well as to the reactive and passionate politics of protest; it refers to economics and to emotions. All of these are implicated in mediated practices.

Connectivity and Participation

The dual themes of speed and space and horizontality and diversity discussed above are also intermeshed with the lauded technical capacity of connectivity afforded in a networked age. The connectivity of the internet can impact upon the internal structure of social movement organizations through the forging of alliances and coalitions across different movements to share best practice and the most effective campaign techniques, which can change the way groups organize and operate. In January 2001, Joseph Estrada, president of the Philippines, became the first head of state to lose power to a smart mob (Deibert et al., 2010) when more than a million Filipinos were mobilized through digital media in four days to assemble at a historic site in Manila. Since then, mass digital mobilizations have become relatively commonplace, having featured prominently in the Orange Revolution in Ukraine in 2004, the Cedar Revolution in Lebanon in

2005 and the Green movement in Iran in 2009 (Curran et al., 2012), not to mention the so-called Arab Spring (see below).

Similarly, the protest activity and alliances of social movements on the ground can affect the way in which the internet is used and structured on the various and multiple websites. Civic and political participation are frequently understood as prerequisites for citizen-based democracies to flourish. But it is not just connectivity that is at play. The interactive dynamics of much of Web 2.0 and beyond is also linked to the more directly political concept of participation. Carpentier (2011: 10) notes that the concept of participation has an 'intimate connection with the political, the ideological and the democratic... that is intrinsically linked to power'. Facilitation of participation is seen to be a crucial factor in transnational internet activism, not least because it is largely understood as putting all internet users on an equal footing, thereby enabling a horizontal politics to be enacted and ensuring that everyone has a voice and can play a part in the movement. In these radical online settings the capacity to maximize connectivity and interaction is seen as the political act. This reflects a further emphasis on participative decision-making and the demand for concentrations of power to be broken down (Gilbert, 2008). The act of participation itself – and engagement with a particular issue – rather than social reform or direct policy impact is often asserted as the political purpose.

This is partially explained through an appreciation of the participation in new social movements being linked to disengagement with traditional party politics. In her extensive interviews with and questionnaires to activists, della Porta (2005) discovers a relationship between mistrust for parties and representative institutions alongside very high trust and participation in social movements. The distinction between institutional politics and social movements rests upon the former acting as bureaucracies founded upon delegation of representation and the latter being founded on participation and direct engagement. This reflects a further emphasis on participative decision-making and the demand for concentrations of power to be broken down (Gilbert, 2008). Similarly, for Benkler (2006), the internet has the potential to change the practice of democracy radically because of its participatory attributes. It allows all citizens to alter their relationship to the public sphere, to become creators and primary subjects, to become engaged in social production. In this sense the internet is ascribed the powers of democratization.

However, connectivity and participation online have also been fiercely criticized as weakening radical politics and offering a pseudo-participation that is illusory rather than actual (Dean, 2009). In other words, rather than the internet signalling a newly vital oppositional political culture, we are witnessing an era of easy-come, easy-go politics where you are only ever one click away from a petition (clicktivism), a technological form that encourages issue drift whereby individuals shift focus from one issue to another or one website to another with little commitment or even thought (slacktivism), where collective political identity has a memory that is short-lived and easily deleted. Collective solidarity is replaced by a politics of visibility that relies on hashtags, 'Likes' and compulsive posting of updates that hinge upon self-presentation as proof of individual activism (Milan, 2015). Online campaigning organizations such as Avaaz often fall prey to such criticisms.

Avaaz describes itself as 'a global web movement to bring people-powered politics to decision-making everywhere' (www.avaaz.org/en/about.php). Avaaz, meaning 'voice' in many European, Middle Eastern and Asian languages, was launched in 2007 and has a core team on six continents and thousands of volunteers. In August 2012 it had 15,378,229 members worldwide in 194 countries and had taken 87,772,473 actions. By September 2014 this had increased to 38,778,130 members and 205,603,598 actions. Avaaz is best known for organizing online petitions that can gain mass global support incredibly quickly, but its activity also extends to funding media campaigns and direct actions, emailing, calling and lobbying governments, and organizing offline protests and events, all with the intention of making the views and the value of the general population matter to decision-makers. It claims to be extraordinarily nimble and flexible in its campaign work, focusing on tipping-point moments of crisis and opportunity. Avaaz decides which issues to focus on through all-member polls. Each week campaign ideas are polled and tested with 10,000-member random samples. Campaigns that gain strong support are then put into action, with hundreds of thousands of members often taking part within hours or days. In January 2012 over 3 million signatures were collected for a worldwide petition opposing an Internet Censorship Bill in the US. Avaaz organized a meeting with White House officials to deliver the petition and claims that, as a result, the White House condemned the Bill and withdrew its support. In August 2012 Avaaz was working with the leadership of democracy movements in Syria, Yemen and Libya to get them high-tech phones and satellite internet modems and connect them to the world's top media outlets, as well as providing communications advice. It has no overriding mission or vision apart from a general and vague ideal that we are all humans and should respect one another and behave responsibly towards the planet. It does not attempt to reach consensus on issues among the diverse membership, stating that this has often led to the fracturing of movements, organizations and coalitions. It simply asks members to support the campaigns they wish to.

A similar organization, 38 Degrees in the UK, has over 3 million members (*The Guardian*, 24 September 2014, p. 42). 38 Degrees is the angle at which an avalanche happens. Its hope is that, through the power of the internet, it can create an avalanche for change. Once more, it is known best for its online activism, such as e-petitions and emailing MPs, but it too uses a range of tactics, from funding newspapers advertisements on its campaigns to organizing meetings with MPs and hosting discussions. 38 Degrees uses its Facebook page, Twitter, blog and website to discuss and vote for campaign ideas, which are then voted on in polls of all the membership. It is important to take this consultation process seriously, as the organization is funded solely from membership donations. Interestingly, one of the things the members are asking for is more offline campaigning. The campaign against the government sell-off of Forestry Commission estates – national state-owned forests – generated a petition half a million strong, hundreds of emails to MPs, adverts in national newspapers, and posters all over the country. After just a few weeks the government dropped its plans. 38 Degrees is keen to point out that 'there is no manifesto and no central campaign direction…it's a campaigning tool, not a movement' (ibid.). Again, its aims are broad: 'We provide simple and effective tools for hundreds of thousands of us to influence the decisions that affect us all. We work together to defend fairness, protect constitutional rights, promote peace, preserve the planet and deepen democracy' (www.38degrees.org.uk/pages/faq/). The organization claims to have over a 50 per cent success with 800 of the 1,500 petitions started in the UK every month, achieving the stated objectives, although politicians have started to complain about the volume of traffic in their email in-boxes and report a tendency to disengage with online petitions as a result (*The Guardian*, 24 September 2014, p. 42).

Other groups, such as MoveOn.org and Change.org in the US and GetUp! in Australia, operate on a similar basis. All focus on single-issue, easily identifiable, winnable campaigns. That means that these must be issues that can be quickly understood in a simple paragraph or two in an email and have an achievable end point. It did not take much persuasion for clicktivists to respond to the idea of privatizing woodland for the benefit of greedy land developers. But where does that leave campaigns on issues that are rather messier, more complicated and not so straightforwardly fixable or gratifying? Campaign populism is a trap that is hard to avoid for many such organizations, which are undoubtedly challenging the powerful and making public concerns heard but nonetheless run the risk of producing a form of radical politics that favours gut reaction and quick fixes over long-term struggle. This is a politics that is all about the short, sharp referendum – a tick-box politics that prefers to avoid the complicated, drawn-out assessment of social and political systems and their consequences and one that is more likely to lead to sticky-tape solutions than to genuine political alternatives. How long will politicians take notice of what can quickly be dismissed as political spam lacking in authenticity and unworthy of consideration? Do these forms of online activism add to an atmosphere of change and possibility that inspires and encourages those among us who desire a better world to continue our struggles and long-fought campaigns, or do they contribute to a politics based on consumerism and choice, that privileges the already privileged, achieving little more than self-satisfaction that one click is all it takes to salve one's political conscience?

The themes of connectivity and participation that flood the literature on new media and political engagement also demonstrate another important lack. The connectivity and participation to which they refer tends to be focused on an online setting and to avoid or ignore the social dynamics of mediated practices. This 'missing social' is well illustrated by much commentary that has been written in relation to the Arab Spring.

The Missing Social

One of the enduring discussions about the role of digital media in revolution is related to the demonstrations and uprisings that began in the Arab world in Tunisia in 2010 (although was not limited to Arab nations), with other revolts happening in quick succession in Algeria, Jordan, Egypt, Libya, Yemen, Syria and Bahrain. The technology available to activists in 2010 was very different to the technology available to the activists over ten years earlier in the Battle of Seattle. In particular, social media had exploded onto the digital scene. Meier (2012) notes how, in Egypt, social media enabled young people to engage in political debate in a manner that had not been possible previously. Howard and Hussain (2012: 111) go further, claiming that social media meant that people interested in democracy could 'build extensive networks, create social capital and organize political action with a speed and on a scale never seen before', and that this made all the difference. Howard and Hussain note how the counter-public sphere online in Egypt was influenced by developments in Tunisia and by a Facebook group, 'We are all Khaled Said', constructed in the memory of a young person dragged out of an internet café and beaten to death by police after he exposed their corruption, which became a focus of collective dissent and solidarity. Social media enabled the expression of alienation and oppression that was then able to be channelled into the strategies and goals of a structured movement.

Barnett (2011) eloquently picks apart much of the ecstatic rhetoric that has circulated around the uprisings in what became known as the Arab Spring. He talks about these remarkable political events as conjuring up a mythical image of 'revolution' with a capital R, undertaken by a utopian figure of 'the people' with a capital P, that obscured the question of who the living subjects of these events actually were and, in consequence, evading what each political and cultural context actually was, preferring instead to evoke the techno-logical saviour of the internet. This is not to diminish the use to which the communicative reach of the internet can be put for oppositional political mobilization. Miladi (2011: 4), talking about the revolution in Tunisia in 2011, claims that

> The mushrooming of social networks on Facebook and Twitter was by far the most instrumental factor in the escalation [of the protests]. Tens of thousands joined Facebook groups and got to know about the news developments and mobilised for further action....Bloggers have proven that they can challenge not only the state media and other independent (self-censored) newspapers and radio stations, but also the government discourse on what is really happening.

We have indeed witnessed many so-called Twitter revolutions, whether in Iran, Moldova, Tunisia or Egypt. Each of these is indeed a social uprising facilitated (but not embodied) by technology (Diamond, 2012). But, by collapsing all of these astonishing events into something akin to 'Twitter revolutions', we fall prey to what Barnett (2011) calls the 'know-nothing-ism' that undergirds such revolutionary universalism. This was given clearest expression by Žižek's interpretation of the uprising in Egypt:

> The uprising was universal: it was immediately possible for all of us around the world to identify with it, to recognize what it was about, *without any need for cultural analysis of the features of Egyptian society*. In contrast to Iran's Khomenei revolution (where leftists had to smuggle their message into the predominantly Islamist frame), here the frame is clearly that of a universal secular call for freedom and

justice, so that the Muslim Brotherhood had to adopt the language of secular demands. (Žižek, 2011)

Barnett's robust rebuttal is that '[t]here is something wonderfully self-aggrandizing about this assertion, which arrogates interpretative authority to a cadre of bombastic philosophical Universalists who don't have to worry about what they do and don't know about other places' (2011: 266). Instead, he points us to the work of the anthropologist Hirschkind (2009), who has provided a deep ethnographic account of the complex relationship between Islam as a political discourse and nationalism. Through detailed documentation of the preaching that occurred during a period of authoritarian rule in Egypt, he reveals how forms of social and cultural practice such as the circulation of taped sermons contributed towards contemporary Islamic counter-public spheres. He shows how the political content of such tapes often included criticisms of Middle Eastern regimes for failing to implement democratic rights and of the United States for imposing a political and economic straitjacket on the region. The cassette, with its portability, reproducibility and ease of evading government control, enabled the circulation of contestatory discourse. Locating the contemporary importance of media technologies in this longer history of social and cultural change, Hirschkind's research reveals how the seeds of Egyptian uprising were sown much earlier and were not dependent on the internet for germination. Hirschkind views the significance of new media such as blogging as enabling the opening up of new spaces of pluralism that could break down old antagonisms between secular and fundamentalist discourses encouraged by the Mubarak regime and offer new conditions for organizing around a common demand for the end to Mubarak's presidency, but he notes how the role of media practices in dramatic political change needs to be understood within a complex history of social and political protest and transformation.

In this vein, Barnett (2011) also points us towards the work of Bayat (2010), who has written about the so-called new post-Islamic social movement politics and the ordinariness of political action in the Middle East. Rather than thinking of the Arab Spring as a wholly unprecedented, unpredictable event or set of events, Bayat's work suggests a need to consider contextual factors, conditions, and causal processes. For Bayat, events in Tunisia and Egypt and beyond are indicative of processes of rapid urbanization and the associated sociocultural developments of increasing literacy, high levels of education, professionalization, changing gender relations, the emergence of a middle-class poor and other new forms of inequality, and, yes, the development of new media cultures. In this perspective, 'the Arab street' (Bayat, 2011) is a complex configuration of ideas and practices about the force of popular opinion, the fragility of state power, and the calibration of formal political processes to material conditions of life. Faris (2013) also points out that, while blogging and digital activism played their part, there had also been a history of sustained protest movements in Egypt, as well as the development of an independent press to provide the political backdrop for uprising to take place. The likes of Bayat and Faris manage to avoid the aggrandizement of ruptural politics as being the only means of social change and focus our attention on more interstitial and complex struggles that emerge over time and provide the political architecture out of which uprisings may occur.

Understanding the social dimensions of political life – what brings people together and why they seek solidarity – is crucial to our understanding of mediated political life. The political cannot be understood outside of relations of power or without the social. Only when we have a sense of what may constitute the political – economically, socially and technologically – alongside a better understanding of the nature of power therein and can interpret these contingent factors through a particular socio-geographic lens, then, and only then, can we begin to address the part played by the internet and its role in the complexity of modern-day living.

Conclusion

This chapter has argued that it is not enough simply to celebrate resistance through the conduit of the internet and the veneration of the potential of some of its technological capabilities. As new communication technologies enable disparate protest groups to forge transnational alliances and affinities, we may be faced with a new politics that is marked by the characteristics of speed and space, horizontality and diversity, and connectivity and participation that demands new ways of thinking about the *means of and the meaning of being political*. The internet may well have ushered in a new form of political activism, but its consequences may not be the ones that were intended or that can necessarily deliver the democratic gains that were hoped for. Networks are not *inherently* liberatory; the internet does not contain the essence of openness that will lead us directly to democracy.

The growing 'civic disengagement' of young people from state politics – the kind of politics that has been developed through modern history to fit and serve the political integration into 'nation-states' – along with the development of new communication technologies, has shifted political interests and hopes to new terrains that are borderless and global – a kind of politics well suited to the internet. New social movements magnified the characteristics of the internet with a switch to a more fluid, issue-based politics with less institutional coherence, where political engagement via the internet offers atomized expressions of social activism that move in and out of focus, reflecting a move to forms of protest politics rather than the delivery of a political project. These forms of online protests and mobilizations remain very much with us, although there are signs that other forms of radical politics that are more project focused and demand driven are emerging (see chapter 6).

Digital media and the internet in particular have dramatically expanded the communicative space available for a radical politics to organize and campaign. But having a voice in a space that is occupied by many millions of other voices does not guarantee that you will be heard, particularly if you are lacking resources and struggling to keep up with the tyranny of new technology, which demands you are always connected and constantly contributing a stream of material on a variety of platforms that will maximize your network power and possibly push you to the top of the search sift. And if you do manage to be audible above the endless hum of multiple digital murmurings, there is of course no guarantee that you will actually be listened to and achieve the response you were hoping for.

Technologies are drenched from conception to realization to practice in the economic and political context of which they are part. They are enmeshed with the systems of power within which they exist – as Feenberg (1995, 2002) argues, technology and capitalism have developed together. Similarly, the practices of new media *may* be liberating for the user but not necessarily democratizing for society. Any argument for the liberating role of new technologies and the enhancement of radical politics needs also to be assessed in the wider context of increasing securitization of cyberspace, which has potentially serious implications for basic freedoms (Morozov, 2012). Radical politics is, of course, about more than communication, about more than participation in communication, and about more than protest: it is about social, political and economic transformation.

In seeking to understand the diversity and horizontality of radical politics in the digital age, we must also be prepared to take stock of representative politics – How *can* one individual represent a multiplicity of different views equally (Fenton, 2011)? Once we ask this question, we are also faced with an interrogation of the assumptions built into the notion of liberal democracy itself. If liberal democracy is deemed to be failing in crucial ways based on the inability of a few elected representatives to account for the views of the many, then it should come as no surprise that radical politics that seeks to challenge such assumptions is emerging. The interrogation of liberal democratic principles on which the notion of the public sphere is based is the subject of the next two chapters.

3

Digital Media, Radical Politics and Counter-Public Spheres

Any discussion of the role of the media in enhancing democracy and political participation frequently falls back on Habermas's (1989) concept of the public sphere. This is understandable, as it is one of the few prominent theoretical frameworks that link the media and its practices directly to the exercise of democracy. This conceptual framing has increased in recent years (Lunt and Livingstone, 2013), with the internet in particular lending itself to discussions around whether or not the space now available online for mass use could constitute a fully functioning public sphere – a space where all debates can be aired and all issues discussed in a deliberative and rational manner. The democratic gain of an ideal Habermasian public sphere is through reaching an understanding based on a consensus view in the process of deliberation that is then responded to by policy-makers through forms of governance. Of course, actually existing democracy often falls far short of this ideal, with societies characterized more by political disaffection (Streeck, 2014) than by a citizenry satisfied that they understand all of the issues they are voting on and that, when they do vote, their views are taken heed of by their elected representatives. As Raymond Williams argued in 'Democracy and Parliament', all too frequently we find ourselves confronted with 'the coexistence of political representation and participation with an economic system which admits no such rights, procedures or claims' (1982: 19).

Furthermore, when a growth in popular mobilizations appears to loom large (as discussed in chapter 2), pleas for the legitimacy of

established electoral systems have often been at the bidding of bourgeois democracy – reform will temper the hunger for revolution. The
danger then is that, by constant recourse to a liberal democratic
frame, situated as it is in parliamentary and other such forms of
democracy where representation and governance are enmeshed and
in which public participation is minimal, we fail to acknowledge fully
the extent to which the contemporary structures of democracy may
have become part of the problem, thereby weakening the critical
capacity of public sphere theory. The quotation above from Williams
alludes to the way in which contemporary forms of democracy are
often disengaged from the economic – liberal democracy depends on
'the vote' rather than the equitable distribution of economic and
social resources, which is one of the reasons for citizen disengagement. Crouch has famously termed our current democratic decay as
a continuing process of dissolution towards 'post-democracy', a state
where 'the forms of democracy remain fully in place', yet 'politics
and government are increasingly slipping back into the control of
privileged elites in the manner characteristic of pre-democratic times'
(2004: 6). Are the interpretations of public sphere theory then captured by a liberal democratic frame to the extent that they cannot
imagine a world beyond the forms and structures of a liberal democratic system? Can a contemporary radical politics that eschews the
functionality of a liberal democratic system be understood through
a Habermasian lens that begins from a normative position that liberal
democracy is the ultimate agreed goal? The rest of this chapter
addresses these concerns.

Liberal Democracy Undone

In an interview in 2006, Stuart Hall articulated the felt experience of
a failed democracy through the lack of political community and the
way in which the social has been transposed into the individual, and
society into the market:

> For the first time I feel like a dinosaur. Not in regard to the particular
> things or the particular programmes I believe in. But there's been a
> shift. The points of reference that organized my political world and
> my political hopes are not around any more. The very idea of the
> 'social' and the 'public' has been specifically liquidated by New Labour.
> ... But what makes it complicated is that there are plenty of references
> in New Labour to building up community. They have bought the
> language and evacuated it. Progressive politics is in their mouth every

day. Community is in their mouth every day. Reform has been absorbed by them and reused in quite a different way. It's that transvaluation of all the key terms, that linguistic move that New Labour has made that presents anyone who is trying to take a critical approach with a tremendous problem. What terms can you use to speak about your objections?...Of course there are sites of resistance but I don't see how they cohere as a political programme, as a philosophy, even a statement. I don't see anyone who thinks they might try to articulate such a statement....I am not so disillusioned as to think that history is finished. But I do think that what Gramsci would call the 'balance of social forces' are very powerfully against hope. (Cited in Taylor, 2006)

The thesis that Hall is hinting at is a complex one that refers to privatization, deregulation and individualization – some of the hallmarks of neoliberalism. It is a debate that resonates with the earlier pessimism of some of the work of the Frankfurt School in trying to understand the surge of mass communications and culture within capitalism and its impact on democratic practice (e.g., Adorno and Horkheimer, 1973). It was this pessimism that Habermas was initially attempting to rally against by arguing that the mass expansion in print culture, and particularly in the press, could bring about increased citizen autonomy and deliberation and hence greater political engagement with and involvement in the political public sphere. The crux of Hall's pessimism in the quotation above indicates the opposite – that the mode of contemporary mediated political communication contributes to a diffuse alienation of citizens from politics. It is an argument that Habermas increasingly adopted (1992, 2006) in response to the development of the press within capitalism as sustaining and maintaining established power relations, relating his earlier work on the public sphere to the contemporary conditions of late capitalism, whereby

the intrusion of the functional imperatives of the market economy into the 'internal logic' of the production and presentation of messages that leads to...[i]ssues of political discourse becom[ing] assimilated into and absorbed by the modes and contents of entertainment. Besides personalization, the dramatization of events, the simplification of complex matters, and the vivid polarization of conflicts promote civic privatism and a mood of anti-politics. (Habermas, 2006: 27)

This is now a common refrain in political communications, that communication has become distorted by the dominance of market forces, in which analysis is subsumed by entertainment, and in which the language of citizens' political engagement has been evacuated from contemporary discourse. This debate often begins with the nature of democracy itself. Within liberal democracies, power is gained by winning elections. Winning elections requires persuasion, which means engaging in impression management on behalf of elite political actors. The media, hungry for news fodder, routinely access and privilege elite definitions of reality and are claimed to serve ruling hegemonic interests, legitimize social inequality and thwart participatory democracy.

There are many other contributory factors to this political malaise. Cottle (2003) claims that commercial television news is primarily a commodity enterprise run by market-oriented managers, who place outflanking the competition above journalistic responsibility and integrity. It is charged with being in the business of entertainment, attempting to pull in audiences for commercial rather than journalistic reasons, setting aside the values of professional journalism in order to indulge in the presentation of gratuitous spectacles and images that create superficiality while it traffics in trivialities and deals in dubious emotionalism. In other words, mainstream news has systematically undermined the crucial arrangement that is meant to operate between a working democracy and its citizens. This, it is claimed, has contributed forcefully to our political disenchantment.

This line of argument has found further purchase in an online world where news media (and the press in particular) have to fill far more space (online and offline) with far fewer journalists, leading to a form of 'churnalism' (Davies, 2008) characterized by the cut and paste, administrative journalistic practice that is conducive to faster and shallower news and ultimately leads to the further deterioration of the public sphere (Fenton, 2010; Lee-Wright et al., 2011). New technology and the struggle of the press industry to find a new business model befitting the internet age, where content is generally expected to come for free and advertising is less lucrative, provide one instance where the prospects of technology enhancing the public sphere have been analysed and found wanting (Phillips, 2014).

However, such critical perspectives are usually preceded by optimism and giddy excitement when a new technology enters the public domain, and the possibility of harnessing the technology for progressive political ends is heralded as a fresh opportunity for reclaiming a newly invigorated public sphere. In this manner, digital media are said to usher forth a revitalization of the public sphere, providing new channels of communication between citizens and institutions of government.[1] In such instances, as with the introduction of radio and then television (Curran et al., 2012, 2016), the reorganization of the space of political mediation forces us to reconceptualize our understanding of what constitutes the political and the political public in contemporary terms. In a context of diminishing voter turnout in national elections (Sloam, 2014), increased political protest (Norris, 2002) and decreased political satisfaction (Hansard Society, 2013; van Deth, 2011), the internet follows the well-trodden path of new technologies that have gone before it in being vested with the hopes and dreams of new opportunities for political participation through the opening of newly deliberative and interactive spaces. Indeed, the sense of optimism with which the internet has been imbued is often so extreme that it offers somehow to transcend the trends of market politics and the logic of late capitalism.[2] In this vein, the new digital media, it is claimed, have reinvented transnational activism and promise the rebirth of a radical politics that is global and participatory (see chapter 2). The internet, with its networked, additive, interactive and polycentric form, can accommodate radically different types of political praxis from different places at different times, offering a new type of political engagement and possibilities for a transnational political realignment amid a massively expanded public sphere.

This chapter addresses some of these concerns in relation to reductive interpretations of public sphere theory and those parts of civil society populated by radical politics and new social movements. It takes as its point of departure the centrality of key notions within public sphere theory that, I argue, have become increasingly problematic for any conception of radical politics to survive and flourish, particularly if they are plucked out of Habermasian theory and applied in isolation.

Many of these concerns relate to the interpretation of information pluralism connected (although it is rarely explained how) to enhanced deliberation that then segues into better democracy (Shane, 2004; Tapscott and Williams, 2008). This elision of pluralism with communicative competency and communicative freedom, which, it is claimed, will deliver, somewhat seamlessly, political gain, too often fails to take account of the many factors that still and increasingly delimit, constrain and undermine public spheres in an online age: surveillance and malware (see chapter 2), censorship and blocking, and corporate exploitation and dominance (see chapter 5). Furthermore, the argument that a pluralistic public sphere can engender forms of radical politics precisely because it is able to embrace difference and diversity, to spew horizontal networks that cross geographical borders and resist universalizing narratives, denies deep political histories and socio-economic contexts. An approach that argues that all democracy requires to function better is an open communicative realm effectively denies the social and political histories from which certain politics have arisen, along with the current social, political and economic contexts in which they exist, and leads us instead to technocratic dead-ends as solutions to all social and political ills – a better, faster internet; more freedom of communication deliverable via technology; increased media literacy and, hey presto, better democracy. A pluralistic public sphere as the solution to political problems blankets over deeper furrows such as the politics of austerity in play since the global financial crisis of 2008, a crisis where:

> those at the bottom are expected to pay disproportionately for a problem created by those at the top, and when those at the top actively eschew any responsibility for that problem by blaming the state for their mistakes, not only will squeezing the bottom not produce enough revenue to fix things, it will produce an even more polarized and politicized society in which the conditions for a sustainable politics of dealing with more debt and less growth are undermined. Populism, nationalism and calls for the return of 'God and gold' in equal doses are what unequal austerity generates, and no one, not even those at the top, benefits. (Blyth, 2013: 17–18)

If we take Blyth's contention seriously, then deliberation is under siege not simply from an impoverished public sphere but also from a particular politics of austerity designed to deal with what Streeck (2011: 29) calls the 'fundamental contradictions of post-war democratic capitalism', whereby states have been structurally required to balance the needs of two sovereigns – 'their people, below, and the international "markets" above'. This balance has become drastically skewed in one direction, leading to the 'dialectic of democracy and capitalism...unfolding at breathtaking speed.' Any discussion then of the possibilities of technology must be situated within the political economy of which they are part. Certainly, in Europe, the politics of austerity since 2008 has translated into programmes of economic bailout, with the proviso of externally imposed conditions designed to restore and secure investor confidence through constantly minimizing the role of the state, leading Streeck to state that, 'more than ever, economic power seems today to have become political power, while citizens appear to be almost entirely stripped of their democratic defences and their capacity to impress upon the political economy interests and demands that are incommensurable with those of capital owners' (2011: 29).[3]

Far from the internet and the glorious information abundance it offers up bringing forth an ever-enhanced public sphere, we see the contemptuous capacity of financial markets to dictate economic and social policy and, through a variety of performative technologies and mediating institutions, to discipline national governments (with Greece being the most prominent example – see chapter 6), which has been partly responsible for the forms of hollowing out and trans-valuation of meanings that Hall refers to above. But it is not just the tentacles of market capitalism that we need to be wary of; we also need to take heed of the nature and structure of the political ecosystems that contribute to political disenchantment and disenfranchisement. This is not to suggest that any such hollowing out is total – far from it. Counter-public spheres engage constantly in struggles over meaning and experiment with and rehearse forms of democratic recovery – it is from these seedlings that hope springs eternal.

The politics of pluralism is closely related to the importance of counter-public spheres and the need to understand a politics of the multitude. New social movements of the past decade and a half, most recently in the form of Occupy, have been marked by commitments to deliberation and map onto a key trajectory of public sphere theory renewal, which argues for grounding 'deliberative democracy in a strong critical theory of communicative action, and [re-emphasizing] oppositional civil society and public spheres as sources of democratic critique and renewal' (Dryzek, 2000: 3). But the likes of the Occupy movement have also drawn critical attention to the relationship between communicative action and the broader democratic process, seeking in their own deliberations to discover a better form of democracy that is horizontal rather than vertical, inclusive and responsive. A politics of the multitude draws into sharp relief the paucity of a (neo)liberal politics that panders to a mythology of pluralism blind to relations of power and the distortions of private interest. When this form of pluralism fails to deliver the promises of liberalism, it is no surprise that political disaffection is the outcome. If liberal democracy is captured by its neoliberal interpretation, then it is surely time to consider the merit of theories that rely upon it.

Homing in on Habermas: Political Mobilization and Counter-Public Spheres

Habermas's discussion of the public sphere is frequently invoked in political communication as an ethical horizon, something that has been lost and should be retrieved. Public spheres, conceived of by

Habermas as operating largely within the confines of the nation-state, were argued to have replaced feudalism based on hierarchy through rational debate that can deliver deliberative understanding. A key aspect of Habermas's understanding of democracy is the right of citizens to engage freely in debate and come to their own rational, critical interpretation. The extension of this act of deliberation in a democracy is that the views of citizens are taken into account in political governance. The principle is that participation in public debate leads to deliberation by a citizenry that can impact upon political decision-making. Habermas describes structural changes in society which led to the development of a public sphere but, in his earlier publications, underplays the part played by social movements, collective action and political conflict in shifting the terrain of political debate and of social policy (Fenton and Downey, 2003; Yla-Anttila, 2006), as well as being criticized for inattention to the power relations of gender, class and racializing structures (Downey and Fenton, 2007; Mouffe, 2005).

Other analyses of the concept of the public sphere stress the competitive relationship between a dominant (or common) public sphere, often interpreted as the mass media, and counter-public spheres (or advocacy domain), now seen as synonymous with alternative media or counter-publicity that exist outside the mainstream (see Dahlberg and Siapera, 2007). Whereas the dominant public sphere and advocacy domains may exist side by side in a liberal polity and contribute to the resolution of competing interests, counter-publicity should be thought of as challenging the legitimacy of the dominant public sphere, as presenting an alternative way of ordering society, as recognized in the work of Negt and Kluge (1972). Part of this counter-publicity is in the act of resistance itself. Through boycotts, petitions and demonstrations, political problems can be pushed on to the public agenda:

> The formation of public spheres at the national level has required the formation of national social movements, with their repertoires of collective action, associational networks and cultural framing of political issues.... collective action can thus be seen as a continuation of debate by other means. Boycotts, petitions, demonstration and other means of collective action co-ordinated on a national scale developed in tandem with the institutions and norms of public debate. (Yla-Anttila, 2006: 425)

Habermas follows a similar line of thought in *Between Facts and Norms* (1996). Here, he adapts his conceptual framework to conclude that counter-public spheres can acquire influence in the mass-media public sphere under certain conditions – namely in periods of crisis: 'in periods of mobilization, the structures that actually support the authority of a critically engaged public begin to vibrate. The balance of power between civil society and the political systems then shifts' (1996: 379). In these circumstances, Habermas concedes, counter-public spheres may provide vital sources of information and experience that are contrary, or at least in addition, to the dominant public sphere, further building civil society and thereby offering a vital impulse to democracy (Downey and Fenton, 2003). But there is a substantive chasm between feeding the democratic impulse and establishing shifts in political culture.

In their review of work on the public sphere, Lunt and Livingstone (2013) examine the impact of the above critiques, firstly by emphasizing the timing of the translation of Habermas's book into English, intersecting as it did with a normative retrenchment in the importance of public media institutions under conditions of Thatcherite assault (Garnham 1992), and then with the burgeoning influence of Foucauldian ideas on the dispersed and multiple workings and effects of power. They argue that 'his account of the media was surely better suited to mass media in the context of post-war social reconstruction and Cold War politics of America and Europe than to the complex, multi-media environments that we now inhabit' (Lunt and Livingstone, 2013: 90). This can be illustrated by returning to the role of media institutions in Habermas's public sphere. In his formulation, media institutions circulate information and are thereby a vital input to the public sphere. Freer and more plural media lead to better democracy. Habermas shows how the geographic spread of trade resulted in information circulated in newsletters that evolved into the political press discussed in the cafés of the bourgeoisie. What he misses is the part played by political conflict and collective action in the development of media institutions – in other words, how democratic practice breeds pluralism from below. As Yla-Anttila (2006) notes, before the French Revolution of 1789 there were 184 papers published; a year later, the number had increased to 335. The revolutions across Europe in 1848 also led to a growth in the press across the continent (Tarrow, 1994: 54). It is not unreasonable to suggest that, where there is political conflict, the means of circulating information will always be a primary aim – this was apparent in the now infamous case of the Zapatista Army of National Liberation (EZLN) in Mexico in the 1990s and the use of the internet to spread information and build solidarity on an international level (see chapter 5). Many transnational new social movements took their lead from the Zapatistas, who inspired the 1999 demonstrations against the World

Trade Organization in Seattle, which in turn led to the development of the Indymedia network around the globe (see chapter 2); the Occupy movement used social networks such as Twitter and YouTube along with an array of websites to organize and document its activities, as did the 15M movement in Spain (see chapter 6).

Counter-publicity often emerges out of political struggles rather than vice versa, making the role of counter-public spheres a rather different one to that of dominant public spheres. The latter, usually characterized as mainstream media in one form or another, may report on conflict and public issues and hopefully include a range of voices in the process, but they are ultimately part of a system that is closely connected to the political systems from which they emerge and the institutional elites that dominate them. Consequently, under normal circumstances the dominant public sphere is more likely (although not always) to sustain the status quo, or key elements of it, rather than undermine it. The mass media, then, may not be the place to look for increased pluralism. Indeed, this is one of the reasons why the internet as an open space, accessible to non-mainstream sources and production, has been invested with so much optimism regarding the proliferation of counter-publicity. But such perspectives also carry other health warnings.

The Limitations of Pluralism and Problems with Liberalism

As discussed in chapter 2 under the theme of diversity and horizontality, theorizations of networked media and new social movements often pivot on notions of pluralism (both of media form and of media content) whereby new (counter-)publics are realized through newly mediated pluralistic public spheres that lead to enhanced participation and thus better democracy. Scholars such as Castells (2009) and Benkler (2006), for example, advance rather different versions of an ultimately similar proposition wherein the promise of plurality that the internet presents is foregrounded as the means to communicative and democratic freedom.

In Benkler's (2006) analysis, the internet has the potential to change the practice of democracy radically because of its participatory and interactive attributes, which engender a more pluralistic public sphere and better civic engagement. Increased capacities to access the internet, and to produce and disseminate media content within expanding and thickening networks, is argued to transform the relations of producer and audience and to enable all citizens to alter their relationship to the public sphere, to become creators and primary subjects engaged in social production. In other words, citizens gain communicative freedom, and the more they gain the more the public sphere expands. In Benkler's words, 'the high capital costs that were a prerequisite to gathering, working, and communicating information, knowledge, and culture have now been widely distributed in the society...[such that]...we have an opportunity to change the way we create and exchange information, knowledge and culture' (2006: 473). The consequence of this ever-expanding networked sociality is claimed to represent enhanced democratization, where the flow of information and possibilities for participation radically expand access to media power and enhance information pluralism, which in turn supports political pluralism and the means to communicative freedom.

Similarly, Castells argues that social movements that engage in oppositional politics – 'the process aiming at political change (institutional change) in discontinuity with the logic embedded in political institutions' (2009: 300) – are now able to enter public space from multiple sources and positions, raising the possibility for major social and political change: 'could it be that the technological and organizational transformation of the network society provides the material and cultural basis for the anarchist utopia of networked self-management *to become a social practice?*' (ibid.: 346; original emphasis). In Castells's argument, the multiplicity of scenarios for intervention and inventiveness coming from a myriad of social nodes combine to create a new symbolic counter-force that can transform social practice. By using both horizontal communication networks and mainstream media to convey their images and messages, social movements increase their chances of enacting social and political change – 'even if they start from a subordinate position in institutional power, financial resources, or symbolic legitimacy' (ibid.: 302). Once again, pluralism and communicative freedom work in tandem and in ever-expanding circles; the more freedom one has, the more plurality is produced; the more plurality there is, the more freedom one has.

So, even though Castells acknowledges that the apparently limitless plurality on offer in an internet age is bounded, offset and challenged by other socio-economic and political factors, ultimately he maintains that the power to overcome these challenges is significantly enhanced. But it is difficult to see how the shifting yet resistant nature of 'digital divides', not only in terms of access to the internet between the global North and South but also in terms of disparities within nations, between the well-educated middle class who are able to direct and contribute to public debate and those who constantly struggle to be heard or who are absent from public discourse altogether (Hindman 2008; Tyler 2013), map onto such a positive rendition. New paradigms of pluralism can only be evaluated when integrated into an assessment of intersecting forms of social, political and economic inequalities, the development of capitalism, and the dramatic consequences of all of these dimensions for representative democratic systems (see Dorling, 2011).

The elision of pluralism with freedom threatens to bypass the complexities of the growth of capitalism and the burgeoning of inequalities and the consequences of both for political citizenship. Streeck (2014: 40) points out that

> [o]nly in the Cold War world did capitalism and democracy seem to become aligned with one another, as economic progress made it possible for working-class majorities to accept a free-market, private-property regime, in turn making it appear that democratic freedom was inseparable from, and indeed depended on, the freedom of markets and profit-making.

Now, however, the linkage between democracy and the free market is questioned, as people are increasingly sceptical as to whether politics can make a difference to their lives in the face of political scandals, corruption and the incompetence of a political elite that has become ever more estranged. These factors, alongside increasing gaps not only in wealth but also in political participation, contribute to diminishing electoral turnout and high voter volatility.

Decline in voter turnout is a markedly general trend across European states (Mair, 2006). As Schäfer and Streeck (2013) note, electoral turnout has further diminished during the eurozone crisis, and notably so for the socio-economically excluded. The UK, for example, went from 4 per cent difference in turnout between high and low earners in the 1987 general election to 23 per cent difference by 2010; the voting gap between the young and old stretched even wider, with a 32 per cent difference in turnout between those over sixty-five and those under twenty-four. When you compound this by comparing the voting habits of the old rich with the young poor, the results become what Lodge, Gottfried and Birch (2013) call 'toxic'. Only a third of those under thirty-five earning £10,000 or less bothered to vote in 2010,[4] compared with almost 80 per cent of those over fifty-five earning £40,000 or more.

Add this to the stark fact that the result of the 2010 UK election was decided by only 1.6 per cent of the electorate (Lodge and Gottfried, 2011) and in 2015 a majority conservative government was returned to Parliament on less than 37 per cent of the vote and with the support of just 24 per cent of the electorate (Garland and Terry, 2015), and the pluralism vested in the communicative freedom on offer in the digital age and the pluralism materialized in representative democratic processes diverge starkly. The counter-argument that young people are not less interested in politics but, rather, have rejected traditional electoral systems in favour of non-bureaucratized, decentred protest politics that speak better to their concerns and experience of a networked society certainly has purchase (Loader, 2007). A 2013 study claimed that 66 per cent of teachers surveyed thought that sixteen- and seventeen-year-olds were more engaged with social issues than past generations (Birdwell and Bani, 2014). However, we cannot ignore the material realities of poverty and inequality that weigh down the imagined subjects of communicative freedom. It is hard to engage fully with the deliberative possibilities of the internet when you are hungry or homeless (see Fenton and Titley, 2015). Similarly, studies (e.g., Blank and Groselj, 2015) now show that the varying forms of political participation online correlate almost exactly with indicators of social class and educational achievement. In other words, although half of the world may now be online, those using the internet for political purposes are still largely middle class and well educated.

In the US, analysis by Hacker and Pierson (2010) reveals that the massive growth in inequality is a result of policy changes relating largely to taxation that supports the mega-rich, trade policies and business regulations that support the market, and the weakening of the trade unions. They report the shocking shift in taxation policy to the benefit of the richest in society, with millionaires paying 43.1 per cent of federal income tax in 1961 and only 23.1 per cent in 2011. Corporation tax fell from 47.4 per cent of profits in 1961 to a mere 11.1 per cent in 2011. Stiglitz (2015) points out that the average wage of male high-school leavers has declined by 12 per cent in the last twenty-five years, whereas the pay of chief executives has soared from thirty times the average worker's wage to 300 times. In the UK, Dorling (2014) notes how rates of taxation have declined since the 1980s while inequality has rocketed. Tragically, Stiglitz (2015) also reports how the economic and employment prospects of the top-performing students of poor families in the US are now lower than those of the weakest performing students of families in the top quartile. Unsurprisingly, research (Bartels, 2008) shows how the poor have no influence over policies and politicians and vote less (McChesney, 2012). Voter participation increases with income simply because the wealthier are more likely to be listened to.

If, as Streeck (2014) argues, the legitimacy of post-war democracy was based on the premise that states could regulate markets in the public interest to prevent their worst excesses, then massive increases in inequality have cast doubt on this, as has the incapacity of governments either to prevent future financial crises or to find sustainable economic alternatives to the financial crash of 2008. Meanwhile,

> the transformation of the capitalist political economy from postwar Keynesianism to neoliberal Hayekianism progressed smoothly: from a political formula for economic growth through redistribution from the top to the bottom, to one expecting growth through redistribution from the bottom to the top. Egalitarian democracy, regarded under Keynesianism as economically productive, is considered a drag on efficiency under contemporary Hayekianism, where growth is to derive from insulation of markets – and of the cumulative advantage they entail – against redistributive political distortions. (Streeck, 2014: 40)

The de-democratization of European capitalism is further entrenched through the decrease of trade union membership and the increase in powers of supranational agencies such as the European Commission and the European Central Bank over national economic policies such as budgets and wages.

It follows from this that those who seek to exemplify the extension of the public sphere through the means and forms of communication must also, if the normative underlying aspiration is democratic, take account of the concentrated and deliberate political and economic assault on the institutions and wares of the public realm. For example, the current UK government's first spending review in 2010 delivered to average voters a loss of 12 per cent – £1,850 – while average non-voters lost 20 per cent, or £2,135 (Lodge, Gottfried and Birch: 2013). In a brutal move that eliminated the educational prospects of the young disadvantaged, the education maintenance allowance was scrapped and supports such as the child trust fund, child benefit, tax credits and cheap travel for the young were reduced. Meanwhile, through the reintroduction of tuition fees, an average £40,000 of debt was piled onto the backs of students, further eroding the 'pluralism' of our university communities (ibid). Dorling (2014) estimates that the full cost of a student loan of £50,000, based on a graduate starting salary of £26,000, will be in the region of £166,000. This is likely to increase with the current UK government currently considering raising the cap on student fees. As educational achievement is directly related to online political participation, the long-term consequences are dire.

When such contexts are elaborated upon, it is clear that any *critical* examination of the democratic potential of new distributions of communicative power must address the material consequences of increasing inequalities in societies and their insidious relationship to vastly impoverished democracies (Fenton and Titley, 2015). As Wilkinson and Pickett (2009: 298) argue – and they provide systematic supporting evidence: 'the health of our democracies, our societies and their people is truly dependent on equality.' Yet plurality in terms of access, and therefore the ability to take advantage of plurality in terms of voice and content, are, it would seem, increasingly reserved for the privileged.

Of course, as Nancy Fraser (1995) notes, inequality is not just socio-economic; it also concerns recognition. Taylor also notes that 'Non-recognition or misrecognition...can be a form of oppression, imprisoning someone in a false, distorted, reduced mode of being. Beyond simple lack of respect, it can inflict a grievous wound, saddling people with crippling self-hatred. Due recognition is not just a courtesy but a vital human need' (Taylor, 1994: 25). Non-recognition and misrecognition in the mainstream media are indeed, as Nancy Fraser notes, 'cultural injustices' that impact upon our political and social selves. In the same way, the notion of democracy is connected both to the mediation of information and to people as thinking, voting and acting publics. Michael Forster, author of the OECD's report *Divided We Stand* (2011), has noted that, in the UK, 65 per cent of people say that inequality is too high, yet at the same time they vastly underestimate its extent. Poverty and the poor suffer constant non-recognition in the mass media (Golding and Middleton, 1982; Redden, 2011), and this has deleterious political consequences. As Tyler has recently argued, increased inequality has been accompanied by the 'heightened stigmatization' in political discourse of 'disposable' populations, to the extent that '*stigmatization* operates as a form of governance which legitimizes the reproduction and entrenchment of inequalities and injustices' (2013: 231; original emphasis). Undoubtedly, these processes of stigmatization are contested and unsettled in multiple ways online. However, this is not the same as contending that pluralism online has provided a prevailing counter to a largely neoliberal hegemony (Fenton and Titley, 2015).

It is sobering to recall research undertaken in the UK by Ipsos MORI (2013) that mapped popular perceptions against reality. According to their survey:

- British people think teenage pregnancy is twenty-five times higher than official estimates;

- 51 per cent of people think that violent crime is rising when it is in fact falling;
- 29 per cent of people think that we spend more money on job-seekers' allowance (a form of welfare benefit) than pensions, when in actual fact we spend fifteen times more on pensions;
- the public think that £24 out of every £100 spent on benefits is claimed fraudulently when it is more like 70p;
- over a quarter of people think foreign aid is in the top two or three items on which the government spends most money when it actually made up 1.1 per cent of expenditure in 2011–12;
- there is a belief that 24 per cent of people in the UK are Muslim when the figure is 5 per cent in England and Wales;
- British people think that 31 per cent of the population are immigrants when the official figures are 13 per cent, and that black and Asian people make up 30 per cent of the population when the proportion is actually 11 per cent.

A global survey conducted in 2014 across fourteen countries (Australia, Belgium, Canada, France, Germany, Hungary, Italy, Japan, Poland, South Korea, Spain, Sweden, Britain and America) similarly found that, on average, people think that 15 per cent of teenagers give birth each year (twelve times higher than the average official estimate of 1.2 per cent across these countries); that all countries massively overestimate the proportion of their population that are Muslim (the average guess being 16 per cent, with the actual figure being 3 per cent); that immigration is at twice the level it actually is; that the population is far older than it actually is; and that the rate of unemployment in their countries is far higher than it actually is (Ipsos MORI 2014).

Accounts that rely upon the elision of pluralism, both in terms of access and in terms of multiplicity of content and content creation with communicative freedom as democratic enrichment, depend on an implicit assumption about the consequential relations between pluralism, networked communication, participation and politics. Introducing inequality – political, economic, cultural, social and technological inequality – to any debate relating to plurality and freedom is critical. It follows from this that narratives that elide pluralism with communicative freedom must account more fully for the concept of power with which they operate.

Castells, in *Communication Power* (2009), devotes considerable time to analysing corporate power in an online context. He argues that 'the media are not the holders of power, but they constitute by and large the space where power is decided' (2009: 242). In other words, as Freedman (2014) points out, media institutions act as hosts of power struggles and invite the real power-holders of international finance, politics and business onto their platforms. The media thereby 'constitute the space where power relationships are decided between competing political and social actors' (Castells, 2009: 194). Therefore, in Castells's argument, if this space is expanded, regardless of whether or not it results in greater concentration of media ownership or further commodification of user data online, competition between actors will be increased and power dispersed, generating 'media counterpower' (Castells, 2009). This understanding of pluralism may not proclaim market forces as a guarantor of freedom, but it does claim that the internet, regardless of its ever-increasing capture by corporate media, will empower sovereign audiences through the creative autonomy bestowed upon them. However, while recognizing that power always exists in multiple forms and that it would be grossly misleading to declare that the corporate purveyors of capitalism prevent counter-power from emerging, it remains crucial to recognize that different types of power have differential influence.

Equating Pluralism with Communicative Freedom

Equating pluralism with communicative freedom is often the approach taken in arguments that circulate around the 'freedom of the press'. The need for a 'free press' for democracy to flourish has a long history and emanates from a diversity of political perspectives. Its centrality and importance has seen it enshrined in political constitutions and many human rights acts and declarations. Such declarations have been translated into normative 'ideals' for media and public communication in fully functioning democracies (Keane, 1991; Curran, 2002).

> These include providing: a source of pluralist and 'objective' information widely available to all citizens, to enable citizens to vote and make other choices; a check ('watchdog role') on the activities of powerful institutions and individuals; as a 'fourth estate' balancing the power of the three institutional estates of government (Executive, Legislature and Judiciary); an arena for public deliberation and debate on the issues and policies affecting wider society; and the means by which a pluralist range of citizens and interest groups may put forward their views. (CCMR, 2011: 3)

The philosophical basis for such ideals was established at a time that differed radically from developed contemporary democratic societies.

It was a time when the state was more powerful, civil society was far smaller and the printed press was the main form of public communication. Today, the landscape looks very different. Electoral democracy and state power find their influences diluted amid competition from a range of other powerful institutions and corporate organizations. These bodies are usually less accountable than their state rivals but wield substantive influence on public media in terms of ownership and content (Miller, 2010). Alongside the complexities of multi-institutional and global corporate endeavours, numerous new forms of media have fragmented and diversified national, public forms of communication. Consequently, ensuring and maintaining a 'free press' that can fulfil all of the above ideals in the face of various institutional, corporate and other pressures is increasingly no simple task.

As Habermas noted, the ideal of a public sphere unfettered by commercial desires and pressures is hard to sustain in the midst of a privately owned press, which is more likely to favour the 'free market' and the 'free choices' of consumers as a means of increasing sales and shareholder returns. Corporate-owned and market-oriented news media may be less inclined to hold large corporations to account or question free-market policies. The lack of critical reporting of the economy and the financial market in the lead up to the most recent financial crash and global economic crisis has been argued to be illustrative of mainstream media that are too close to the system they are supposed to be holding to account (Berry, 2013; Davis, 2005). In other words, commercial media are more likely to be driven by a market rationale, leading to cheaper and shallower news coverage that may give rise to large audience figures but in the process diminish and demean decent coverage of a range of public issues.

In the UK context, over several decades, news journalism has been forced steadily to become more productive, rational and market-oriented. The Coordinating Committee for Media Reform (CCMR, 2011: 4) (now renamed the Media Reform Coalition) reports that, since the 1970s, there have been a range of trends that all point in the same direction. There is substantially more news but also greater competition and fragmentation, with fewer consumers per outlet (Tunstall, 1996; Franklin, 1997, 2005; Curran and Seaton, 2003; Davies, 2008). Global competition, market segmentation and entertainment alternatives have resulted in a steady decline of advertising revenues for most single, commercial news outlets. Consequently, national news producers have presided over a gradual downturn in audience figures over the period. In an effort to remain profitable, papers have raised prices well above inflation and increased both outputs and news sections while simultaneously cutting back on staff. Tunstall (1996) estimated that, between the 1960s and the 1990s, individual output had at least doubled. Davis (2002) recorded that, between the mid-1980s and the mid-1990s, the *Financial Times* and *The Sun* increased their pagination by just over 60 per cent but their journalist numbers by between 15 and 22 per cent. *The Times* increased in size by 125 per cent but added just 22 per cent to its editorial staff. More recently, Davies (2008) concluded that journalists now have to fill three times as much news space as they did in 1985.

The tremendous growth in the number of free newspapers, the emergence of 24-hour television news, and the popularization of online and mobile platforms, which has seen advertising revenue migrate to the likes of Craigslist and eBay, have presented the newspaper industry with some real challenges. Maintaining profit margins and shareholder returns is increasingly dependent upon the use of fewer journalists doing more work in less time to fill more space than ever before. Furthermore, for the majority of reporters in employment, working conditions have clearly become more difficult, as union recognition has declined, journalist rights have been eroded, and new working conditions have been imposed. In 2006 (NUJ, 2006), 31 per cent of journalists were found to work part-time or were on 'flexible hours' and 41 per cent were 'freelance' (see Franklin, 1997; Davies, 2008). A similar picture can be found around the globe. In the US, the Pew Research Center (2012) reported that the newspaper industry had suffered a loss of 28 per cent of journalists' jobs and 43 per cent of newspapers since 2000, with an average of fifteen papers going bankrupt each year.

Surveys of working journalists and news content suggest that both newsgathering and production have suffered in a variety of ways. One of these is the increased dependency of journalists on outside 'information subsidy' supply, in the form of public relations material and news wire copy. A study by Lewis et al. (2008) of 2,207 newsprint items and 402 broadcasts found that 19 per cent of press stories and 17 per cent of broadcasts were entirely or mainly reproduced PR material; 49 per cent of press stories were either entirely or mainly dependent on news wire agency copy, much of which had also come from press releases. Wide-ranging interview-based research with journalists (Fenton, 2010; Davis, 2010; Lee-Wright et al., 2011) also showed a series of worrying trends in the way news was gathered and reproduced and that a variety of traditional corners were being cut. These included a general propensity to rely on press releases and other PR material (often unattributed); greater pressure on multiskilling and the reproduction of stories on multiple media platforms;

rising newsroom pressures and stress levels and the replacement of experienced journalists with cheaper, inexperienced counterparts; relentless efficiency drives, leaving less time to communicate with sources directly and check information/quotes; a widespread propensity for monitoring rival news operations and then cannibalizing that coverage; and a decline in foreign, investigative and other costly forms of news coverage.

McChesney and Nichols (2010) noted that 40 to 50 per cent of newspaper stories in the US originated from press releases, with a mere 14 per cent the product of reporters' efforts. Critics have labelled the new end product 'Newszak' (Franklin, 1997), 'Infotainment' (Delli Carpini and Williams, 2001) and, most recently, 'Churnalism' (Davies, 2008) – a practice that is antithetical to deliberative engagement and the kind of public-interest values upon which the democratic public sphere depends. If the dominant public sphere is tainted by commercial imperatives, then the assumption is that democracy flounders.

However, as Habermas argued in his revisions to his public sphere thesis (1996), under such conditions civil society steps into the breach, with counter-publicity likely to emerge. We can point here to a flowering of small, cause-specific and alternative news websites that have emerged online. The problem is that counter-publicity is less likely to be heard and taken account of by political elites. Counter-public spheres are by their nature outside of and antagonistic to the dominant political system in any one instance.

So, while we may have had no end of political demonstrations with many thousands of people – Norris (2002) reports a massive increase in demonstrative politics across liberal democracies in the West, and we have witnessed more counter-publicity than we ever thought possible on the internet – yet we have more inequality (Piketty, 2013), more surveillance (Morozov, 2011; Diamond and Plattner, 2012) and more centralization of power than ever before (Jones, 2014). Even acknowledging the explosion of counter-publicity in a digital age does not necessarily translate into counter-public spheres if the point at which '[t]he balance of power between civil society and the political systems [then] shifts' (Habermas, 1996: 379) is never reached. If we focus on the enhancement of the process and quality of deliberation, but the deliberation under question has little or no impact on the 'political administrative complex', isn't the public sphere once more simply hollowed out (Fenton and Titley, 2015)? Furthermore, the political struggles that form part of the explosion of counter-publicity are often far from rational and encourage affective rather than critical responses. Civil society is not always civil. It complies better with the description of a politics of antagonism forwarded by Mouffe (2005) than a deliberative liberal pluralism suggested by Habermas (1989).

Seen from this perspective, then, equating a healthy democracy with a multiplicity of counter-publicity would appear severely misplaced. Indeed, the idea of liberal democracy stresses pluralism to such an extent that the point at which the balance shifts and power is then shared is frequently ignored. It is deemed to be enough simply to display a supermarket of views and perspectives and so present an illusion of political choice. As Tormey (2005: 399) contends, rather than integrate multiplicity and conflict into its very fabric, liberal democracy 'makes a fetish of diversity and plurality of ends', asserting the need for multiple voices to be heard and resolved through the institutions of the state that are not, in the end – in neoliberal societies at least – conducive to responding. In this manner,

> The contest of ideas and ideals is not at the heart of liberalism. It is at the heart of the rhetoric of liberalism. Values and ideals may be contested; but this does not mean that we can meaningfully contest the 'freedom' of the market, the rationality of representation, the monopolizing nature of anti-monopoly legislation, the tyranny of 'choice'. (Ibid.: 400)

Part of the problem then with a Habermasian model is that it is simply too neat both when the public sphere is deemed to be working well and when it is deemed to be failing. When it is deemed to be working well, it still cannot take account of the multiple pressures and complexities of modern political mediated life. Actually existing democracy rarely follows the rational, logical pathways that a public sphere thesis suggests. When it is going badly, it is similarly unable to account for the contemporary configurations of public life in a digital age. From a political economic perspective, we can argue in a Habermasian vein that the public realm is ever more under threat from the privatization and marketization of public services, which bring forth competitive pressures and private financial considerations into public institutions (Barnett, 2003, 2010). In the UK, the increasing privatization of higher education (Freedman and Bailey, 2011) and the National Health Service (Leys and Player, 2011) illustrates this all too well. As the quotation from Hall at the beginning of this chapter argued, it is easy to drown oneself in pessimism and claim that the direction of this particular political economic perspective wipes out all in its wake, sweeping aside discourses of citizenship and replacing them with discourses of the consumer. Market logic is argued to colonize human experience to such an extent that the ability to develop counter-rationalities, to think beyond what we know as global capitalism, is severely restricted. The public sphere, in such an analysis, is bereft.

Neoliberalism and its practices tell us that we are all individuals and should be treated as such except when we act with others (usually for free) to relieve the state of its duties. As individuals we are given rights that are translated into choice based on consumption – we have the right to choose what school our children may go to and the right to complain when our individual needs are not met. Of course these rights are not equal to all, but the rhetoric is one of equality because each person is treated as a private individual (regardless of class, gender, race or religion). Hence we are left with the contradiction that, while the discourses of equality have increased under neoliberalism, the material reality of inequality has in fact rocketed (see chapter 1) because neoliberal practice refuses to take account of the socio-structural causes of poverty.

The crucial point within neoliberal ideological frameworks of politics and their lived practices is that the individual, and hence the political individual, is defined almost entirely in economic terms, while the inadequacy of economic structures is simultaneously denied – part of the selective amnesia of neoliberalism. As accurate as this may feel, it inflates the degree to which the social has been abandoned for the economic and skips over the very many contradictions that make up the lived experience of life under neoliberalism. As such we fall foul of political economic reductionism, where the political is only ever construed as a politics of control and consensus that can be argued to contribute to the rhetoric of the unstoppable dynamic of global economic competition (even when it creates national bankruptcy).

Capitalism and Its Contradictions

Of course, anyone who has ever been involved in oppositional politics will know that these experiences are often marked by a refusal to consent to capitalism's supposed logic. Andrejevic (2013) argues that, in an information society, information produces both potentials that undermine competition and at the same time new forms of domination and competition. In other words, global, informational capitalism produces threats and opportunities. The opportunities at hand may allow for the realization of co-operation – solidarity forged through contradiction. The threat is complicity with a neoliberal stance based on market rationality. The reality is often somewhere in between. If we accept the social constructivist premise that we are all products of our environment, then it is simply impossible to locate either a 'pure' radical politics unmarred by the march of capitalism or a politics of consumption that straightforwardly reproduces capitalism's logic without recourse to a history of radical progressive political thought and action. The politics of choice that has emerged in the last two decades is based on issues of consumption, which translate into consumer activism that extends from sustainability and environmental politics (Lekakis, 2013), to politics of sexuality, to demands for changes in modes of health-care provision and other welfare services. These are indicative of the changing relationship between the individual, the state and the market. Although they are concerned largely with the moment of consumption rather than the point of production, they should not be misconstrued as straightforwardly de-politicizing (although they may be this as well). Rather, they are a part of the repoliticization of the distribution of social goods that emerges from new political economics of public life (Murray, 2004).

Nonetheless, to be a force for structural change, the spaces in which such repoliticizations can take shape must be struggled for and created in a co-ordinated and systematic fashion in order to transcend the highly co-ordinated, deftly administered and systemic limitations of the structures of capitalism. At some level the neoliberal political economics of public life must be ruptured to forge a space for the reimagination of co-operative and collective social practices to emerge. And this raises a problem. In the online mediated world of radical progressive politics, where counter-public spheres are claimed as enabling a more expansive deliberative democracy to materialize, the prospects of a co-ordinated and deftly administered counter-politics being formed often seem some way off.

Even if we accept that, through political conflict, associational networks can emerge and civil society can be established as a force for change, the problem remains: How can fragmented and multiple oppositional groupings function together for political ends? And, crucially, this must be political ends in the plural. One end point may well be the pursuit of protest in and for itself; another may be to progress from a resistant identity to a political project that is sustainable and likely to produce social change. Put another way, it is either a conception of democratic participation that conforms to the existing rules and conventions of debate or one that challenges those rules. This is the subject of constant discussion within radical oppositional political groups and organizations. Put crudely, should they be reformists accepting of the rule of representative democracy and the structures of the nation-state or revolutionaries who refuse to play by established rules and conventions, preferring to challenge and question the basis on which those rules are enacted and normalized?

This can also be related to the relevance of a Habermasian public sphere for such debates. Reformists will generally feel right at home in the conceptual space of the liberal public sphere – if you campaign hard, your voice will be heard and legal frameworks will bend to accommodate the demands that can garner the most popular support. But if the oppositional politics in question embraces a more anarchic spirit, the liberal democratic model will offer no such sense of comfort. The question these political groupings may pose is: Whose revolution and whose ideas of reform? Many contemporary counter-public spheres reject the reduction of political action to the construction of a single end point that infers a rational, exclusionary approach whereby all other potential end points are dismissed as ill-conceived or wrong. Paradoxically, then, although multiplicity and pluralism are viewed as key to a fully functioning public sphere, no such con-ferment is granted to the actual practice of the politics itself within the Habermasian liberal democratic frame.

Political action understood simply as the delivery of a homogeneous ideal (such as a democratic public sphere) removes uncertainty and unknowability and reduces politics to the 'administration of things' (Bhabha, 1994). It is seen as removing creativity from political action and ultimately sustaining the status quo. Contemporary political activists talk of constructing autonomous spaces of imagination and creativity[5] that are contingent, open and unpredictable – an attempt to escape ideological politics and move to a dialogical politics where we continually acknowledge difference and learn from others. The political premise is one of anti-reductionism that refuses a monological process or vision. Such forms of resistance are often united by a shared perception of an injustice rather than a common, determinate vision of a 'better world' that may follow.

But, as feminist theorists have noted (Fenton 2000; Spivak, 1992; Braidotti, 1991), for political efficacy there must be more than the apparent freedom that comes with embracing difference and diversity, more than just an increase of instances of mediated protest or opposition. Even if we accept the possibility for fragmented and multiple oppositional groupings that can create their own political interventions via the internet, we still have to broach the next stage: How will a politics of solidarity in difference be realized and sustained? Social solidarity can be described as a morality of co-operation, the ability of individuals to identify with one another in a spirit of mutuality and reciprocity without individual advantage or compulsion, leading to a network of individuals or secondary institutions that involve the creation of social and political bonds such as the anti-globalization movement. There must be a commitment to the value of difference that goes beyond a simple respect and involves an inclusive politics of voice and representation. It also requires a non-essentialist conceptualization of the political subject as made up of manifold, fluid identities that mirror the multiple differentiations of groups.

Such mediated solidarity is evident in the research of social movement theorists. As noted in chapter 4, Tarrow and della Porta (2005: 237) refer to people and groups situated in specific national contexts but involved in transnational networks of contacts and conflicts that operate both online and offline as 'rooted cosmopolitans' with 'multiple belongings' and 'flexible identities' (Keck and Sikkink, 1998; della Porta and Diani, 1999). Tormey notes that the politics at play here favours a praxis of micro-power and a micro-politics of and in everyday life directed against the master-signifier of ideological thought and 'by extension the coalescence of revolutionary struggle around some agreed place that it was the task of the "movement" to build or construct' (Tormey, 2005: 403).

We can also see this perspective echoed in Deleuze and Guattari's *A Thousand Plateaus* (1988: 469–73), which argues against 'majoritarianism' – the notion that there must be some scheme, project, goal or telos around which 'we' can be united, preferring a minoritarian stance that pursues 'univocity' and rejects the ultimately essentialist and pointless search for a universal blueprint. In order to resist incorporation into the dominant ideal, there is a necessity to generate spaces in which micro-politics can become established and thrive. Such spaces of affinity and creativity, according to Deleuze and Guattari, have the potential to develop an activist rhizomatics – a network of micro-politics that can converge, multiply and develop without an ideology or a strategy – a space that is predicated on learning, solidarity and proliferation. In response to the anti-globalization movement, this has been referred to as 'swarming', whereby networks of affinity and association integrate and form multiple resistances and actions. In other words, the *space* of political activity is enlarged and the rhizome extends outwards, drawing in difference and plurality and embracing uncertainty. Solidarity spreads on the basis of a shared sense of injustice rather than a shared vision of an alternative world. Similarly, Virno (2004), in his theorizations of the 'multitude', claims such spaces as the 'right of resistance' – a community that is antagonistic in its collectivity.

Networks of resistance are criticized for being fragmentary, for being without a political project and therefore politically ineffective – where can they go to without a unifying narrative to take them there? – when so often a unifying narrative is precisely what such groups and alliances want to resist. These networks speak to a passion of disagreement, conflict and antagonism – a post-foundational politics that proffers a different experience of being political that does not fit with our standard liberal democratic interpretations of what politics should be.

These arguments, many of which I have sympathy with, suffer from one major limitation – they are framed by a particular understanding of democracy that accepts existing institutional structures of representational politics and applies a liberal pluralism model of democratic practice inherent in certain established approaches to Habermasian thought. Arguments such as these are based on an understanding of liberal democracy that functions primarily through established political parties, which are directly at odds with a radical politics that has rejected establishment politics and so will never be able to explore their political strengths or adequately interpret their lessons.

Contemporary transnational social movements are a combination of collective action and public debate. The spaces of action and debate take place on many levels, often all at once – from the hyper-local, to the regional and national, to 'global' counter-summits – all mediated by the internet (alongside other media forms). As noted in chapter 2, one of the striking differences between the counter-publicity of contemporary transnational social movements and the counter-politics of the nation-state is the lack of common identity and the rejection of unifying meta-narratives of organization. It is a movement of movements, a network of networks.

So how do we begin to take account of the contemporary radical politics of the multitude? How can the left learn from these hopes and desires for rethinking democratic formations? Stengers (2010) points to the very real dangers of translating the joys and compulsions of multiplicity into either liberal tolerance of difference that prevents substantive questions from being asked (such as who holds the balance of power and whose voice gets heard) or anarchic, autonomous and ultimately individualistic politics that prevents substantive change from happening because it insists on existing outside of institutional frameworks and constitutional structures. Stengers's vision in her discussion of science is radically democratic: science is not a transcending 'truth' but one of many 'interests' that constantly need to negotiate with one another. This can only happen if all the competing interests are taken seriously (not merely tolerated) and are actively able to intervene with and against one another on an equal footing. In this critical democratic constellation, the myriad mediations of radical progressive politics may refuse both to offer a vision of a unified collectivity and to stand for a solidarity premised on individual peculiarities and desires (the reverse of solidarity) and insist, rather, on the painstaking and organized struggle to reclaim the state as a force to be used against neoliberalism and its corporate beneficiaries.

Conclusion

What public sphere theory can tell us is that we should not isolate any one particular medium (e.g., the internet), with its own technical characteristics, from the entire social and political context and communicative realm. However, the tendency in public sphere frameworks to elide pluralism with communicative freedom, and to posit the linear correlation of access-communicative freedom/pluralism-political participation, relegates the influence of 'power over' in an overenthusiastic embrace of the 'power to'. This runs the risk of reducing power to an individual resource that is purely relational and behavioural, and one that will always overemphasize technology to the detriment of social, political and economic context. In its poorest manifestation, this descends into 'clicktivism' – signing online petitions, writing dissenting blogs and sending political tweets that, as Dean has argued, are fully recuperable in a context where 'rhetorics of access, participation and democracy work ideologically to secure the technological infrastructure of neoliberalism, an invidious and predatory politico-economic project that concentrates assets and power in the hands of the very, very rich, devastating the planet and destroying the lives of billions of people' (Dean, 2009: 23).

However, we also know from Williams (1961) that agency and intention are crucial aspects of change and cultural evolution. Expanded communicative freedom, working in a non-stratified and diffuse manner, can unsettle and destabilize power relations under certain conditions. These multiple, often contradictory practices of counter-politics bear witness to a Foucauldian micro-politics or a Deleuzian rhizomatic politics rooted in the knowledge that every person is a plurality, every group a multitude of differences, all operating at varying levels in a complexity of matrices at any one time. It is easy to see how this strikes a chord with a networked politics of the digital age built on recognition of individual difference but common cause, however loosely articulated. But it is difficult to imagine how this will converge into new forms of democratic thinking without a fuller, integrated account of the concomitant assault on the public evacuation of representative democratic agency.

As Norval (2007: 102) reminds us, we must avoid 'assum[ing] the existence of a framework of politics in which in principle every voice could be heard, without giving attention to the very structuring of those frameworks and the ways in which the visibility of subjects is structured.' Creative autonomy is pretty difficult to express under conditions of material poverty, exploitation and oppression. Individual particularities and political desires alone, even if they are articulated together and facilitated by new communication technologies, will not reclaim and rebuild the institutions necessary to reveal and sustain a new political order.

Benkler (2006) points to a further problem: as we see an expansion in terms of available communicative spaces for politics, we also encounter extended ideological breadth and reach. In focusing on a politics of identity and difference that feeds a myriad of counter-public spheres, we can easily lose sight of larger issues of power in society and the world, fostering an inwardly oriented fixation on the individual groups' interests. Moreover, if carried too far, such patterns threaten to undercut a shared public culture; various groups develop little contact with – or understanding of – one another and become less capable of building alliances that could be politically effective, resulting in what Sunstein (2001) calls the 'Daily Me' that renders the public sphere a very personal one and undermines its efficacy.

Approaches that recognize the many ways in which individuals are creatively empowered and emphasize the astonishing array of micro-politics at play at any one time remind us that the politics of recognition and the importance of voice (Couldry, 2010) are critical to the felt experience of politics. It can also increase contestability through broadening the range of conflictual content online – a vital political act. But acknowledging this should not give way to a fetishization of notions of plurality and communicative freedom that remain encompassed by the wider politics of neoliberalism. Democracy conceived of as access to a range of communication and information can only ever take us so far. Pluralism, as a value and set of practices, poses no threat to the neoliberal discourses that can be seen as a powerful and largely successful attempt to reshape the direction of travel of the political for a whole generation, normalizing the individualizing subjectivities that saturate much life and action online, even though this may be constantly under challenge. Pluralism does not automatically transcend global capitalism, and communicative freedom is not a given, even in the digital age.

Discussions that return to notions of the public sphere, to pluralism, and to communicative freedom must take account of the contemporary transformations in global capitalism and representative democratic systems. Unless these consequences are named, claims to enhancing freedom and supporting democracy remain limited to the 'media side' of an equation that must be critiqued in its totality. This does not mean that we should revert to a political-economic form of determinism but, instead, points to a need to attend with care to the relations of power among people, state institutions, corporate bodies and markets. The rhetoric of liberal democracy that insists we have more choice and more creative control, and that the public sphere is radically expanded, must confront how neoliberal hegemony organizes 'states and subjects...by market rationality' (Brown, 2005) in ways that place considerable stress on established ideological imaginations. Only then will we be able to liberate ourselves from the strictures of liberal democratic insistences that have been evacuated of almost all democratic intent and start the difficult job of translating the passions and desires of radical progressive politics into new material political and democratic formations. It is to these abiding passions and desires that the next two chapters turn.

4

Passion and Politics: Radical Politics and Mediated Subjects

The previous chapter argues that many studies that seek to investigate the political in relation to the media have taken as their approach a particular type of Habermasian framework. In doing so, such studies are restrained by a type of liberal deliberative democratic practice as the main aim or end point for political engagement, which poses a limitation on the possibilities for understanding what it means to be political and cannot take account of any politics that situates itself outside of liberal democratic frameworks. A Habermasian approach to the public sphere rests on an understanding of liberal pluralism as ultimately a quest for consensus politics – a desire to discuss and deliberate on public issues and reach a common understanding of the way forward, based on 'a procedure to which all consent' (Habermas, 1996: 496). The process is one of reaching constitutional agreement. But what if the politics under consideration is based on the notion that agreement is not always possible or even desirable?

This chapter points to further limitations in public sphere theory regarding both the conceptualization of the political subject as a rational individual and the political system as a rational process that functions on the basis of consensus and the assumption that this will then result in policy reform that conforms to the will of the majority. Retaining an emphasis on multiple viewpoints or a plurality of political cultures or potential solutions (as in much contemporary radical politics) does not fit with a model of deliberative democracy. From a Habermasian perspective, to insist on the multiplicity of subject positions and to resist socialization into a common political culture is to break down into fragmentation and dissolution of the political – one group's oppositional politics is neutralized by another's in a reductive competition of activism. To avoid interpreting multiplicity as fragmentation and dispersal of political efficacy and, rather, to define it as an inclusive politics of difference and diversity, we need to consider concepts of democracy and forms of politics that may well be deliberative and participatory but are also *agonistic* (see Mouffe, 2005). To be able to deliberate we must have the ability to choose between different types of political praxis; to be able to participate fully we must have both the socio-economic capacity and the cultural capital. If we think of protest as being a crucial element in political deliberation – political struggle and agonism as being at the heart of politics – then we may also begin to reimagine democracy as a radical and plural project.

This chapter will discuss this argument in detail and, in doing so, will not only challenge liberal deliberative concepts of democracy as being appropriate to critiquing certain forms of radical, progressive politics but also stress the necessity for understanding the intersubjective bases for experiencing politics as part and parcel of understanding democratic participation better. Previous chapters have stressed the importance of deep context and the need to situate any examination of radical politics in socio-economic, political and technological histories. But politics is also about passion. It refers to individuals' personal histories as much as it does to the context in which such personal journeys take place. As such, politics is always social. The practices of both mainstream and radical politics are bounded and structured in particular ways that limit and constrain the politics in play (this is discussed further in chapter 6).

Nonetheless, we cannot miss noticing that radical politics is all around us: the protests in Hong Kong for democratic elections, the 15M movement in Spain and the growth of the left-wing Podemos party (see chapter 6), even the referendum for Scottish independence in the UK and the election of Jeremy Corbyn (a self-proclaimed socialist with an anti-austerity platform) as leader of the Labour Party. We know that there are many attempts to create spaces protected from colonization by capital calculation – alternative spaces for progressive political voices such as the Occupy movement and public-sector strikes. And much digital content also provides the means not only to legitimate but to challenge, resist and counter the hegemony of a neoliberal political-economic order. These constitute alternative bids for political meaning and value and, swimming against the rip-tide of global capitalism, often seek to establish politics in common – the ability and will of 'the people' to come together, organize and construct a collective politics for the general good, against an individualist and corporate agenda. Such alternative bids are necessarily affective. They stir political passions. Social practices cannot be reduced to more or less resistant effects of reproduction as shaped by the interests of capital. Gramsci's phrase 'pessimism of the intellect, optimism of the will' (1971) speaks to this paradox. We need to understand where and how this optimism is maintained; we need to appreciate the passion of politics in order to understand better our political futures. Key to understanding the relationship between radical politics and social change, and the role of media therein, is recognizing the part of the individual and their responses to and motivations regarding radical politics.

The Political 'Subject'

The notion of the 'subject' is part of a long-standing philosophical debate. Descartes' famous phrase 'I think, therefore I am' expresses the idea of a sovereign subject totally transparent to itself and firmly rational and is one of the foundations of modernity and a cornerstone of the Enlightenment. It also underlies many nineteenth-century emancipatory movements, such as liberalism, Marxism and anarchism, which see autonomous, free-thinking, agentic individuals in full possession of their independence as the key to our liberated futures. There are, of course, important differences between these movements in how they construe the subject in other ways. In *The German Ideology*, Marx proposed that, as we are historical beings, our subjectivity is composed from particular social arrangements that constitute our basic material productive relations. Subjectivity is then a dynamic process in which the subject comes to itself from an engagement with the external social environment. Because our consciousness and our sensibilities as moral and intellectual beings are constituted in the socio-structural environment over time, all subjectivity is intersubjective (Nelson, 2011) and open to change. This is part of what endows Marxism with a transformative politics – new kinds of subject can emerge as a consequence of our conditions and experiences of them.

Other Marxist theorists see subjectivity from a more totalizing ideological perspective. Dean (2014) points out that, for Althusser, subjectivity is an effect of the larger ideological structure. Thus the subject for Althusser relies on a conception of the 'unitary "identity" of the individual' (Hirst, 1976: 400) that does not acknowledge class struggle and hence cannot account for clashes of political identities and views. In this vein, Rancière claims that Althusser misses what was clear to Marx: ideological forms 'are the forms in which a struggle is fought out' (2011b: 149). Althusser also stands accused of seeing the subject (a thinking being with the capacity to act based on their own decisions but situated in social contexts with others and in structures and systems that shape their subjectivity) as interchangeable with the 'individual' (otherwise conceived of as a singular person dissociated from conditions that are social and collective and disembedded from histories of systems of exploitation). This is why ultimately, for Althusser, an individual is, in the face of ideological structures of capitalism, without agency.

The theorization of liberalism takes the notion of the individual largely as atomistic and ahistorical and places it at its centre. Liberalism decrees individual freedom and personal autonomy as fundamental moral priorities. It sees the protection and enhancement of the freedom of the individual to be the central problem of politics and the purpose of government, while also recognizing that government can itself pose a threat to liberty. The extent of the role of government in the protection and enhancement of freedom is what distinguishes the various strands of liberalism from each other. At one extreme, libertarians believe that, the less 'interference' from the state, the better and more 'free' the individual, whereas modernist liberalism is rather more interventionist, understanding the removal of poverty, disease, discrimination and inequality as key to government's role in the promotion of freedom. A central tenet of modern liberal thought is that our capacity for rational thinking has given us the unique ability to separate ourselves from our socio-historical conditions. We are not subjects constructed by socio-historical context; rather, we are able to make conscious, rational choices as individuals unhindered by what has gone before and what now is.[1]

To understand people's relationship to any politics, then, requires an understanding of the intersubjective basis of meaning and rationality, as this will influence how we conceive of democracy. If we believe, for example, in the autonomous-rational subject as the active agent in a political democracy, and we believe that a complete transparency of meaning is always possible, then our politics can concur with the pursuit of consensus via representation. Citizens of the world read and analyse all the information around them and come to a view that is communicated to their various political representatives, who then rationally take it into account. But, if we accept that as political subjects we are rarely autonomous and often irrational, and that complete transparency of meaning may be an aim but one that is constantly undermined and frequently distorted by vested interests, then the pursuit of a politics of consensus and the ideal of representative politics becomes more problematic.

Feminist theorists (see Scott, 1996) have long since criticized the notion of rationality as the defining feature of the subject for embodying an entirely male-gendered concept of the subject and one that emphasizes individual subjectivity over collective subjectivity (Dean, 2014). No one individual exists in isolation from others, and the notion of freedom will differ for each – one person's terrorist may indeed be another person's freedom fighter, and one person's feminism may not be to another's liking. In other words, there is no single unitary, rational subject. Adorno and Horkheimer (1973) underline this point by illustrating the many ways in which 'reason' has been complicit in some of the worst crimes against humanity, such as the gas chambers in the Second World War. So the subject as something possessing a singular and rational identity has been challenged from many quarters.

A unitary, rational subject has also been heavily criticized for being essentialist – in other words, for assuming that this is the 'natural' way to be and a state to which we are all born in equal measure. The move away from an essentialist position has been hugely important to feminist theorizing in denaturalizing patriarchy (male domination is not a given) and problematizing traditional conceptions of sexual identities. The distinction between 'men' and 'women' is a historical construct that cannot hope to account for the complexity of the sexual situation of any one individual at any one time. For Judith Butler (1990), all sexual identities are unfixed, floating categories to the extent that the notion of identity itself is problematic, as in denaturalizing some identities we often find ourselves naturalizing others. This results in vexatious categories that trap individuals in sexual identities and practices that limit our potential. By extension, a non-identity politics cannot have a unitary subject. This can be further illustrated by reference to the development of feminism as a movement that in its earlier formations sought to be representative of all 'women' as an oppressed unitary category. The notion that one version of women's oppression can represent all women has been deemed deeply problematic and exclusionary to the extent that Butler rejects all forms of representational politics (see chapter 5), preferring to focus on the overthrow of the structures of oppression rather than on the subjects of politics. For example, she is critical of demands for gay and lesbian marriage that threaten to reinforce an institution on which patriarchy is based and exclude those who may be more oppressed as a result; she argues instead that no special civil or fiscal rights should be conferred by marriage.

Identifying the political and the subject of the political is itself a deeply political act with consequences for how we conceive of political systems. Classical Marxism presented a unified theory with the working class as *the* political subject; this was then developed into the notion of a planned economy as an alternative to capitalism (see chapter 5). At the poststructuralist extreme there is no unified political subject; rather, we find a type of Deleuzian truism that every person is a multiplicity, every group a myriad of differences, all operating at varying levels in a complexity of matrices at any one time. In other words, the subject is conceived not as rational and singular but as multiple and contradictory.

Many contemporary theorizations of oppositional political movements take a poststructuralist view that 'decentres' the subject (Terranova, 2004; Day, 2005), which in turn reflects on their practice of politics. There are, of course, a great variety of types of radical politics and political activists. But the likes of Occupy (see chapter 7) did eschew the notion of membership or citizenship more readily associated with the liberal democratic model. Indeed, the Occupy movement was premised on the belief that legislative models of governance or a representative model of election had failed. It was partly a rejection of conventional liberal democratic processes that attracted activists to it – it was different from conventional state-bound politics and it also endeavoured to embrace difference in its practices and configurations (although how successful it was is debatable) (Castells, 2015). If an emergent politics could be identified within Occupy, then it was a politics of non-representation that refused to accept that one view can encompass all and sought to instil into its decision-making practices a multiplicity of experiences that were recognized as contradictory and contingent.

However, the danger in this embrace of multiplicity is the poststructuralist political conundrum that all distinctions threaten to collapse into 'a boundary-less primeval soup of either the impossibility of knowing anything or a relativistic knowledge that everything counts' (Hughes, 2011: 428). This may well allow for different identities and social organizations to co-exist, but it cannot explain how and why a particular set of hegemonic norms emerges from such a constellation. Neither, then, can it deliver democratic political systems or new economic orders. As Brown has said, Foucault, in giving us such a sophisticated and elaborate interpretation of the powers that structure and constrain us, has made it very difficult to imagine how we can democratize those powers apart from at the level of individual conduct and ethics through micro-powers. If micro-power is everywhere it is difficult to locate anywhere. As a consequence, we find ourselves seduced by a Foucauldian, Derridean, Levinasian and Deleuzian thinking that has 'derailed democratic thinking in that it has pushed it off onto a path of thinking about how I conduct myself, what is my relation to the other, what is my ethos or orientation toward those who are different from me' (Brown, in Celikates and Jansen, 2013: 5). Nonetheless, such thinking has provided an important impetus for many contemporary social movements keen to avoid the authoritarian tendencies of a left politics of old (Whyte, 2013). But it has also infuriated those impatient for change and who see as politically pointless the refusal even to seek to claim political power through electoral processes in preference to a healthy commons from which a strong, inclusive, civil society can influence political cultures and decisions (Holloway, 2002). Micro-power is no match for corporate capitalism.

In the most extreme interpretation of Foucault's theory of micro-power, Badiou (2012, 2013) at once claims a revolutionary revival, with the raft of protests, riots and uprisings that erupted in many parts of the world in 2011, which quickly turns to radical pessimism as he sees the resistance shown being generated and used by power, in the face of which the left, he claims, is impotent. This dreary outlook is shared by many radical theorists who were initially cheered by the possibility of a resurgence of the left, only to find themselves retreating to a position of gloom and cynicism as they reflected on the subsequent lack of progressive political transformation. Žižek (2012: 127) wrote that 2011 (the year of the Arab Spring uprisings) 'was the year of *dreaming* dangerously ... now a year later, every day brings new evidence of how fragile and inconsistent that awakening was.' Although Žižek (2013) went on to adjust his evaluation to embrace a rather more hopeful outlook with the success of the Greek Syriza party (see chapter 6) in the Greek national elections in 2015, his initial gloom is echoed in Caygill's (2013: 208) concluding sentence to his book on resistance: 'Resistance is engaged in defiant delegitimization of existing and potential domination but without any prospect of a final outcome in the guise of a revolutionary or reformist result or solution ... The politics of resistance is disillusioned and without end.'

This general pessimism falls back on the structuring forces of neoliberalism and the lack of any real political alternative emerging. Rancière (1999) outlines the possible ways in which politics can deteriorate. He refers to 'archi-politics', whereby internal contradictions are rendered invisible, as in totalitarianism (of the left or right). He also talks of a 'para-politics' that sees the depoliticization of public issues, such as when neoliberal solutions are proffered as the 'only' rational response in an attempt to remove the conflictual dimension of politics and so squeeze it dry. One example here would be the free-market response to an economic crisis that is partly the result of the very same economics. A third potential threat is meta-politics – in this formulation there may be some form of recognition of the existence of irreducible conflicts in the community, but these are then situated outside of politics.

Meta-politics is probably the most common form of political degradation in nations with advanced capitalism. A contemporary example of this would be the Transatlantic Trade and Investment Partnership (TTIP) – a comprehensive free trade and investment treaty currently being negotiated – in secret – between the European Union and the US. The main goal of TTIP is to remove regulatory 'barriers' which restrict the potential profits to be made by trans-national corporations on both sides of the Atlantic. These 'barriers' are some of our most prized social standards and environmental regulations, such as labour rights, food safety rules, regulations on the use of toxic chemicals, digital privacy laws, and even new banking safeguards introduced to prevent a repeat of the 2008 financial crisis. Yet, in a corporate neoliberal pact, democratic institutions become economic ones captured by the requirements of transnational traders and at once remove any sense of politics and therefore of the public from some of the most crucial decisions that govern our lives. At the time of going to press, it is not yet clear whether TTIP will succeed, but it threatens to embed further the structural division between the public power of the polity and the private power of the economy.

Miller (2014) takes this a stage further, noting that elite and corporate power often occur behind our backs. His argument stresses that power is built in places we do not know about rather than those we actively or even unconsciously consent to. So theories that see publics as holding a fundamental legitimating role in liberal democracies entirely miss the point that, in fact, our consent is now needed only in particular circumstances. More often, strong, popular, widespread, even global protest can be and frequently is entirely ignored by the powerful. Miller points to the global protests over the Iraq War, involving millions of people worldwide, having no effect. These are conflicts which have no political place or consequence or, worse, which serve up an illusion of democracy and a fantasy of politics – a convenient distraction for those involved from where power really lies.

As politics is frequently undermined by the above processes, we can deduce that actual politics and genuine democracy are rare. But, while subjects will always be subjected to dominant power, individual and collective subjectivities similarly emerge from relations of power. Individual and collective identities emerge from resistance:

> When an unemployed youth realizes that his condition is a symptom of the disease of the socio-economic system and not his own failure; when a sans papiers immigrant realizes that her predicament is the symptom of a political and juridical system that divides and excludes; when a lesbian realizes that the suppression of her sexuality is a symptom of a system of disciplining and controlling bodies; at that point, subjects of resistance emerge. (Douzinas, 2015: 92)

The emergence of subjects of resistance is usually accompanied by a huge sense of injustice of a wrong that must be righted. It is wrong that my family should live in poverty and go hungry because of austerity measures that are nothing to do with me; it is wrong that I have no access to free health care; it is wrong that the state should destroy a public park or increase bus fares; it is wrong that I am discriminated against because of my race, sexuality, gender, religion, etc. This does not usually arrive with a formally worked-out plan of how justice can be claimed and applied universally, although it may result in specific claims relating to particular concerns. So it should come as no surprise that a unified left radical front does not immediately spring forth. But it is only through particular acts of resisting local configurations of power that the seeds of an alternative normative position can be sown, that the realization that 'another world is possible' can come into being which then requires the engagement of a broader public.

The indignation that begins this process of resistance is the felt experience of the resisting subject against abuses of power and the injustices of the existing order. Being outside of power, disenfranchised and excluded is where we can find an agonistic universality, since many and diverse people are in such positions. As Douzinas (2015: 96) states, 'Collective resistance becomes political and may succeed in radically changing the balance of forces when it condenses different causes, a multiplicity of struggles and local and regional complaints, bringing them together in a common place and concurrent time.' Condensing different causes and a multiplicity of struggles will always incur dissymmetry and agonism. In Foucault's (2004: 39) words, 'The subject that speaks is a warring – I won't even say a polemical – subject.' But this dissymmetry and disagreement importantly does not preclude collective political subjectivity; rather, it is fundamental to it.

Political Affect

Theories of affect have become increasingly popular as a way of conceptualizing and analysing the interrelational production of forms of
subjectivity (Clough, 2008; Blackman et al., 2008; Venn, 2009;
Blackman, 2012), largely on account of the ways in which they seek
to theorize the complex relationship between the social and the psychological. My own first awareness of the importance of affect came
as an undergraduate student studying Ernst Bloch. After what felt like
the endless pessimism of much of the Frankfurt School, here suddenly
was a theorist with hope, and a desire to understand what hope meant
and where it came from, and could therefore engender hope in me.
Bloch (1988) saw the subject as constantly unfinished and being made,
and hence the future as not yet known. As a wonderful antidote to
pessimism, my own immediate response to Bloch was to be affected,
which led me to recognize for the first time the importance of social
and political imaginaries – dreams of what might be as a means of
encouraging the disruption and transformation of what is.

  Bloch distinguishes between dreams that are more abstract and
immature (utopia as wishful thinking without any wilful application
to change) and those which are more concrete and focused on real
possibilities. Levitas (1998: 67) argues that, '[W]hilst abstract utopia
may express desire, only concrete utopia carries hope.' For Bloch, the
process of extracting concrete hope from the abstract, wilfully turning
abstract hope into concrete proposals, is what he calls *docta spes*: 'a
methodical organ for the New, an objective aggregate form of what
is coming up' (Bloch, [1959] 1996: 157). So, as hope is socially constructed, it is also not yet determined. This unfinished feature of hope
brings together feelings and cognition, as well as opening up the
necessity for experimentation, and leads Levitas to state that 'it operates as a dialectic between reason and passion' (1998: 70). Levitas
goes on to argue that the *docta spes* is a highly normative concept
that relies on a notion of the good society and what should comprise
it. This makes sense, but then much of the work of the Frankfurt
School openly acknowledged the need for normativity to do critical
theory (see chapter 1). Critical theory is, after all, evaluative. What
Bloch's approach encourages is attention to the *process* of thinking
about social and political change in which hoping for something
better disrupts the here and now through the endless possibilities of
what could be. The frequently asserted motto of the anti-globalization/
global justice movement of 'another world is possible' clearly speaks
to this hopefulness. As Giroux argues: 'Rather than seeing it as an

individual proclivity, we must see hope as part of a broader politics that acknowledges those social, economic, spiritual and cultural conditions in the present that make certain kinds of agency and democratic politics possible' (2004: 38; cited in Ellis and Tucker, 2011: 443).

Of course, the need to move from abstract to concrete utopia with the wilful application of ideas for change has been one of the (often unfairly attributed) criticisms of the Occupy movement and the anti-globalization movement before it. A different way of approaching this via Bloch would be to understand that such movements emerge from particular socio-economic configurations which themselves form an affective engagement with what might be and offer hopeful surges into the future. Protests contain a mixture of anger, frustration and sadness amid a cornucopia of feelings of injustice. They may contain moments of joy and elation as well as fear and intimidation. They may change nothing. But they may signal other not yet realized possibilities – just as the Zapatista movement was said to inspire the anti-globalization movement, which was said to inspire the Indigna-dos in Spain, which was said to inspire the Occupy movement, which was said to inspire pro-democracy movements across the Middle East. Whatever we think, it is hard to deny that affect somehow plays a part and cannot be glibly discounted.

There are many differences between Bloch and the contemporary theories of affect (which are themselves highly differentiated).[2] Most contemporary approaches are based on the notion that 'activity is produced through relational forces that exist between bodies, rather than driven by internalised drives' (Ellis and Tucker, 2011: 436). Many theorists have focused on how this process ends with a posi-tioning of the subject. Massumi (2002), however, prefers to concen-trate on the movement within the process. In doing so, he emphasizes the relations between people as key, the 'not yet' known as opening up the possibilities for change within the process. Bloch was trying to do something similar through proposing a process-oriented under-standing of subjectivity that is open and forward-looking – a process that involves both reason and passion.

Recognizing that passion is a critical element of politics means also accepting that passion is simultaneously part of reason. Deleting one then deletes much of what the other consists of. Passions motivate and inform all political life. Politicians clearly understand this, and political rhetoric is employed in an attempt to maximize affective political responses. Indeed, both pessimistic and optimistic accounts of radical politics outlined in this book are fed by their own affective responses which feed into philosophical rationales. When dealing with affect, we must similarly take account of the very many ways an affective register is called upon to legitimize and sustain contemporary neoliberal politics of austerity. Lauren Berlant (2010a: 3) describes how

> The attempt to associate democracy with austerity – a state of liquidity being dried out, the way wine dries out a tongue – is fundamentally antidemocratic. The demand for the people's austerity hides processes of the uneven distribution of risk and vulnerability. Democracy is supposed to hold out for the equal distribution of sovereignty and risk. Still, austerity sounds good, clean, ascetic: the lines of austerity are drawn round a polis to incite it toward askesis, toward managing its appetites and taking satisfaction in a self-management in whose mirror of performance it can feel proud and superior.

As the capacity to affect and to be affected is situated in history, so it is not equally available to all or distributed evenly. Theorists of affect still, then, point to structures of power as able to naturalize social relations and reproduce dominance – there is bad affect just as there is good affect (Berlant, 2010b; Thrift, 2007). As Gilbert (2014: 68) notes, we are still left with the 'problems of populism and the facts of fascism'. But the dual emphasis on 'becoming' and process also points to disruption, interruption and suspension, with the possibility of recasting power relations. However, the dangers are not dissimilar to those that have gone before – theories of affect can be employed in any form to suit any approach, taking us in ever-increasing circles but never getting anywhere; as the affective has been used to reproduce power, so it can be used to express agency, but this affective agency in and of itself does not transform political systems. What theories of affect can do is help us to understand what motivates, accelerates and sustains political activity of a particular kind, to enable us better to appreciate political participation and the nature, form and consequences of contemporary oppositional politics. What theories of affect cannot do is recast democracy with its liberal limitations removed and take on board anti-essentialist ideas, agonistic approaches and what the practical interpretations of a radical plurality might be.

The Social Media Mix: The Political Is Personal

One of the resounding successes of the feminist movement has been to force the recognition that the personal is political. This is closely related to the above debates. If a political subject exists in the public sphere only as in the earliest formulations of a Habermasian ideal of liberal democracy, then it excludes many women. The feminist movement fought hard to gain acknowledgement that what happens in the domestic or private lives of citizens is political – the division of labour within the home, the economics of the household and domestic abuse are a few of the very many issues that contribute to the oppression of women and require political solutions.

The public sphere is also implicated in the debates outlined above on the private self. The neoliberal subject is the basis for the promotion of and quest for individual economic self-gain. The stress on the individual in theories of liberalism erodes the practices and values of non-commercial society and institutions – those that rely upon collectivity, solidarity, trust, cohesion, social duty and responsibility. A market society, just like any other society, requires norms, values and practices to hold it together, to provide the stability that is required for capitalism to thrive. The conflict between the public and the private individual, the public and the private spheres, creates tensions and contributes towards a political dynamic that is bound up with the difficult relationship between the social and the communal. As the contradictions in neoliberalism become ever starker with the increasing mismatch between the discourses of freedom – anyone can be a television star; anyone can be a business tycoon or an internet entrepreneur – and the reality of gross inequality and lack of freedom become more and more apparent (see chapter 1), so the tension between our private and collective selves is ever greater manifest.

The internet and cultures of convergence are also said to add to the tension and contradictions between the private and the public. The conflation of symbols and/or practices we have come to associate with the realms of the social, cultural, economic and political is argued to blend and blur, so that they become more open to disruption and change (Andrejevic, 2004; Castells, 2009). The thoroughly mediated space of citizenship is colonized by activities that combine the social, commercial, political and cultural but do not define them in isolation. So blogs may offer politically concentrated coverage and link to an array of video and/or photo sharing sites, but they do so from a highly personalized perspective (Papacharissi, 2010b). This is not, of course, a new trend, but it is intensified by the architecture of the online world, which renders these categorizations more easily fluid and slippery. What was once reserved for the hard news sections of certain newspapers now litters our social media.

The thoroughly mediated spaces of our contemporary citizenships are colonized by activities that combine the social, commercial, political and cultural all at once. In other words, to search for spaces or activities that are purely political is probably meaningless. Just as feminist theory has pointed out, politics is everywhere and touches on all aspects of life. The personalized media environments typical of blogs and social media postings may have a limited contribution to the 'greater good' objectives of the public sphere. But the unique contribution of such mediated interventions may lie not in enabling progressive political transformation but, rather, in challenging the premises upon which mainstream politics rests. Their function is expressive first and deliberative by accident. And, as the boundaries between the public and the private bleed, blur and reform, it is argued that a new set of socio-political habits develop. This brings to the fore, once more, debates on the very notion of what is meant by 'the political'. Mouffe (in Miessen, 2007: 2) argues that liberal thought has never been able to identify the

> specificity of the political. When liberals intend to speak about politics, they think either in terms of economics – and that would definitely be the aggregative model – or in terms of morality, and this represents the deliberative model. But what is specific to the political always eludes liberal thought. I consider this as a serious shortcoming because to be able to act in politics one needs to understand what is the dynamic of the political.

Understanding the 'dynamic of the political' certainly requires a more complex grasp of social change. In an attempt to do just this, Bauman (1999, 2000) describes a world where affiliations with discourses of state, religion, morality, etc., are no longer static – where relationships with social practices are constantly re-examined and re-formed. In this liquid modernity the political becomes more elusive, as there are no longer sites that are anchored to politics. This leads Bauman to express concern over the narcissism involved in the politics of self-interest. The liquid citizen, possessing autonomy and flexibility, is deeply and constantly dissatisfied because their autonomy is given only on the basis that it is groundless. It is not related to anything specific but elusively floats around an ever-changing amalgamation of everything without anywhere to anchor. This is an ever-moving autonomy without institutional foundations. The digitally enabled citizen may have found new forms of political expression which may, as yet, develop into new forms of political consciousness, but with no resting place for this consciousness to settle and take root. In other words, Bauman desires an anchor where none exists, in a similar way to Caygill's desperate denunciation of current politics of resistance being 'without end' (2013: 208).

Others see this liquid citizen as gaining control in an online world. Papacharissi (2010a), following on from Benkler (2006), argues that we exist in a social realm of mass-produced images and symbols dominated by consumption wherein the self is the one constant that has some control in shaping these experiences. Donath (2007) argues that the communicative experience of social media is based on a sense of participation which is claimed to offer a sense of ownership that incurs emotional involvement through a commonly shared understanding of protocol and conduct that frames the network and speaks to identities that are reflexive, mobile and performative. Communicative involvement is the primary motivation, and its aim is to perform the self anywhere at any time. Clearly, communication is never just about the act of communicating, and communicational desires and informational requirements often overlap. But in social networking the need to be linked in, to feel at once connected and in control of your forms of interaction and means of self-expression, and, ultimately, for the creative promotion of self, is argued to gain in importance.

This resonates with many people's knowledge and practice of social media and brings to the fore the affective dimension of communication that is critical to our understanding of contemporary mediated experiences. Social media, communication led rather than content driven, highlights the psychological and personal incentives of interaction and participation over and above the politics of media content for public consumption. It is a form of communication that is, above all, connective, and this has tended to dominate much of the early writing on it. Because it is social and is felt to begin with the individual user choosing to communicate with whomsoever they desire, it also confers a high degree of autonomy to the communicator. This apparent increased sociality is said to give rise to new understandings, as we are subjected to a wider range of viewpoints and encouraged to deliberate freely within a variety of networks. The enhanced autonomy is said to engender improved levels of power and control to the user. This in turn is said to bring about a type of cultural citizenship in response to a crisis of belonging attributed to a decline in traditional forms of civic engagement, the erosion of the news sphere, and the permeation of consumption into all aspects of everyday life (Miller, 2008).

If we accept the argument that digital media work to blur the boundaries of the personal and the political as we click and link our way through our days, this brings forth the possibility of the sociability of the private sphere opening up new civic habits and new political rituals that cannot be understood through the prioritizing of rational deliberative discourse. The claims to self-realization through social media mean that, in an environment where representative democracy is failing, citizens retreat to the private sphere and a means of communicating over which they feel they have more control. I am angry; I don't know what to do, so I write a blog. This is argued *not* to be indicative of a lack of political interest but, rather, to signal a relocation of that interest to domains that are more intimate. This is resonant of Sennett's argument that dead public space (public space that may be visible but is no longer collective) is one reason why 'people seek out on intimate terrain what is denied them on more alien ground' (1974: 15). This could explain why people have been shown to enjoy participating in online polls and circulating political jokes and cartoons over and above the rather more traditional content of news releases (Cornfield, 2004). This does not mean that the political is cancelled out but that multiple roles are performed as the user plays out a range of roles in a world of political infotainment. This can be participatory but it can also be passive; it can be collective but, equally, it might be introspective. This is a form of 'the political' that resists definition by means of transferable policy (re)formulation or rational deliberation.

So, it would seem fair to surmise that the daily rituals of the internet and social media bring people into contact with the political, but through habits which do not fit neatly into the structure of democratic institutions, the function of media campaigns or the traditions of political information dissemination that view uses of technology as too frivolous or entertainment oriented to be truly civic. Indeed, representative democracy and the organizational and hierarchical structures it embodies simply cannot contend with these new forms of social telling that legitimize the hybridization of capitalist and public-interest objectives, which, in Habermasian analysis, are responsible for the demise of the public sphere itself. But it could be they also suggest that the public sphere is not the most meaningful lens through which to evaluate the democratizing potential of online technologies. These modes of civic engagement speak to a more fluid model of citizenship.

The tendency to situate any analysis of the political in relation to the media in a particular type of Habermasian framework poses a limitation on the possibilities for understanding what it means to be political. These limitations are bound in particular by the requirement to be rational and to reach a consensus, on the assumption that this will then result in policy reform that conforms to the will of the majority. This leads to our political desire and hope for change being channelled into a notion of liberal democracy that is trapped within the institutions of mainstream political parties – and is then actually incapable of being used to understand the type of political activity which circulates around social media and that operates frequently outside of a liberal deliberative democratic framework. Habermasian liberal deliberative democrats seek to prioritize representative institutions and legal systems of liberal democratic states as the exclusive or even the main home of political deliberation, leaving us with a dubiously narrow conception of both democracy and politics. As the market, globalization and the media all exert their pressures on state democracy, a reliance on this form of democratic practice alone grows ever more insubstantial.

As I have argued above, the particular model of the public sphere assumed in much of the debate fails to conceptualize adequately the intersubjective basis of meaning and rationality and hence of the political. In other words, the model posits a naive theory of the autonomous-rational subject and the transparency of meaning that rests ultimately on consensus. The politics of the likes of the anti-globalization and Occupy movements, based on difference and diversity, polycentric networks that resist a universal voice, cross geographical borders and work against universalizing narratives – a movement of movements, a network of networks – does not fit easily in a liberal democratic frame favoured by many public sphere theorists (see chapter 7).

Papacharissi (2010a, 2010b) argues that, along with the collapse of public and private boundaries, we also have the collapse of the capitalist and creative imaginaries. She cites the example of YouTube, which contains vast amounts of independently produced and commercial content presented in an amorphous format that is almost impossible to monitor or regulate. Some of this content reproduces material already copyrighted by others, potentially violating copyright, reworks material positioning the audience as producer, or pitches a campaign against commercial creative industries in favour of independent production with the ultimate aim of achieving commercial success. One example is provided by Jon and Tracy Morter, who decided to set up a Facebook group to advocate voting for a track by the rap metal band Rage Against the Machine rather than a song by the 2010 winner of *The X Factor*, Joe McElderry. They succeeded through the online votes they mobilized in preventing the Christmas number 1 slot being taken for the fourth time running by the winner of the show. The lead singer of Rage Against the Machine, Zack de la Rocha, claimed it was a victory for 'real', not 'corporatized' music (*The Guardian*, 21 December 2009), through an 'incredible organic grassroots campaign [that] says more about the spontaneous action taken by young people throughout the UK to topple this very sterile pop monopoly. When young people decide to take action they can make what's seemingly impossible, possible' (BBC News, 20 December 2009).

YouTube also features other original political content, which ranges from digitally capturing political moments to planned filming of protest marches. Such commercial public spaces may for the most part simply provide background noise. But they do afford space where individuals can, if they desire, engage in interaction that may be political and may have civic intent. Importantly, however, they are also performing other tasks in the process – not least, entertaining. Papacharissi (2010a, 2010b) argues that these spaces are essential for maintaining a politically active consciousness which may, when necessary, facilitate a sizable oppositional voice in response to all manner of public issues. While distinct from the Habermasian notion of the public sphere, these tendencies to hybridity (mixing the public and the private) may present a more accurate reflection of the contemporary public's experience of social media.

The claims that social media offer a new form of social telling (Fenton, 2016) that cuts across the social, cultural and political is closely aligned to the argument that liberal democracy, relying as it does on rational deliberation and consensus, has not paid enough attention and cannot account for the intersubjective basis of 'the political' and cannot therefore adequately account for transformative capacity. Lyotard (1984) argued that Habermas overemphasized rational accord as a condition for a democratic public sphere and insisted that it is anarchy, individuality and disagreement that can lead to genuine democratic emancipation. Lyotard's dissent was founded in Derrida's (1997) deconstructivist approach that emphasized undecidability as the necessary constant in any form of public deliberation. Similarly, Mouffe (2000) proposed agonistic pluralism as an alternative that better accounts for a vibrant clash of democratic political positions guided by undecidability and is more receptive to the plurality of voices in society than is allowed for by the deliberative model. Specifically, the agonistic approach 'acknowledges the real nature of its frontiers and the forms of exclusion that they entail, instead of trying to disguise them under the veil of rationality or morality' (2000: 105). This fits much better in an online context of cultural politics. These shifting spaces of public discourse are claimed to be more hospitable to a range of diverse issues and views, conflicting approaches and reflexive modes of representation (Holt, 2004). Here we can see identity politics played out where individualistic, pluralistic and collective priorities overlap, contradict and conflict –

all part of the contemporary digital mêlée of public and private spaces. Discussing her latest book, Papacharissi suggests that we should

> not waste time looking for immediate, legislative, economic, political impact to emerge out of the ways in which we put these technologies to use. The impact lies elsewhere. For publics that are convened online around affective commonalities, impact is symbolic, agency is claimed discursively and is of a semantic nature, and power accessed is liminal. . . . symbolic impact is important because it liberates the imagination. (Interview with Jenkins, 2015: 1)

The notions of 'liberating the imagination' and 'discursive agency' can be readily criticized for being politically reductive and amounting to precisely nothing in terms of social and political transformation. It is a type of politics that Gramsci (1971) would call apoliticism and avoids questions of power relations and material inequalities. But, nonetheless, such notions encourage us to consider transformative capacity as suggestive of an enlargement of how we think of politics and the mechanisms of social change. It speaks to what Bloch would call 'abstract hope' ([1959] 1996: 157). Many new social movements have taken pride in their practices being open-ended. There are no meta-narratives that shape the beginning, middle and end of a particular ideological approach. As such they are ever incomplete, tacit and experiential, with an emphasis on horizontal sharing and exchanging of knowledge – a highly self-conscious and self-reflexive form of action and struggle that functions in an endless dynamic of experimentation and search for synthesis. Borrowing from Raymond Williams (1961), Papacharissi (2015) talks about social media platforms as soft 'structures of feeling' that reflect social experiences – the culture, feeling and mood of a particular moment in time. She discusses how collaborative narratives that coalesce around hashtags on Twitter work as structures of feeling which connect different types of people around subjective and highly affective expressions and impulses. It is not the technology but, rather, the stories that come out of these structures of feeling that connect or divide us. Importantly here, Papacharissi is shifting emphasis from the ability of the technology to forge networks to the actual content of the social media in use. A consideration of who is saying what to whom then comes back into focus and requires us to critique the nature of the storytelling in play.

A virtual space may enhance discussion, but does it enhance democracy? As discussed above, this depends on what model of democracy you are measuring it against. As people integrate online media into their daily habits and practices, it may be that political activity is expressed and experienced in a manner that is not conducive to a Habermasian public sphere built on rational deliberation but has more in common with contemporary public impulses and the desires of a liquid citizen moving through fluid contexts, and so requires a different way of thinking about the conditions for democracy to thrive. But even if we look to different types of democratic renewal, such as agonistic democracy (Mouffe, 2000), direct democracy (Fishkin, 2011) or participatory democracy (Elster, 1998), turning to the internet as an expression of their fulfilment is still deeply problematic. This is largely because attributing to any technology the powers to deliver a democratic nirvana extracts the internet itself from the ideas, values, systems and structures of which it is a part. Focusing on the content of social storytelling in the digital age is one thing, but in order to make sense of the stories that are told we must situate them in the deep contexts of which they are a part.

Boltanski and Chiappello (2005) write convincingly of a change in the contemporary 'spirit of capitalism' which co-opts critiques as a source of reinvention. This 'new spirit of capitalism' has integrated elements of the 'artistic critique' of the new left based on the counter-cultural desire for autonomy and creativity, and in so doing it has been able to justify its essentially amoral purpose – the unlimited accumulation of profit by peaceful means – and to motivate managers to embrace it. In the process, it disqualified the quest for equality and security which proponents of capitalism's 'social critique' (for example, trade unions) had been advancing: autonomy, in their thesis, has been exchanged for security. The new spirit of capitalism promotes new, liberated and even libertarian ways of making profit as well as the realization of the self, of the individual's most personal aspirations. In this connexionist universe, what matters above all else is establishing good links that will enable individuals to shift from project to project. Successful individuals are always busy, always active, drawing no difference between work and play; alienation has been overcome. So, just as politics and culture converge and overlap in a YouTube setting where irreverence and humour injects vitality into political conversation trapped in conventional formulas, so too do work and play combine and intermesh.

This convergence, seen as playful work, is easily regarded as holding the potential for creative counter-culture. But when it is seen in reverse, as workful play, we are faced with a more critical stance towards an internet ideology of free content and free labour. In this approach the creative, autonomous self, rather than challenging the capitalist system, has provided the means to sustain and rejuvenate it. Notions of creativity and autonomy now pervade developed liberal democracies and are not the sole preserve of counter-cultural activity. Rather, they are part of the dominant paradigm of today's market economies, which emphasize fixed-term project work, portfolio careers, alongside the necessity for constant reskilling and networking to retain flexible, insecure employment. The 'flexibility' that is demanded of workers to respond to changes in the political economics of labour markets may allow individuals to increase their self-development, to develop a cultural presence, but it also requires them to be ever present at the interface. The connexionist universe epitomizes a converged work–play ethic where to be successful demands non-stop activity: successful bloggers 'post' constantly – they survive through their ability to connect, so they must always be turned on and tuned in. Seen in this light, the work practices embraced by counter-cultural political activists, such as high productivity, endurance and unconventional time patterns, support rather than contradict those idealized by the new spirit of capitalism.

One example is the strategies of participatory management often practised in new technology industries which encourage the integration of play into labour. In places such as Microsoft, work is constructed as fun – a place where workers develop new ideas, realize their creativity and enjoy free (productive) time within the workplace. The boundaries between work time and free time, labour and play, are blurred. Work acquires qualities of play, and entertainment in free time becomes labour-like. Working time and free time become inseparable. At the same time, as work permeates all down-time and monopolizes our daily rituals and head space, work-related stress intensifies. Microsoft has been called a 'Velvet Sweatshop' as a result of the long hours and frequent burn-out experienced by employees (Andrews, 1989).

In a similar vein, Dean (2009) suggests that, rather than deliver messages, the internet creates an endless circulation loop that entraps those who use it into constant linking, forwarding, storing, commenting and contributing without expectation of response. The circulation loop constantly seduces us to search for information that is perpetually out of reach. This may mean that we are ever engaged in high levels of productivity that confirms our creativity, but in a context wherein our labour power is likely to be exploited by capital and resistance is minimal. Thus we fall foul of communicative capitalism.

Despite the potential for participatory democracy, our digital existence is enmeshed in global capitalism. The emancipatory potential of the internet is at the same time subsumed under capital. The paradox is that, while it creates and embeds forms of capitalism, it also raises the prospect of new forms of post-capitalism. It is neither all one nor all the other. The *potentials* of resistance are evident, and when the conditions are right they can help bring about radical political movements. But too frequently people overestimate the resistive potential and forget about the fact that it, too, is enclosed by global capitalism. There are positive potentials and projects for an alternative participatory internet, but the contemporary internet is largely shaped by powerful corporations, which derive material benefits at the expense of internet users, commodify the internet, and appropriate the internet commons. The internet produces more dominance of major corporations and more competition in a capitalist market place (Freedman, 2014). But it also produces information and co-operation that can potentially undermine competition. If the techno-historical developments of the last decades are transforming social experience, the one thing we can say for sure is that they are doing so in multiple and often contradictory ways.

Of course, all creative human activity holds the potential for political transformative capacity, but to understand how this potential can be translated into a reality requires an appreciation of the enduring social and political relations that surround and pre-exist certain individuals and their relations with others. Put simply, we need a deep and radical contextualization of our online mediations to reach a critical understanding of media changes and political ontology in the new mediascape. Only when we can reach a full appreciation of our online mediations and their contingent and multiple relations to *structure and agency* can we assess the *feasibility* of achieving a new hegemony, of transforming the existing political order either partially or radically and the role of mediation therein.

Conclusion

This chapter began by arguing that politics involves passion. I have suggested that, to understand new media and radical politics, we also need to understand the motivations and barriers to being political. I have also argued that, if we restrict ourselves purely to a political economic analysis that tends to understand the world from the perspective of the reproduction of the logic of capital, then we risk misnoticing or misrecognizing much that is political. To deny the passion in politics is to misunderstand what politics is. There is no politics without contention; there is no contention without feelings of injustice, unfairness, sadness and anger. Radical politics cannot survive and flourish without passion to provide the momentum. Therefore, theoretical frameworks that cohere around conceptions of democracy that cannot account for this and overemphasize rationality cannot understand radical politics in any form.

But, in our rush to embrace a passionate politics and smother it with love and joy, in the excitement that ensues from turning away from the dour demeanour of much political economy, we must also resist swinging too far to the other side and falling flat on our faces. What I have tried to argue in this chapter is that the macro-pessimism found in much political economy can and should be combined with the micro-optimism of much cultural theory (similar to what Deleuze refers to as the molar and the molecular). Both are crucial to understand fully the relations between new media and radical politics. Yet all too frequently one dominates to the detriment of the other, leaving us stuck in overly simplistic ruts of the good, bad or downright ugly consequences of new technology. Accepting that both are relevant does not absolve us of the difficult political questions that remain. In fact it brings them to the fore. How are the multifarious publics that could constitute a political commons actually generated? How do they come together and effect social change when operating alongside 'the individualizing logic of contemporary consumer culture…and the mechanics of neo-liberalism [that] work to inhibit the emergence of any political collectivity whatsoever' (Gilbert, 2014: 28)?

Dahlgren (2009) notes that civic cultures are shaped by an array of factors: family and schools, group settings, relations of power (including social class, gender and ethnicity), economics, the legal system and organizational possibilities are all relevant, and the resources that people can draw upon are more abundant among the more privileged. Dahlgren describes how the media directly and routinely impact upon the character of civic cultures via their form, content, logics and modes of use. In terms of the internet, he points out that its significance is found not simply at the level of social institutions but also in lived experience. Lived experience is messy and contradictory.

If passion is at the heart of political subjectivity, it is also part and parcel of political organization (Amin and Thrift, 2013). Just as we cannot understand new media and radical politics without an appreciation of the political subject, so we cannot understand any type of politics or political system without attention to organizational dynamics. It is to this facet of radical politics in the digital age that the next chapter attends.

5

Radical Politics and Organizational Form in Theory and in Practice

In chapter 2 the key characteristics of digital media (and in particular of the internet) linked to radical politics were described as speed and space, connectivity and participation, and horizontality and diversity. Notions of communicative space, citizen participation and political activism in those spaces, and the diversity of communications that this then brings, speak to the overarching notion that in the digital age there is an abundance of highly diverse sources of information which a wide range of citizens/activists can make use of and contribute to. This in turn is said to be conducive to a particular type of post-foundational politics. Chapter 2 outlines the many ways in which such claims are refuted. Claims of a multiplicity of voices in transnational mediated spaces also link to the larger debate about the nature of the public sphere that was discussed in chapter 3, a debate that emanates from the history of liberal thought. In interrogating the nature of the public sphere we have highlighted the need to critique the assumptions surrounding liberal democracy – in particular the notion of rational deliberation inherent within them (see chapter 4) – that much radical politics has lost faith in and rallied against. This chapter leads on from those discussions to pose the question: If a rational deliberative model of liberal democracy cannot account for the new forms of radical politics emerging in the digital age, then how can we better understand them? To do this, we return to the notion of multiplicity and the concept of the multitude.

One of the striking differences between the counter-publicity of transnational social movements and the counter-politics of the nation-state is the lack of common identity and the rejection of unifying meta-narratives of organization. It is a movement of movements, a network of networks. This chapter unravels how the rejection of meta-narratives of political ideas and values such as socialism and communism has emerged and how this is related to the notion of multiplicity in contemporary configurations of radical politics. While this discussion hopes to proffer understanding of certain currents in contemporary radical counter-politics, it also raises concerns over new problems that surface through the parallel promotion of the notion of individual creative autonomy.

The first half of this chapter returns to some of the defining characteristics of the internet discussed in chapter 2 and restated above – horizontality and diversity and connectivity and participation. It then develops this discussion in relation to the debates in chapter 4 around the political concerns of commonality and difference regarding digital media and radical politics. Can an oppositional politics based on multiplicity and difference can be conceived of or perceived as universal? Although each of us may have a different political identity, can we have a politics in common? Can a politics based on difference that embraces multiple viewpoints and a variety of political identities ever forge solidarity powerful enough to bring about social change?

The nature of struggles online and the diversity of social relations that they embody reveal a multiplicity of relations of subordination and opposition. But when does multiplicity shift from being an inclusive politics of difference to one of fragmentation and dispersal of political efficacy? What does it mean in practice to argue for a political subject that is made up of manifold, fluid identities that mirror the multiple differentiations of groups? How can a politics of solidarity in difference be realized and sustained? Do we weaken our various struggles and dilute our solidarity through constant recourse to the multitude? Or are such contested spaces, as Virno (2004) claims in his theorizations of the 'multitude', the 'right of resistance' for communities that are necessarily antagonistic in their collectivity?

Interactivity, Participation and Autonomy

Civic and political participation are frequently understood as prerequisites for citizen-based democracies to flourish. Facilitation of participation is a crucial factor in transnational internet activism. The interactive and participative capability of the internet to speed up and increase the circulation of struggle has been argued as key to the success of some campaigns such as the anti-globalization movement

(Cleaver, 1999), as well as the spread of pro-democracy protest in the Middle East in 2011 (Ghannam, 2011; Miladi, 2011). The nature of participation promoted by many contemporary forms of radical political mobilization online is promulgated upon a particular notion of individual autonomy connected directly to the celebration of multiplicity and difference: the ability to act and speak for oneself while also being part of a collective movement over which no one individual, or central hierarchy, has control.

This multiplicity is also inflected by another concept – autonomy – the principle that no one speaks for the collective, that each takes control of his or her own political activism. The rise of the notion of autonomy for communicative subjects in the digital age is at the heart of the networked politics of many radical groups/social movements. Through addressing the political issues raised by the multiplicity of voices in transnational mediated spaces and the rejection of meta-narratives of political ideas in favour of autonomous political subjects and values, this chapter discusses how these key characteristics of the networked politics of radical and progressive groups/movements relate to the concepts of (political) representation and hegemony.

The principle that no one speaks for the collective, that each takes control of their own political activism, that each activist is autonomous, has become increasingly prominent in the new wave of radical political movements since the anti-globalization movement, although it has a history that predates this.[1] One of the first social movements explicitly to embrace and endorse such an approach through the use of digital media was the Zapatista Army of National Liberation (EZLN) in its political rebellion against neoliberal capitalism and, in particular, against the North American Free Trade Agreement (NAFTA) in pursuit of the liberation of Chiapas in Mexico. From the outset, the Zapatista struggle, established in 1994 and led by Subcomandante Marcos, differentiated itself from previous political movements through a disinterest in state power and hierarchical structures and a clear focus on autonomy and direct democracy (Klein, 2002; Graeber, 2002). Direct democracy in this context emphasizes horizontal autonomy, indigenous leadership and collective organization, which means listening to each voice in the community to build individual social systems that suit everyone's needs. In accordance with these principles, the Zapatistas refuse the identity of a political party and reject the notion of claiming power through government office, which they argue would do no more than perpetuate a system that they repudiate (Marcos, 2001). Concurrently, they also place importance on interconnectedness and networking, using the internet to create a collective political identity that has spread across the globe

(Atton, 2007; Castells, 1997; Kowal, 2002; Ribeiro, 1998). Subcomandante Marcos deliberately resisted the status of leader and refused any name that would identify him as an individual. The conflict in Chiapas gave rise to the People's Global Action network (PGA), which led to the 1999 Seattle demonstrations and the creation of the movement for global justice (Day, 2005; Graeber, 2002; Holloway, 2002), with the internet cemented as part of the repertoire of political action (Traugott, 1995; Fenton and Barassi, 2011). The internet was also seen as evidence that radical politics can arise horizontally and take the form of networks, rather than hierarchical hegemonies as in a traditional trade union politics of labour.

The notion of the 'network' as an ever open space of politics has been given heightened significance through the work of Hardt and Negri (2004, 2009). They present the network as far more than the connective dynamics of linked individuals. For them, it confers self-constituted, unhierarchical, transnational and affinity-based relationships, premised upon 'autonomy' (everyone's right to express their own political identity) and 'solidarity' (to overcome power/ neoliberalism) (Graeber, 2002: 68). As discussed in chapter 2, this is partially explained through an appreciation of participation in contemporary radical politics being linked to disengagement and disillusionment with traditional party politics (della Porta, 2005). Those who distrust mainstream political parties and representative institutions most are more likely to trust and participate in social movements. The former are seen as bureaucratic, with the democratic process delegated to elected representatives, whereas the latter are based on participation and direct engagement. All Western democracies follow a variety of systems of representative politics. But any representative democracy of a liberal pluralist kind always raises the issue of who speaks for whom (and who does not speak for whom).

Representational politics grants a lot of power to a small number of individuals who are supposed to represent the interests of the rest and, in doing so, necessarily homogenize the unique situation of each. Badiou's radical critique places liberal democracy in direct relation to capitalism, whereby everything on the market is equal in value to everything else: 'If democracy is representation, it is representation first and foremost of the general system that bears its forms. In other words electoral democracy is not representative except to the extent that it is the consensual representation of capitalism, today rebranded "the market economy"' (Badiou, 2010: 122). For Rancière, representation is 'fully and overtly an oligarchic form' and 'the exact opposite of democracy' (2011a: 60). It is representation by a minority endowed with the title of custodians of our affairs. Douzinas (2015:

81) reports on a newspaper interview with Badiou in 2014, where he also professes that

> The Left is part of a 'structural imposture'... The Left, an idea created in and by the state, has made an agreement with the oligarchy with whom it wants to alternate in power. It has abandoned its commitment to radical change and promotes the myth that parliamentary elections can be used for 'revolutionary' purposes.

On the other hand, the notion of a more participatory or even direct democracy encourages us to think in terms of a decentred democracy that rejects the modernist version of a political project, with a single coherent aim of social reform decided upon by consensus (see chapter 3); this would allow a more fluid and negotiable order to emerge, 'with plural authority structures along a number of different dimensions rather than a single location for public authority and power' (Bohman, 2004: 148). This requires a radical rethinking of the theory and practice of politics. Digital media – and the internet in particular – as a consequence of their participatory and interactive attributes that enable citizens to be, at once, connected, creative and autonomous, are claimed to be well suited to the extension of such a democratic endeavour.

Disorganization or Fragmentation?

But participation rooted in autonomy is hotly contested on grounds of political efficacy, with the network society seen as producing localized, disaggregated, fragmented, diversified and divided political identities. Earlier work by Castells (1996) saw the fragmented nature of digital media as limiting the capacity of new political movements to create coherent strategies on account of the increasing individualization of activists. Similarly, in an approach based on *disorganiza-tion*, problems of quantity and the chaos of information challenge the way analysis and action are integrated in decision-making processes – how issues are debated and decisions reached can be at best unclear and at worst unfathomable. If, like Castells (1996), we view an inclusive approach to a diversity of perspectives within a particular political response or mobilization as no more than fragmentation and dissolution of solidarity, we are led ultimately to the conclusion that this is a form of politics that lacks direction and political agency. It is unclear why Castells changed his mind by 2009, but it is likely related to the increase in volume and intensity of such activity.

But even if we accept that representative democracy has failed (see chapter 1) and that, through political conflict, associational networks can emerge, civil society be established and social change occur (see chapter 2), the problem remains: How can fragmented and multiple oppositional groupings function together for political ends? The key to understanding this approach to what has been termed a 'post-foundational' (Marchart, 2007) radical politics is to keep in mind that any end point has multiple possibilities and there are many different routes to get to each. The reduction of political action to the construction of a single end point that infers a rational, exclusionary approach whereby all other potential end points are dismissed as ill-conceived or wrong is considered by many to be unacceptable. Why would someone participate in a politics that is established on someone else's terms and tries to flatten disagreement and stifle dissent – the markers of a failed and stale representative politics? Participation on someone else's terms is understood as the misguided delivery of a homogeneous ideal that attempts to remove uncertainty and unknowability and reduces politics to the 'administration of things' (Bhabha, 1994). It is seen as removing creativity and autonomy from political action. Contemporary political activists talk of creating autonomous spaces of imagination and creativity that are contingent, open and unpredictable – an attempt to escape ideological politics and move to a dialogical politics where we continually acknowledge difference and learn from others. The political premise is one of anti-reductionism that refuses a monological process or vision. Such forms of resistance are united by a shared perception of an injustice rather than a common, determinate vision of a 'better world' that may follow.

But, as many feminist theorists have noted in relation to the development of feminism as a political movement (Fenton 2000; Spivak, 1992; Braidotti, 1991), for political efficacy there must be more than the apparent freedom that comes with embracing difference and diversity, more than just an increase of instances of mediated protest or opposition. Even if we accept the possibility that fragmented and multiple oppositional groupings can create their own political interventions via the internet, we still have to broach the next stage: How can a politics of solidarity (based often on a consensus of what people do not want) forged through difference (based often on what people do want) be realized and sustained? Can a commitment to the value of difference and an appreciation of everyone's right to dissent sustain a cohesive radical politics? Can the 'multiple belongings' and 'flexible identities' that Tarrow and della Porta (2005: 237) speak of, the micro-politics of the multitude, extend beyond a protest politics to give rise to societal transformation?

In attempting to progress a radical politics beyond what many theorists have come to see as a radical left political impasse, Rancière (1999), Badiou (2008) and Žižek (Žižek and Daly, 2004) all share a desire to revive a form of universalism in counter-politics, albeit in different ways. Rancière is committed to a universality that is always 'local' and 'singular': '[a] political subject is not a group that "becomes aware" of itself, finds its voice, imposes its weight on society. It is an operator that connects and disconnects different areas, regions, identities, functions and capacities existing in the configuration of a given experience' (1999: 40). Rancière takes the movements of Algerian and French militants who worked in solidarity for Algerian independence in the 1950s and 1960s and compares the backing they received with the relative lack of support for those massacred and displaced in Bosnia in the 1990s. In the former, the recognition of the cause of the other as relating to one's own cause expressed as solidarity brings about the emergence of equality – the recognition of the other on equal terms.

For Badiou, universalism is closely connected to subjectivity and is a condition of its possibility. He argues that we have moved beyond the revolutionary politics of old that was constituted via parties that would confront the state, take control and instigate its demise. This, he argues, was a politics built on the 'paradigm of war' (2007: 44), which led to brutal atrocities before the revolutionary parties routinized themselves and became party-states. For Badiou, the crucial question for contemporary politics is whether a revolutionary politics without a party is possible. A party-less politics does not, in his terms, infer a politics without organization – far from it. But it does mean a politics without any relationship to the state.

Žižek's plea for a reinstatement of universalism is somewhat different and draws on the figure of Lenin, who, he argues, had the necessary courage to assume effective leadership of the state (Žižek and Daly, 2004). Controversially, he maintains that the necessary translation of a revolutionary politics into an enduring social and political order always carries a cost. All of the above operate with some version of autonomy linked to their own conceptualization of the political subject as discussed in the previous chapter, but each recognizes the necessity for a type of universalism that will not cancel out diversity but will engender solidarity.

Autonomy, Anarchism and Counter-Hegemony

Just as there are different ways of conceiving of the political subject, so there are different ways of conceiving of autonomy. The conceptualization and enactment of autonomy in the networked sociality of contemporary radical politics has been forged through a connection to anarchism, the autonomous movement and autonomous Marxism. As Barassi (2015b: 33) notes:

> The Italian Autonomous Movement finds its roots in the movements of the late 1960s and established itself during the 1970s, when different political realities started to organize moved by a quest for political autonomy. On the one hand, there were the autonomous worker groups such as *Autonomia Operaia* (AO) that sought to assert their grassroots independence from both the management of factories and the unions, which were linked to the Italian Communist Party (PCI). On the other hand, the movement owes its legacy to the feminist, student, and youth collectives that during those years were seeking to establish their autonomy from the Italian political and social context, which was defined by a system largely influenced not only by capitalist exploitation but also by blatant patriarchal costumes, and the legacy of fascism.

Autonomous Marxism developed as a political movement on the Italian left after the Second World War. Although it has been seen as synonymous with the autonomous movement, Barassi points out that the two are actually very distinct. Autonomous Marxism emerged from a movement called *operaismo* (loosely translated as 'worker-ism'), which found a political place somewhere between the Stalinist leadership of the Italian Communist Party and the radicalized young workers and intellectuals that existed on the edges of the party. The *operaismo* was immersed in the so-called years of lead:

> In the last years of the 1970s the Italian government approved a law allowing the police to open fire on protesters. Repression reached its peak, different sections of the autonomous movement organized in guerrilla-terrorist groups, which led to the armed struggle. In 1978, one of these groups, the Red Brigades, kidnapped and killed former Christian Democrat Prime Minister Aldo Moro. The 1970s and the early years of the 1980s were years of violence, repression, armed robberies, kidnappings and exile. They were bloody years for Italian politics, and have been known as the years of lead. (Barassi, 2015b: 48)

At the risk of gross oversimplification, *operaismo* emphasized the self-motivation of workers' struggle that did not flow through or from parties or leaderships and could not be attributed straightforwardly to exploitation. Rather, this self-activation was a result of workers making their own struggle against capital. The autonomous movement extended beyond a focus on workers and opted increasingly for small confrontations with the state rather than mass actions of the working class. Those involved saw themselves as separate from established structures of political control such as the state, the main political parties and also the trade unions.

Approaches that have built on the autonomous movement have evolved in different directions in different countries, but increasingly across the board autonomism came to be more closely associated with anarchism. The horizontalism it embraced progressed from an organizational principle to an anti-state anarchism premised primarily on the freedom of the individual and their actions and choices rather than the relationship of politics to society that led to larger issues of economy of scale and social power.

This leads Day to claim that the rise of the movements for global justice based on anarchist political strategies and autonomous discourses that refuse a singular social totality implies that the 'logic of hegemony' has been exhausted: 'Gramsci is dead' (2005: 203). Such a claim does, however, rather gloss over the post-Marxist shift in Gramscian theory. If we take heed of Laclau and Mouffe's (1985) formulation of hegemony as entirely relational and contingent in context, then we must accept that it is not defined as a fixed structure or as a particular social relation as Day implies. Yet Day harks back to classical Marxist conceptualizations of hegemony that view society as a totality with a central locus of power, thereby assuming that deference to a single ideology can be the only outcome of political projects that seek to subsume minority concerns into liberal society.

The eulogizing, from the likes of Day (2005), on the emancipatory qualities of new social movements as indicative of the end of hegemony, based on their autonomy from state power, is deeply problematic. When a politics of new social movements resides in autonomy as freedom for oneself disconnected from everything, including its own history, then autonomy becomes a limitation rather than a freedom. Through its insistence on relationality and contingency, later developments in hegemonic theory encourage us to acknowledge the complexity of power relations at any one time. To do otherwise is not only to deny that relations of influence occur between different components or factors in a political process; it is also to deny the complexity of social and political relations that develop between contemporary political movements and dominant political institutions (Barassi, 2010).

Indeed, as Barassi (2010) points out, transnational social movement organizations are very much interlinked with dominant political institutions such as local and national governments (McCarthy, 1997; Kriesberg, 1997) and cannot be understood in isolation from them. Barassi (2010) also points to the work of Starn et al. (2005) among the *ronda campesinas* in northern Peru, in which he shows how the movements were simultaneously developing a politics based on the idea of autonomy while also being aided by the influence of the Church (Gledhill, 1994). As Barassi argues, emphasizing autonomy as the defining characteristic of NSMs risks essentializing not only the movements themselves but also understandings of the reach of the state. Approaches that foreground individual autonomy, and suggest that the liberation or enabling of this autonomy opens up a space for a new politics of the global, frequently fail to take account of state autonomy and hence of broader relations of power. When they do, they often come with an anarchist reading that the international realm is one of freedom and possibility, precisely because the autonomy of the individual is not constrained by the autonomy of the state. Indeed, it is argued that 'anarchism is not the political ideology of disorder, but of autonomy, and a framework for understanding how groups and individuals can relate without the need for states' (Prichard, 2010: 24). This bifurcates the world into individuals and structures and robs us of an understanding of collective agency, whether in the form of trade unions, social class, NGOs or multinationals.

Autonomist approaches all too frequently overlook the critical contextual factors of state boundaries, prevalent political infrastructures, and ever dominant economic constraints that raise critical questions regarding the political efficacy of many contemporary forms of radical politics. Frequently, such approaches either disregard the impact of the politics of the organizations and movements on a state polity or base the success of such movements on their ability to function external to a state polity. As a consequence, they are not well placed to assess the nature and consequence of the political act in a broader context of political structures, leaving wide open the critical question posed at the beginning of this book: How open to contest and revision is politics today?

Equally problematic is the frequent oversight on behalf of much theorizing over hegemony to analyse in depth the organizational, as well as the social and political, *conditions* required for counter-hegemonies to take root and for political transformation and actual democracy (however conceived) to become established. This is as relevant for forms of counter-political organization – how members of a group can function together for political ends – as it is for the functioning of political systems. Understanding how we do politics well together on a small, group-based or local scale is as important as understanding how democratic political systems can emerge. Autonomy that is ultimately detached from everything, including our political friends as well as sovereign states, is, as Brown (2011: 49) notes, 'politically meaningless': 'Democracy detached from a bounded sovereign jurisdiction (whether virtual or literal) is politically meaningless: for the people to rule themselves, there must be an identifiable collective entity within which their power sharing is organized and upon which it is exercised.'

Such conceptualizations of autonomy associated with post-hegemony autonomist theorists deny the thorny issues of collective power, social institutions and political strategy. The conceptualization of autonomy as expressed by post-Marxist discourse theorists, which operates within a hegemonic frame, needs, then, to be clearly distinguished from that of the post-hegemony autonomist theorists (e.g., Day, 2005; Holloway, 2002), which is more closely associated with the autonomist movement. The former follows the theoretical trajectory of the Italian Marxist Antonio Gramsci but develops it a stage further by stressing articulation and contingency and recognizing that, although the singularity of multiple voices must be respected, ultimately it is neither feasible nor desirable that each of these singularities occupies a permanently unified space, politics or language. In other words, while the singular authenticity of many individual voices is constitutive of the whole, it is necessary to transcend the particular concerns of each individual to form a collective identity and ultimately to establish counter-hegemony (although, as a consequence of its accepted contentious disposition, this counter-hegemony will necessarily always be in flux and under challenge):

> In this way, a counter hegemony can be constructed, although it will be marked by an ineliminable tension between the singularity of the various demands and voices included within the counter hegemonic bloc and their representation within an overarching ideology or programme. The representation does violence to singularity, but the singularities also disrupt the functioning of the representation. (Thomassen, 2007: 120)

As such, Thomassen recognizes a necessary dialectic relationship between the individual and the collective, between autonomy and solidarity. It is only through appreciating the dynamic relationship between the two and the constant and contingent struggle to build upon the articulation of differences that any counter-hegemonic force can be sustained. What does this mean for radical politics when we pause to take account of the media in the digital age?

Digital Media, Radical Politics and Autonomy

It is always surprising to me that much political theory and philosophy fails to take account of or seriously underplays the extent to which democratic procedures and outcomes (of both mainstream and alternative politics) are shaped by the 'actions of those with access to the media, to mechanisms of representation and to political parties' (Tormey and Townshend, 2006: 224). In our thoroughly mediated democracies, this too frequently feels like an inexcusable oversight. However, approaching social and political transformation by starting with the media is also prone to problems of techno-centrism if not technological determinism.

This has been a particular difficulty with many of the theorists who begin with the wonders of the internet and its ability to extend political engagement, which then automatically engenders an enhanced networked sociality for political citizenship more generally (e.g., Benkler, 2006). Autonomy makes a frequent appearance in this debate. Castells (2009: 136) refers to the concept of 'creative autonomy' in relation to the internet. According to Castells, 'Web 2.0' brought about a historical transformation of communication practices with considerable consequences for social organization and cultural change. He argues that a new form of communication has emerged: the 'mass communication of the self', made possible particularly through social media platforms, where self-generated messages created by individuals can reach global audiences (ibid.: 58–71). This unprecedented opportunity for creative individuals to communicate to potentially millions of people online gives the audience control over communicative practices and affords them unprecedented levels of autonomy imbued with emancipatory possibilities. Castells believes that self-expression through new media platforms can act as a tool of resistance, and he maintains that 'the construction of communicative autonomy is directly related to the development of social and political autonomy, a key factor in fostering social change' (ibid.: 414).

On one level, Castells would appear to be right in relation to new social movements and their online practices: through the mass communication of the self, new media enable the participation of citizens in politically significant ways – the Green Revolution in Iran is but one example (see Khiabany, 2010), and the series of uprisings that were labelled the Arab Spring are another. But Castells's approach does not help us to understand what happened politically in these instances. It is important to remember that Castells is writing from the position of an anarchist. Political participation is construed via the role of the individual. It is the individual subject that is asked to develop new techniques of the self as acts of resistance, encouraged to mobilize in favour of political issues, or persuaded to get involved in the debates that precede political elections (Castells, 2009: 299–364).

Castells (2009) focuses on an approach that prioritizes the importance of self-expression that originates from an individual formulation and act – creative autonomy. Individual political subjectivity is central to political engagement, but we should also remember that political participation is frequently defined by and takes place in relation to and in co-ordination with others. It is not enough simply to say that this is a new, networked form of politics. Every social, cultural or political identity is always fragmented and characterized by its multifaceted relations to others. Indeed, any social transformations that could be called hegemonic can be achieved only through a process of connection/disconnection and articulation/rearticulation with others. Foregrounding creative autonomy of the self in relation to new technological forms negates the collective dimension of political participation so prevalent in the wave of social movements and political uprisings around the globe, and thereby dissipates the political properties of the participatory communicative act itself.

Networks of Power and Networks of Counter-Power

Castells (2009) argues that it is of fundamental importance to highlight the networks of power that are constructed by global multimedia business and to understand how these relate to national and international politics. He sees the contemporary historical situation as being shaped by a conflict of networks. On one side, we have the networks of power, the ones constructed around multi-media businesses. On the other, we have the networks of counter-power, the ones shaped by the mass communication of the self. But the practice of the self, through the form of creative autonomy he advocates, bears little relation to the deeper and broader social and political contexts in which it takes place. And this brings us directly back once more to concepts of hegemony. A consideration of social and political contexts brings to bear a critical consideration of the dominant framings of acceptable political action and social organization, as well as the broader positioning of political activity within neoliberal discourse. In this contemporary political configuration, participation is framed in terms of individualistic values that are clearly identifiable in much of the life and action in digital media, and in social media in particular. Hence, the creative autonomy of individuals enabled by new communication technologies that Castells proclaims as libera-tory can equally be interpreted, drawing on Castoriadis (1991), as 'individualistic autonomy' conducive to neoliberal practice.

Indeed, Castoriadis's (1991) discussion of different levels of auton-omy is particularly helpful as a corrective here. He makes a crucial distinction between individualistic autonomy, social autonomy (through equality of participation) and autonomy as political subjectivity (that liberates the imagination). Castoriadis confronts autonomy within the system of neoliberal capitalism (individualistic) with autonomy that seeks to challenge the system (social) or transcend the system (through political subjectivity), arguing for better recognition of the social-historical conditions for, and the social-historical dimensions of, the project of autonomy (Papacharissi, 2010b). Of course, while these theo-retical distinctions are useful in enabling us to interrogate the term, in daily life, facilitated by converged media, we may well engage in all three forms of autonomy at once. We may go on to a social networking site and comment on the latest celebrity gossip story, then click and link our way to a petition on ending child poverty, while updating our blog that tells everyone what we've just done and how we think the world could be a better place.

This chimes with Habermas's understanding of 'the co-originality of private autonomy and public autonomy' (1996: 104) – though they may be opposed, they are internally related and 'reciprocally presuppose each other' (ibid.: 417). The one does not exist without the other. In other words, it acknowledges the deep context in which any form of autonomy or creativity is situated and seeks to under-stand its various manifestations in relation to it. The problem with Castells's (2009) notion of creative autonomy and the emphasis in new social movements on autonomous individuals is the prioritiza-tion of the individual over the political and collective context, which resists problematizing the notion of autonomy in relation to broader social and political contexts.

And here we come back to the conditions required for political organizing and new political systems. Claims that the starting condi-tions for social and political action have been radically changed by digital communications are difficult to take seriously when they rely solely on the creative autonomy of the individual and largely ignore how these individuals are themselves situated in particular social orders that enable some social and/or political responses and disable others. If we take Laclau and Mouffe's (1985) proposition that poli-tics is a struggle between complexes of meaningful social practice as well as ideas, we must also insist on political economic concerns as one set of practices. We are then reminded that the internet does not transcend global capitalism but is deeply involved with it by virtue of the corporate interests it supports and the discourses of capitalism and neoliberalism in which the people who use it are drenched.

It is irrefutable that the growth in social networking sites and their usage has been phenomenal. In March 2015, Facebook had an average of 936 million daily active users (http://newsroom.fb.com/company-info/) compared with 250 million in 2010, with an average of 12.58 daily unique page views per visitor for an average of 19.37 minutes per day (www.alexa.com/siteinfo/facebook.com). Nielsen's research (2012) shows that, in 2012, people spent 20 per cent of their total time online via their personal computer on social media and 30 per cent via mobile devices. However, assumptions of radical political possibilities based on usage quickly fade into insignificance when we consider the political-economic context in more detail. In 2014, Facebook had an annual turnover of \$12.466 billion and quarterly advertising revenue of \$3.594 billion (representing a 7.6 per cent share of the US digital advertising market), while Twitter had an annual turnover of \$1.403 billion and quarterly advertising revenue of \$432 million. So social networking may further promote forms of mediation that could be used for radical political ends, but these are deeply commodified. The sociality inscribed within these platforms also enables corporations to extract value from our personal data while encouraging a form of sociality that foregrounds the self and self-promotion. In other words, in developed Western democracies, where social media exist within social and political contexts that foreground individualization, embedded in technological developments that encourage pervasive communication and an ever-connected online presence, social networking sites are seen as extending neoliberal ideology rather than contesting it (Fenton, 2016).

One of the ways in which neoliberal ideology is extended is through the discourses of the 'network'. The network promises flexibility in the practices of living and working, speed and efficiency in domestic and professional worlds, as well as the rewards of a limitless archive and an abundance of information that comes from being connected. Networked capitalism insists on always being switched on and being online in order to live the network, but rarely acknowledges that, as Couldry (2010: 33) states, 'networks are only possible because of underlying practices of meaning.' In a neoliberal context, the overriding practice of meaning is the market, which has made a virtue out of the necessity of mobility and connection that the network brings. But the network also 'presents itself as the negation of categories to which people are attached on a permanent basis, and thanks to which they can construct collective norms setting limits on their individual passions' (Boltanski and Chiappello, 2005: 432). In this manner, not only must the internet be seen as deeply commodified while being conducive to sociality and to the facilitation of political networking, but networking itself must be understood as a resource for capitalism that enables the exploitation of labour through constant access to the worker and the erosion of some of the social conditions such as stable contexts for affiliation, co-operation and organization necessary for alternative discourses to emerge.

Therefore, even in the context of radical political activism, the network can be as hierarchical as communications of old, as Coretti (2014) demonstrates in his analysis of the Purple Movement in Italy (see chapter 2). If the political organization is set up for non-dialogic politics, then it is highly unlikely that network capability is going to change that. Politics and political organization emerge from histories that do not evaporate in the face of technology. Thus, the possibilities for political organization and a left transformative politics will be different in each context. In the developed democracies of the West, establishing the conditions for political collectivity and co-operation to thrive requires countering the consumerist and individualistic ideology of neoliberalism that exists across all of our daily practices and experiences – offline and online. In laying claim to autonomy that seeks to challenge and transcend the system of which it is part, we must first recognize that our political subjectivities form part of the social order and exist in relation to others. Personal autonomy based on self-will too quickly collapses into individualistic autonomy of an asocial ego that is conducive to rather than affronting the capitalist order. Such an approach may be able to offer respect for diversity, but it can never offer a means of living better together through radically democratized political systems.

Seen from this angle, the multiplicity and autonomy that have been proclaimed as revolutionary take on a different complexion, as we are forced to recognize and take account of current relations of power in an online context that encircles (but does not enslave) the agency of individuals. We are also encouraged to recognize and take account of communicational life without fetishizing the media forms that may enable it. In resisting a fetishized media centrism, we are also encouraged to rethink the complex of relations and organizational dynamics involved in any political movement in a critical contextual frame in order to understand mediation and its relationship to our social and cultural practices.

Participating in Digital Networks

The notion of autonomy that is somehow thrust upon us in an online world has an ally in the form of the celebration of participation.

Žižek (1997) has called this 'inter-passivity', by which he means that our online involvement gives the illusion of activity, a circulation of endless opinion resulting in the fetishization of contribution that is ultimately passive. This resonates with Dean's (2009) analysis of communicative capitalism – a techno-scientific form of democracy that talks without responding, a communicative politics that resides in an obsession with voice – where everyone has one but few get heard and even fewer are responded to in a manner that could ever be heralded as politically significant. The flip side of course is, when you want to be ignored, new media makes that impossible too, as all your digital comings and goings can be tracked, and even the smallest whisper can be policed, monitored, traced and criminalized (Khiabany, 2010).

We also have to ask ourselves: Does the autonomy endowed upon us in this participatory nirvana, and the multiplicity of voices it facilitates, expand the extent and range of contention? And, then, who gains preferential treatment as the favoured subjects and matter of politics, and who and what are disfavoured, or made less likely? The micro-blogging platform Twitter has been hailed as a democratic medium for the dissemination of marginalized political views. It is rarely acknowledged, however, that 90 per cent of Twitter traffic is generated by 10 per cent of respondents who have managed to amass a multitude of followers, often as a consequence of their celebrity status (Heil and Piskorski, 2009). In 2014 in the UK, the most followed person on Twitter was Harry Styles of the pop group One Direction, who had 22.8 million followers; in second place was the generic One Direction account, with 21.5 million followers; the pop star Adele was in third place, followed by Liam Payne (yet another One Direction member) and then Louis Tomlinson (you guessed it, One Direction again). The rest of those in the top ten, apart from @BBCBreaking (a trusted but dominant mainstream news source, which came in at ninth place) (Allan, 2014), were also celebrities or pop stars. A US study of Twitter during the 2012 presidential campaign conventions and debates similarly found a slavish retweeting of elites, media stars and established news outlets (Lin et al., 2014).

Furthermore, the proliferation of types of popular subjects and matter that dominant media institutions are predisposed to recognize implies that expansions in so-called participatory networked media are no more than echo chambers for hegemonic discourse. Dean (2009) also suggests that the mythic attribution to social media of openness and participation inculcates its own hegemonic discourse based on the rhetoric of liberal pluralism, which happens to coincide with extreme corporatization, financialization and privatization across the globe.

In the UK, a report by the Carnegie Trust (2010) remarks on diminishing arenas for public deliberation, along with the marginalization of dissent, especially in relation to those who lack power or confidence to voice their concerns or those who have non-mainstream views. This narrowing of the public sphere appears to be happening despite the expansion of mediated space and the multiplicity of media platforms and claims regarding interactivity, speed and the international reach of online communications. So, rather than simply celebrating digital media as multiplying contestation, amplifying dissent and thereby enhancing autonomy, it is also important to consider the critical question raised by Dean (2009: 25): 'Why, at a time when the means of communication have been revolutionized,...why has democracy failed as a political form? And then to ask the pertinent question of why neoliberalism continues to thrive as a political project.'

But we could equally point to an amplification of protest and a proliferation of political uprisings that are suggestive of a broader historical context, where the residues of other politics – such as the redistributive politics of the welfare state in the UK and many parts of Western Europe – combine with the affective dimensions of counter-political networked communication that may enable empathy and care and expand co-operation and collaborative working, extending to corners where capital has yet to reach. Indeed, it is ever more important to do so. If we understand the world only from the perspective of the reproduction of the logic of capital, we run the risk of misnoticing or misrecognizing political opportunities. Capital does not always win out. And, when it fails, we need to understand what is particular to the circumstances and histories of cases that 'obstruct capital's lines of flight' (Skeggs, 2014: 15). We need to identify resistance to corporate capitalism in order to analyse what it is and how it can bring about a progressive politics. To understand radical politics and resistance, we need to appreciate that this involves individuals, their identities and their passions, as much as it does organizations and institutions, their structures and their strictures. And this is where the issue of political organization becomes key.

New Politics or Anti-Politics?

The work of Hardt and Negri (2000, 2004) embodies many of the debates above in their attempts to broach a politics of the multitude. Their work has become a source of validation and direction for many (young) people involved in contemporary radical politics and transnational social movements. Hardt and Negri call on us to reclaim the concept of democracy in its radical, utopian sense: the absolute democracy of 'the rule of everyone by everyone' (2004: 307). The multitude, they argue, is the first and only social subject capable of realizing such a project. They propose a description of the multitude as 'an open network of singularities that links together on the basis of the common they share and the common they produce' – a union that does not, however, in any way subordinate or erase the radical differences among those singularities. It is a network analysis well suited to the webbed communication of the internet.

Empire, by colonizing and interconnecting ever more areas of human life, creates the possibility for democracy the likes of which we have never seen before. Brought together in multinodal forms of resistance, different groups combine and recombine in fluid networks expressive of 'life in common' (Hardt and Negri, 2004: 202). In other words, they form a multitude. The multitude is a heterogeneous web of workers, migrants, social movements and non-governmental organizations – 'potentially...all the diverse figures of social production' (ibid.: xv), 'the living alternative that grows within Empire' (ibid.: xiii). The multitude is not the people per se but, rather, many peoples acting in networked concert. Because of both its plurality and the sharing of life in common controlled by capital, it is claimed that the multitude contains the composition of true democracy.

Hardt and Negri argue that the shift from industrial to post-industrial societies has been accompanied by a shift in the dominant form of labour, from industrial labour to more 'immaterial' forms of work – the production of social relations, communication, affects, relationships and ideas. It produces and touches on all aspects of social, economic, cultural and political life. Hardt and Negri call this 'newly dominant model' 'biopolitical production' (2004: xvi). This shift is profoundly reorganizing many aspects of our lives, including the very ways we interact and organize ourselves. The authors propose that this labour increasingly produces 'the common' – a central concept to their thesis and the basis upon which any democratic project will be built. The multitude's ability to communicate, form alliances and forge solidarity – often through the very capitalist networks that oppress it – allows it to produce a common body of knowledge and ideas that can serve as a platform for democratic resistance to Empire, a union which does not in any way subordinate or erase the radical differences among those disparate groupings. As Oswell (2006: 97) states, 'If the people are defined by their identity, relation to sovereignty and represented homogeneity, the multitude in contrast is defined through its absolute heterogeneity and through its being a congregation of singularities.'

Hardt and Negri (2004) see one of the political manifestations of globalization as the declining autonomy of the nation-state, with power shifting simultaneously towards intergovernmental organizations such as the United Nations and the World Trade Organization and downwards towards regional and local assemblies (Held, 1999). The shrinkage of the state through initiatives such as privatization, marketization and deregulation means that decision-making has flowed away from public bodies and official government agencies that were directly accountable to elected representatives and devolved to a complex variety of non-profits and private agencies operating at local, national and international levels. It is claimed that it has become more difficult for citizens to use conventional state-oriented channels of participation, exemplified by national elections, as a way of challenging those in power, reinforcing the need for alternative avenues and targets of political expression and mobilization. Hardt and Negri point to anti-globalization and anti-war protests as exercises in democracy motivated by people's desire to have a say over decisions that impact upon the world in which they live – operating at a transnational level.

However, Hardt and Negri's call for a 'new science of democracy' (2004: 348) is difficult to pin down. Exactly how the multitude can stand up and be counted is never set out. Badiou (cited in Bosteels, 2011: 318) referred to the idea of the multitude as a 'dreamy hallucination', something to 'enjoy without doing anything, while taking special care to avoid any form of discipline, whereas we know that discipline, in all fields, is the key to truths.' Laclau (2004) has called the notion of the multitude the antithesis of politics – an agency that does not articulate, represent or strategize. This is utopia without architecture and universality without meaning. A movement of antagonistic constitution does not offer direction as to how such a community of diversity is organized; it merely enacts the right of resistance. But, as Mouffe (2005) contends, enacting the right of resistance, revealing political struggle and conflict in a diversity of forms, is crucial to the actual practice of democracy and can lead to multiple forms of unity and common action. The more acts of resistance, the more various the forms of struggle, the better possibility there is for appeal to a wide a range of political actors and thus to the potential for many instances of unity.

Mouffe (2005) argues against an understanding of democracy that operates under the illusion of consensus and unanimity, believing that this results in a lack of political struggles with which people can identify – a void which is then open to other forms of identification such as those of an ethnic, nationalist or religious nature. It also leads to a direct association of liberal democracy with 'actually existing liberal democratic capitalism', whereby the political dimension is instilled within the rules of law and the sovereign nation-state. Rather, Mouffe contends,

> There is no threshold of democracy that once reached will guarantee its continued existence. Democracy is in peril not only when there is insufficient consensus and allegiance to the values it embodies but also when its agonistic dynamic is hindered by an apparent excess of consensus.... A healthy democratic process calls for a vibrant clash of political positions and an open conflict of interests. If such is missing, it can too easily be replaced by a confrontation between non-negotiable moral values and essentialist identities. (2005: 6)

Mouffe seeks a radical plural interpretation of liberalism that will break with rationalism, individualism and universalism and see the political as a complex of power relations that is necessarily plural and discursively constructed. Translating a plural politics of agonism into forms of political organization takes supreme effort and much time. Taking account of all views, insisting on inclusivity, debating, considering, referring and reconsidering is a lengthy and often arduous process that works against fast capitalism. It is precisely *not* something that can be done at the click of a mouse online. In the same manner that Sennett (2008) argues that the work of the craftsman represents an oppositional value system that has struggled against industrialization and capitalism, so the work of the radical democrat represents counter-political values that struggle against the commodification of politics into tick-boxes in sporadic elections in a liberal democratic system.

Conclusion: Organization Is Politics[2]

A post-foundational politics that seeks to move beyond the strictures of the 'isms' of old and embrace individual creative autonomy reminds us that all creative human activity holds the potential for political transformation. But to understand how this potential can be translated into a reality requires an appreciation of the enduring social and political relations that surround and pre-exist certain individuals and their relations with others. Broadening radical political imagination to think outside of existing neoliberal frameworks can never be a solitary project; it must be a collective endeavour. This is not to deny the role of individuals in singular acts of political intervention. Rather, it is a plea to recognize and appreciate the extent of the struggle required to counter the practices of domination that are embedded ever deeper in the means of communication.

Multiplicity and autonomy alone offer no way of fathoming the means to transcend and replace dominant hegemonic discourses. Only when we can reach a full appreciation of our online mediations and their contingent and multiple relations to structure and agency can we assess the *feasibility* of achieving a new hegemony, of transforming the existing political order, either partially or radically, and the role of mediation therein. Despite the claims of multiplicity and autonomy, we need to be reminded constantly that politics and its transformation rest on material conditions and their consequences, both for individuals and for organizations and institutions. Without this critical contextual anchorage, a focus on multiplicity, interactivity and participation runs the risk of being translated into either a liberal tolerance of difference, which in fact prevents substantive questions from being asked, or an anarchic, autonomous and ultimately individualistic politics that prevents substantive change from happening (Fenton, 2012a).

The contemporary political constellation also requires us to appreciate that organization *is* politics. A politics requires a practice. Autonomous movements attempt to embody their politics in horizontal organizational forms that eschew leadership. Leninist revolutionary politics has invariably taken the form of democratic centralism, which functions with rules and norms in a bid to build revolutionary workers' organizations. The politics at play influences the organization's relationship to the media and to their own mediated practices. The politics of the autonomous movements are well suited to the networked architecture of the internet, whereas the desire to control the message in a Leninist politics is challenged by a less disciplined and less easily orchestrated issue-affinity approach of the politically engaged in a digital age. Organizational habits are then as much politically inflected as they are socially constructed. We cannot understand the nature of the organization without understanding its politics; we cannot understand the politics without appreciating its processes and organization. Yet so many studies do just this. Social movement studies dedicate much research and analysis to organizational form. In doing so, they articulate the relationship between modernization, technological change and organizational variation. Della Porta and Diani (2006) discuss how organizations were once required to be tightly structured to get their message across, whereas in the digital age a loosely knit organization can do just the same; but such studies rarely critique how the actual politics evolves in these dynamic processes.

It is worth underlining that the consequences of material conditions for political organizations can be severe. Put simply, creating an organizational infrastructure for political transformation when you are hungry and homeless is deeply problematic, even if you are angry and have a passion for social change. On the whole, economic progress benefits the organizing capacity of social movements: 'as the amount of discretionary resources of mass and elite publics increases, the absolute and relative amount of resources available to the SMS [social movement sector] increases' (Zald and McCarthy 1987: 25). Crucially this will include people's time and money, but it also refers to political freedom, the means of communication and transportation (della Porta and Diani, 2006; Kaun, 2015). As these develop, the resources available for new groups and movements to emerge also increase, and so economic development leads incrementally to more professional, formal groupings (Zald and McCarthy, 1987). This, in turn, will impact upon the groups' access to power. But if economic development means increasing inequality and an ever-greater degree of poverty (see chapter 1), it will also impact on the organizing capacity of radical political groups and movements. This is when the low entry cost of new technology is considered paramount.

Paradoxically, Tufekci (2014) has argued that the lower costs associated with communication and mobilization via digital connectivity have both empowered social movements around the world and disempowered them by pushing them into the spotlight without the requisite organizational infrastructure to be able to deal with what comes next. Barassi (2015a, 2015b) also notes how the immediacy of online communication 'is affecting processes of political reflection, discussion and elaboration in negative ways[,]...creat[ing] a type of "political participation" that relies on weak affinities and strong emotions' (2015b: 99). So it is undeniable that social media have enabled movements to spread and grow and to put into practice aspirations of a seemingly leaderless and horizontal politics, but this has also contributed to a lack of organizational depth – an oppositional politics that is speeded up but spread thin. An over-reliance on online organization is also an easy target for repressive regimes keen to censor and scrutinize the online world for insubordination, then 'seek to divide, polarize and counter its influence by joining it, with their own supporters or employees, or by beating it, via demonization and/or bans, which do not completely block motivated citizens but help keep government supporters from using and trusting it' (Tufekci,

2014: 8). The wave of political uprisings and new social movements of the last decade has not pushed back austerity policies in Europe (despite Syriza's election victory in Greece); the Occupy movement may have publicized the gross inequality between the 99 percent and the 1 per cent, but it has not directly changed the underlying policies that sustain it; and within one year of the massive protests in Gezi Park the ruling AKP party won two elections comfortably. But why would we expect anything different? The impact of mobilizations will always depend on a whole range of deeply contextual and contingent factors (see chapter 4).

Tufekci (2014) suggests that we should adopt Amartya Sen's (1999) approach from development economics that focuses on capabilities and apply it to political movements. So, rather than focus on outputs, we consider the functions that give a group and the individuals within it agency and capability to carry out other acts. If we think about this in relation to technology, we see the capability of digital media to respond quickly to events and mobilize mass demonstrations with speed – functions that once required much more formal and lengthy organizing. This is fantastic for protest politics, but in the race to respond there is a danger that the movement runs roughshod over the slower process of political organization, which also built the capacity to deliberate, establish close relations and trust between participants, and consider long-term objectives, strategies and tactics – all of things that political activism requires to collaborate effectively. Hence, movements find themselves too quickly in confrontation, without prior experience of how to manage what comes next. The trade-off between speed and long-term organizational capacity-building also threatens to diminish the slow burn of skills development of activists who help push a protest politics towards being a political movement. As Tufekci notes, it is often at the end of street protests, when the initial excitement and energy fades, that protesters accustomed to organizing horizontally and online are often unable to decide what to do next:

> Toward the end of the Gezi Park protests...the government requested a delegation to negotiate on behalf of the protesters. Some protesters felt that this was a disingenuous move, while others were willing to negotiate. However, the park had no formal leadership mechanism that was universally recognized by all protesters. A loose coordinating committee had taken to running many aspects of the movement, but lacking formal recognition, it also lacked formal legitimacy. There was much contestation over who should serve as delegates, and it ended up being the government that, on two occasions, invited different

cohorts of delegates to represent the park. The first was composed of fairly irrelevant people within the movement and was seen as less than legitimate by movement participants. The second invitation was extended to people who appeared to have had a long record of involvement with the movement and were active in highly visible roles, which thus garnered more approval. However, this too had no formal mechanism for recognition. In the end, the second delegation was unable to negotiate or devise a strategic plan to move forward…In the end, no real resolution was reached because some formal institutions that had taken part in the protests decided to end them, leaving behind a symbolic tent, while many individuals and some other collectives wanted to stay. This caused even more confusion, and the government moved in shortly after with a massive police presence and disbanded the camp by force. (Tufekci, 2014: 14)

The capacity of the Gezi Park movement was clearly limited beyond its impressive ability to organize a protest. Tufekci then compares this to the civil rights 'March on Washington' in 1963, whose participants had wanted to remain leaderless and operate as a horizontal movement. However, because the means of communication were simply not available to them, had they completely refused leaders or organizations, the large march might never have happened, since it would have been too difficult to pull off at the practical level. When it did happen, it illustrated to those in power how impressive its organizational capacity was and hence the level of threat it posed. The same cannot be said of the Occupy movement, which, although it was huge in scale (taking place in over 900 cities worldwide), was organized in a very short space of time and did not lead to any discernible policy changes – the organizational capacity it signalled based on ease of mobilization does not pose the same danger to those in power.

Communicative means are important, but of course they are not the only factor that determines the forms, intensity and longevity of political movements. Organizational form shapes political action and politics just as political action and politics shape organizational form. A politics of protest can end up being no politics at all if the politics has not been in gestation before the protest takes place and the organizational infrastructure is absent. Protest happens first and foremost as a response to symptoms – an often visceral response to problems in the prevailing social system. As such, a protest politics rarely presents a challenge to the social order because it has no alternative proposition to make other than remedial solutions. Bookchin (2015: 180) notes that '[a] revolutionary Left that seeks to advance from protest demonstrations to revolutionary demonstrations must resolutely confront the problem of organization.' This means asking what forms of organization are likely to be enduring and develop a programme for social change that can be translated into everyday practice. What are the conditions required (including the communicative conditions) for political organizations to endure and build capacity? Has the understandable desire for leaderless (dis)organization fetishized multiplicity and difference to the point of political hindrance?

Without an understanding of organization and of the politics that informs it, we are left with a naive view of the relations between technology and politics. In one of the most complex and empirically detailed studies of digital media and oppositional politics, Bennett and Segerberg (2013) talk about organizational form and its relationship to technology in terms of connective action and collective action and the characteristics that define each. But what is surprising and replicated in study upon study is that at no point do they discuss the actual politics involved. This is tantamount to studying a body by looking only at the skeleton and how the joints fit together without ever getting to grips with the beating heart that powers it or the brain that tells it what to do. Ultimately, by ignoring the actual politics, we end up depoliticizing counter-politics because we offer precious few suggestions as to how we can do democratic politics differently (on both the small and the large scale). Chapter 1 discussed what defines critical theory – it must be explanatory, normative and pragmatic. In other words, it must shed light on what *is* with a clear sense of what *should be* and then suggest a way to bridge the two. Without an understanding of the organization on which a left progressive politics can develop, the politics itself will remain nebulous and ill-defined. And we will have no one to blame but ourselves.

6

On Being Political and the Politics
of Being

This chapter brings together the debates in the previous two and argues that the way in which we discuss the notion of the political (in media, communication and cultural studies in particular) is often lacking because of the tendency to separate politics into *being political and the politics of being*. There is a conceptual difference that is tangible and measurable between 'being political' (often translated as the practice of politics that may occur within or in opposition to a conventional political system) and 'the politics of being' (the more subjective aspect of our political selves described in chapter 4), which is more nebulous and difficult to pin down, though the two aspects are intimately connected.

The notion of 'being political' is dominated largely by approaches that stress active participation and citizenship, defined most frequently through voting or engagement in the public sphere, which is at the very least inflected by the terms of its mediation – often found in the subfields of political communication or social scientific approaches and usually framed by political economy. What I am calling the 'politics of being', on the other hand, refers to the more subjective, affective and irrational dimensions of the political, often related to being resistive and exhibiting agency that invariably falls under the banner of cultural studies. For example, the active audience *is political* not usually by virtue of an engagement with a state or non-state/societal polity, but by dint of an affective response to dominant social and political structures that speaks to the lived experience of the political. In the field of media, communication and cultural studies, being an oppositional or active social agent has invariably come under the banner of 'resistance'. The active audience resists the hegemonic representation in the text. People are able to manipulate imagery and information for their own ends, to build their own identities and local politics from the vast array of mediated bits and pieces they have at their disposal. Through this, social and political agency occurs and subcultures form acts of resistance, displaying their profound aversion to particular socio-political conditions in various ways.[1] We look for resistance in every element of mediation and every act of consumption to satisfy ourselves that we are not cultural dupes beholden to the edicts of the market and the state. We rarely, however, extend the identification of subjective resistance (which is itself often contested) into the actual development and deliberation of a new politics and the world of the political public sphere.[2]

Traditionally, political economy has tended to read the state and other superstructural forces from the specific configuration of capital at any one time and insists that this is the starting point of social analysis.[3] Cultural studies reminds political economy that the substance of its work, the analysis of communication, is rooted in the needs, goals, conflicts, failures and accomplishments of ordinary people attempting to make sense of their lives. Cultural studies has recognized the energizing potential of multifaceted forms of social agency, each of which brings with it dimensions of subjectivity and consciousness that are vital to political praxis. Often this has been displayed through research that focuses on media consumption. But cultural studies conceptions of power have a tendency to be rooted in individual subjectivities, their identities and collective action, rather than, as political economy would have it, structured in the institutions of society (Fenton, 2007).

Most of us feel a profound sense of politics when we experience or empathize with a sense of injustice. Being political is, as we know, not solely or even largely about the act of voting – a rational, accountable and representative form of politics structured by consensus; it is so much more than that. Yet the way we discuss the notion of the political is often lacking because of the tendency to separate politics into discrete aspects that may better map onto particular theoretical perspectives but lose a holistic sense of the felt experience and practice of politics in the process: being political is then disengaged from the politics of being, and radical progressive thought struggles to move forward.

In both aspects, 'the political' refers to the nature of representation (whether cultural and/or political) and the way in which politics is

administrated and mediated (discussed in terms of political organization in the previous chapter), but rarely do they come together to
provide a more sophisticated understanding of political life. Neither
approach takes full account of both the difference and the relationship between being political (the act of doing politics) and the politics
of being (the subjective experience of the political), and neither can
therefore reach a full understanding of radical politics. Yet it is hard
to imagine a more important task at a more relevant time. We are
now at a critical historical juncture where we have experienced both
the collapse of socialist regimes and the dramatic crash of the markets
that support global capitalism. But it appears that so many thinkers
are struggling to find alternatives to neoliberalism and are bereft of
a social imaginary that embodies any sort of radical political hope.

Chapters 4 and 5 have argued that focusing on creating the optimal
conditions for being political is vital but will only ever reach a limited
understanding of political behaviour and the transformative power
of agency. Fixing our sights solely on 'being political' ignores the
affective, irrational, antagonistic characteristics that mark out 'politics as being' – the dimension of the political that inspires, frustrates,
exhilarates, angers and mobilizes. Similarly, focusing only on the
affective dimensions of 'politics as being' often disconnects political
agency from any political end point(s) (whether this translates into
institutional forms or not) – it removes the purpose of radical politics
(to achieve socially progressive transformation).

My argument is straightforward: it is not enough simply to celebrate agency and resistance through the conduit of the internet and
the veneration of horizontality and difference or to detail the macro-
structures of power and political economy; nor is it enough to identify
and distinguish individual autonomy without appreciating the social
construction of political identity. Rather, we must do both at once
and, in the process, find a means to interrogate contradiction and
control, the global and the local, the mainstream and the alternative.
These two polarized debates, which suffer from the centrifugal tendencies of approaches that deal with either 'structure' or 'agency',
are then brought together through a discussion of 'being political and
the politics of being', via the lens of contemporary radical politics
and political/social movements, to argue for a broader and deeper
understanding of what 'the political' means and the context required
for an adequate assessment of the terms of its mediation. Approaching analysis in this holistic manner then opens up political critique
and leads me to suggest that a potential way forward for radical
politics is to look towards *repoliticizing the economy* and *resocializing the political*.

One way to bring these two polarized debates together is through a consideration of power – who has it and what should be done with it. We need to explain and evaluate power and its relationship to the political in order to do critique. We need to understand who holds power, how it is wielded and in what forms it exists, whether visibly or invisibly, to understand how those who have it influence the decisions that structure and organize the distribution of resources throughout societies. How power is used is related to the political vision it stems from and whether this is generally right wing and possibly neoliberal or left wing and possibly progressive and radical. The power to influence the way society is governed is massively limited and determined largely by money – through either wealthy individuals or corporations. In this context we need also to understand what powerlessness feels like. We cannot do social and political critique of any sort without an appreciation of how these pieces fit together. To understand radical politics better and extend the possibilities for radical progressive thought, we need to interrogate the relationship between radical politics and power and test power against equality. This will require a broader and deeper understanding of intersubjectivity and difference, solidarity and contestationary politics – or the relationship between '*being political and the politics of being*'. Yet few theorists consciously and constantly make power, and the claiming of that power into political systems that can sustain equal power relations, a consistent part of their analyses. On this basis, this chapter is a bid to understand radical politics and power both as concepts and *as practices*, without which critique is fatally flawed.

Of course, *being political* has never been just about voting in formal elections or being part of formal party politics. The idea of 'being political' is a deeply social one, often (although not always) aligned with joining, being committed to, or obligated to political action through various forms of collective responsibility or connective affinities (Bennett and Segerberg, 2013; Bennett et al., 2014). Being political can involve a range of intermingled practices that will have something to do with living together in a world of difference and about how and why resources get shared. It may involve self-sacrifice as your political duties displace (or even take over) activities connected to personal gain. It may be self-consciously (or even actually) heroic in the pursuit of social good, or it may be something you do in a spare five minutes online. It will likely involve conflict of some kind and regular disagreement, and so it will also involve compromise, negotiation and bargaining. In this sense, being political is constantly performative and embodies *a politics of being* – an activity that confers identity through practice and display. This is important, as it is only through display and practice, through making a politics visible, that it can be both contested and put to the test. And it is only under these circumstances that politics can edge towards being a radical politics.

Alain Badiou (2005) rightly insists that politics is a type of thinking; its 'truth' emerges in political action. But this 'truth' must also be constantly challenged in order to continue being radically political. Doing radical politics, then, involves a process of becoming but of never arriving; in order to be progressive, one must continually challenge the here and now. But being political often operates under severe constraints; this leads Rancière (1999) to note that real politics is extremely rare. These constraints are multiple and refer, not least, to the vastly unequal access to resources required to do politics at the level of intensity required to effect change – the time, money and cultural capital that is more available to the middle and upper classes. But the contemporary political economies of our worlds bring with them further structural limitations that constantly frame and constrain our political practices. Two of these meta-constraints are outlined below. They have been selected for the particular ways in which they enclose and enfold politics and for the linkages between those ways (each involves massive consolidations of global capital). Both have been the subject of much campaigning and oppositional politics through the media reform movements worldwide[4] and the anti-austerity politics of the current financial crisis (spurred by the Indignados movement in Spain).

The Constraints of Being Political: Politics Subordinated to Media Power

The political playing field is not just tilted towards those who already hold economic and social power; its slant is positively vertiginous. It has long been acknowledged that democracy is linked to capitalism while also being at odds with it (Streeck, 2012, 2014; Bauman and Bordini, 2014). This is brought into sharp relief when we consider the wily entanglement between political elites and media elites exposed in the phone hacking scandal in the UK in 2011 (Fenton, 2013).

In the summer of 2011, the *News of the World*, owned by Rupert Murdoch, stood accused of illegal, unethical behaviour through the systematic phone hacking of politicians, members of the royal family, celebrities, and murder victims and their families. Murdoch subsequently closed down the paper, and several ex-editors and journalists found themselves under criminal investigation. The prime minister, David Cameron, publicly embarrassed by having employed, as his director of communications, Andy Coulson (a former editor of the *News of the World* between 2003 and 2007), who was arrested by the Metropolitan Police in July 2011 on allegations of corruption and phone hacking (and charged in June 2014), then called for a public inquiry chaired by Lord Justice Leveson to investigate the issue. Eighteen months later the report by Lord Leveson (2012) into the culture, practices and ethics of the press was published. It revealed a sordid relationship of kowtowing and mutual back scratching between politicians and media owners and raised serious doubts as to whether certain newspapers in the UK could ever claim to be contributing to democratic sustenance.

Hackgate, as it became known, portrayed in lurid technicolour, through live web-streaming of courtroom evidence, the mechanisms of a system based on the corruption of power – of both governing and mediating elites and the relations between them. During the Leveson inquiry it was revealed that a member of the cabinet had met executives from Rupert Murdoch's empire once every three days on average since the coalition government had been formed.[5] The inquiry also heard about the close personal relationships between senior members of government and senior Murdoch employees. On 7 October 2009, the day before David Cameron addressed the Conservative Party conference, Rebekah Brooks, then chief executive of News International (2009–11) and herself a former editor of the *News of the World* and *The Sun*, sent Cameron the following text message:

> But seriously I do understand the issue with the *Times*. Let's discuss over country supper soon. On the party it was because I had asked a number of NI [News International] people to Manchester post endorsement and they were disappointed not to see you. But as always Sam was wonderful – (and I thought it was OE's [Old Etonians] that were charm personified!) I am so rooting for you tomorrow not just as a proud friend but because professionally we're definitely in this together! Speech of your life? Yes he Cam![6]

The Brooks–Cameron relationship is particularly indicative of a culture of press–politician mutual interest in which media executives and party leaders work together to 'push the same agenda', in Cameron's words. But we also heard four successive prime ministers give evidence to the Leveson inquiry into the press admitting they were 'too close' to the big media players because the political stakes were so very high. The inquiry also revealed the systematic invasions of privacy by headline-hungry journalists which wrecked lives of ordinary people on a daily basis (Cathcart, 2012); the lies and deceit of senior newspaper figures; and a highly politicized and corrupt police force also in league with media power. Rebekah Brooks admitted having paid police for information in a House of Commons Select Committee in 2003 but denied it in 2011 (BBC News, 15 April 2011), and we discovered that over a quarter of members of the police public affairs department were previous employees of the *News of the World* (Warrell, 2011). In such circumstances, political parties, the police and other institutions are reluctant to investigate wrongdoing in the news media, to hinder the expansion of large media conglomerates, or to introduce new regulation of news organizations and journalistic practice.

The problem of phone hacking reaches much broader and deeper than any slippage in ethical practice would seem to suggest and rests not with the individual journalists but with the system of news production of which they are part. The reasons hinge, first, on the increasing entanglement of political and media elites as news coverage has taken on an ever more important role in policy-making and elections (Davis 2002; Coleman, 2012) and fewer and fewer people vote; second, on the failure of the Press Complaints Commission (the newspaper industry watchdog)[7] to uphold ethical standards and enable adequate self-regulation of journalists (CCMR, 2011; Couldry et al., 2010); and, third, on the broken business model of newspapers with plummeting circulation and readership figures and the migration of classified advertising to online sites such as Craigslist in the US and Gumtree and eBay in the UK (Fenton, 2010; Levy and Nielsen, 2010) (see chapter 3).

At a time when resources are scarce and when there is pressure to meet multiple deadlines across a whole series of news platforms, it is easy to see how the already constrained autonomy of journalists and their freedom to act ethically towards the collective gains of the profession can be eroded for the competitive gain of the commercial newspaper. Combine the faster and shallower corporate journalism of the digital age (Lee-Wright et al., 2011) with the need to pull in readers for commercial rather than journalistic reasons, and it is not difficult to see how the values of professional journalism are quickly cast aside in order to indulge in sensationalism, to trade in gratuitous spectacles and to deal in dubious emotionalism. These economic drivers cannot be underestimated, but they do not tell the whole story. Rather, the concerns spring from a thoroughly marketized and deregulated newspaper industry, many parts of which have long since relegated to the sidelines the motive of the press as fourth estate speaking truth to power. As Trevor Kavanagh, associate editor of *The Sun*, noted in his own evidence to Leveson: 'news is as saleable a commodity as any other. Newspapers are commercial, competitive businesses, not a public service' (*The Guardian*, 6 October 2011). News in these formulations is conceived of as being primarily for profit – a market place that operates on market principles. But, of course, news is no ordinary commodity: it offers the possibility of directing the public conversation and hence is of relevance to politicians keen to convince voters of the benefits of their particular policy formulations. This puts news proprietors in a particular position of power. As the owner of the *London Evening Standard* and *The Independent*, the Russian billionaire Evgeny Lebedev tweeted after his appearance at Leveson: 'Forgot to tell #Leveson that it's unreasonable to expect individuals to spend £millions on newspapers and not have access to politicians.'

When news proprietors accumulate excessive power and influence, the problems associated with this power are exacerbated. In the UK, a thoroughly marketized and deregulated newspaper industry has led to unchecked media concentration over several decades, allowing some media groups to amass vast amounts of revenue along with social and political influence,with adverse consequences for ethical journalism and democracy. As this book goes to press, just three companies control 71 per cent of the UK national newspaper market. When online readers are included, just five companies dominate 80 per cent of market share (Media Reform Coalition, 2015). Rupert Murdoch 'and family' were recently positioned at number 33 on *Forbes* magazine's list of the world's most powerful people, with a net worth of $13.4 billion.[8] The work of Davis (2002) and Dean (2011) shows how such patterns of dominance and influence have also contributed to certain public policy areas – law and order, drugs, asylum-seekers, immigration, the economy – being avoided or dealt with differently for fear of either hostile reporting or media owner conflict.

In evidence to a House of Lords select committee in 2007, Rupert Murdoch said that he simply acted like 'a traditional proprietor' in regard to *The Sun* and the *News of the World*: he didn't interfere except 'on major issues, such as which party to back in a general election or policy on Europe' (House of Lords, 2008). On 21 April, *The Independent* reported that Murdoch had told journalists at *The Sun* that, if Miliband got into power, the future of the company was at stake. He then directed them to be more aggressive in their attacks against Labour and more positive about the Conservative Party.

Such market dominance of news media results in an excess of power and unruly political influence that breeds fear – fear in politicians scared of their careers being wrecked and lives ruined by negative publicity along with their parties' chances of re-election, and fear in employees too intimidated to stand up to a bullying culture where market-oriented managers place commercial priorities above journalistic responsibility and integrity. With the threat of yet more compulsory redundancies at *The Independent*, Michelle Stanistreet, general secretary of the National Union of Journalists, commented that a workforce that is paid 'bargain basement salaries...is fearful and compliant' (*Press Gazette*, 2 August 2013).

Of course, it is not only journalists whose freedom is circumscribed by corporate compliance. Our ability to exercise our own democratic freedom as ordinary members of the public is premised on the basic fact that governments are not distorted by the private interest of multi-media conglomerates. When governments as well as journalists are beholden to corporate power, then freedom is hard to come by for all but the most powerful. Politics and the opportunity to be political are beholden to public knowledge. Despite the abundance of information available online, the mainstream established news outlets still dominate our news consumption across all platforms with increasingly homogeneous content. In a nine-country study of news websites, Curran et al. (2013: 887) note that 'leading websites around the world reproduce the same kind of news as legacy media. These websites favour the voices of authority and expertise over those of campaigning organizations and the ordinary citizen.' The power of multinational media corporations is not dispersed in the age of new media; rather, new forms of media capital come to the fore. This is only one of the many ways in which public knowledge is under constant and increasing threat (Davis, 2015).

For those who think the mainstream media are ever more irrelevant in the new digital world of information abundance, McChesney (2014) notes how the global power of new digital distributors has created the greatest monopolies in economic history, with new digital industries moving from competitive, to oligopolistic, to monopolistic at a furious pace until the internet now rests in the hands of a very few giant global corporations. McChesney argues that the hyper-commercialism, advertising and monopoly markets we now find online enhance rather than disrupt the contours of capitalism; they lead to rampant depoliticization and undemocratic, commercial media policy as the point of government regulation pivots on helping corporate media maximize their profits rather than advancing the public interest. Freedman challenges the view that digital networks have shifted power from 'the centre to the periphery and from elites to ordinary users and creators', outlining how they have privileged 'accumulation strategies that are designed to reward corporate interests more than to empower individual actors' (2014: 101). He goes on to note that the power imbalance between states and those who oppose them remains vast and that, when it comes to digital surveillance, states are complicit with the world's largest communications providers. The ever-increasing entanglement of media and communications corporations with politicians and state agencies constrains the opportunities and possibilities for being political through limiting public knowledge and policing dissent, whether covertly or not.

The Constraints of Being Political: Politics Subordinated to The State Subordinated to Capital

A simple imagining of the politics of the nation-state begins with the idea of the people. A state consists of people, whether they are conceived of as already present or as a project for the future – the people to be called into being. If a state can somehow embody the collective will of its people, it is felt to be legitimate. But, when it comes to the economy, the sovereignty of the state has been transferred from national institutions to supranational authorities such as the European Central Bank, the International Monetary Fund and the World Trade Organization. These institutions have removed the political agency of the state in terms of the economy. They have made the economy their business and none of ours.[9] Such supranational organizations offer no pretence of being democratic. Therefore it is hardly surprising that successive and global protests against the WTO have met with a deafening silence. Meanwhile, the main space for political struggles to win ground remains at the national level. This political disjuncture, the way in which the global flow of capital has been severed from politics, puts acute constraints on the possibilities of being political to effect radical and progressive social change. Although the economy functions on a global basis, trade is relatively free to operate, and multinational corporations float above nation-states, often paying less in corporation tax than smaller local businesses, politics – the ability to effect political change to systems of governance – remains state-bound while states have lost the power to do anything about it.

Bauman and Bordini argue that states have been stripped of much of their power to shape the course of events. Many of our problems are globally produced, but the volume of power at the disposal of individual nation-states is simply not sufficient to cope with the extraterritorial problems they face. This divorce between power ('the ability to get things seen through and done') and politics ('the ability to decide when things ought to be done and which things are to be sorted out on the global level' (2014: 11)) produces a new kind of paralysis. It weakens the political agency that is needed to deal with the crisis, and it depletes citizens' belief that governments can deliver on their promises. The impotence of governments goes hand in hand with the growing cynicism and distrust of citizens. States are simply not equipped with the capacity to manage the new social and economic realities of finance, investment capital, global labour markets and the circulation of commodities. Hence the current economic crisis is at once a crisis of agency (governments no longer have the ability to choose a course of action and enact it), a crisis of representative democracy (because elected officials do not have the power to get things done) and a crisis of the sovereignty of the state (which is subservient to the global power of capital). Bauman notes that, 'seriously drained of powers and continuing to weaken, state governments are compelled to cede, one by one, the functions once considered a natural and inalienable monopoly of the political organs of the state into the care of the already "deregulated" market forces, evicting them thereby from the realm of political responsibility and supervision' (Bauman and Bordini, 2014: 20). The Transatlantic Trade and Investment Partnership (TTIP) – a comprehensive free trade and investment treaty (discussed in chapter 4) – is a good example of a current attempt to remove regulatory 'barriers' which restrict the potential profits to be made by transnational corporations on both sides of the Atlantic. These 'barriers' refer to social standards and environmental regulations and even new banking safeguards introduced to prevent a repeat of the 2008 financial crisis.

Bauman and Bordini's analysis resonates with Crouch's notion of a 'post-democracy' – whereby the representative mechanisms that underpin the state have been hollowed out as corporate power and influence has crept in. The state has then abdicated what power it had to counterbalance insidious economic forces and has become 'an institutional idiot' (2004: 41). The only role left to it is to attempt to manage public opinion as best it can. Crouch's (2004, 2011) analysis takes an extreme view and tends to overlook the areas where it has been argued that the state has increased its powers largely through its disciplinary and policing roles. In this analysis, the state, having lost control over the broader economic dynamics that operate outside and above its territory, is left with attempting to sort out the problems this leaves behind. Wacquant argues that, as the state has privatized its social welfare provisions, so it has also strengthened its 'penal fist' (2009: 289) as it seeks to contain those who cannot work and discipline those who can, thereby weakening the capacity of subordinate groups for political action. Wacquant goes on to show how welfare policies in the US and the UK increasingly marginalize the poor. These policies exist alongside an enormous increase in others designed to pre-empt dissent (see chapter 1), including surveillance, anti-union legislation, the criminalization of protest and incarceration. As the state increasingly renounces responsibility for the poor (through the likes of benefit capping and the sell-off of social housing), employers also push responsibility onto the individual. And we see a massive surge in insecure employment contracts, creating a new class faction – the precariat (Wacquant, 2008). The precariat, ever anxious of where the next job will come from, exerts a downward pressure on wages and limits the possibilities for industrial action. Wacquant refers to this as 'desocialized wage labour' (2008: 265).

Precarious labour increases as unemployment, particularly among the young, rises. There are currently over 5 million young people (aged under twenty-five) unemployed in the European Union, which represents a rate of 23.2 per cent in the eurozone. The differences between countries are stark. In those countries where the financial crisis has cut deepest, youth unemployment has soared. Spain has a shocking rate of 53.8 per cent and Greece 53.1 per cent, while Germany is at 7.8 per cent (European Commission, 2014). Jobs are a consequence of economic growth. If there is no growth, there are no new jobs. The International Labour Organization (2014) reported that the number of unemployed people globally grew by 5 million between 2012 and 2013, reaching nearly 202 million, and this figure is projected to grow to 215 million by 2018. Economists such as McKinsey and Company (2014) advocate yet more neoliberal policies to deal with the problem – the labour market, we are told, needs to be more 'agile' and more 'flexible', with more transferable skills and more mobility – in other words, more insecure and less well paid. The business lobby in the UK also argues for lower levels of employment protection in order to create jobs (Lanning and Rudiger, 2012). And so the fallout from a crisis brought about by financial institutions beyond state control is left to states to manage without having the tools to do the job. The state can no longer regulate the economy, and so its ability to provide social services and redistribute wealth is severely diminished. Piketty (2014) argues that the rise in inequality is indicative of markets working well – the more perfect the market, the higher the rate of return on capital in comparison to the rate of growth of the economy. The higher the ratio is, the greater inequality is. If capital incomes are more concentrated than incomes from labour, then personal income distribution also becomes more unequal.

Bordini (Bauman and Bordini, 2014: 140) lists the chief characteristics of post-democracy:

(a) deregulation – that is, the cancellation of the rules governing economic relations and the supremacy of finance and stock markets;

(b) a drop in citizens' participation in political life and elections;

(c) the return of economic liberalism (neoliberalism), entrusting to the private sector part of the functions of the state and management services – which before were 'public' – with the same criteria of economic performance as a private company;

(d) the decline of the welfare state, reserving basic services only for the poorest – i.e., as an exceptional circumstance and not as part of a generalized right for all citizens;

(e) the prevalence of lobbies which increase their power and direct policies in their desired direction;

(f) the show-business of politics, in which advertising techniques are used to produce consensus; the predominance of the figure of the leader, which relies on the power of the image, market research and a precise communicative project;

(g) a reduction in public investments;

(h) the preservation of the 'formal' aspects of democracy, which at least maintain the appearance of the guarantee of liberty.

All of these factors are interlinked, but the first sends shock waves through the rest and leaves us with greatly enfeebled nation-states which have little power (and sometimes little will) to deal with the problems they face and democracies that are increasingly bereft. The dynamics of political power and the depoliticization of the economy have contributed to the rise in inequality in advanced economies. Piketty (2014) states that the only way to halt devastating inequality in wealth is to impose a global progressive tax on wealth. A global tax would prevent the transfer of assets to countries without such taxes, restrict the concentration of wealth, and limit the income flowing to capital. But states do not have the power to bring this about.

The above examples of constraints on our political lives are set out not to spread misery and hopelessness – far from it. They are discussed in an attempt to appreciate the broader context in which a radical politics must play out. It is only by situating radical progressive politics in such a context that we can begin to ascertain what might be required to be radically political and to achieve progressive social change. In recent times, two political organizations in Europe have challenged dominant power relations in particular ways that have sought to rethink how a radical politics is possible.

The Case of Syriza

In Athens, on 6 December 2008, the police murdered a sixteen-year-old student, Alexis Grigoropoulos. This spurred a huge uprising of students and workers, who took to the streets and over the coming weeks took part in an astonishing array of dissident activities, from rallies and marches, sit-ins of police stations, the occupation of a state TV studio during a news broadcast, and the disruption of theatre performances to engage in discussion with audiences, to looting and rioting. Amnesty International accused the Greek police of brutality in their handling of the riots, as they bombarded the protesters with tear gas and flash grenades. Four days after the death of the student, the General Confederation of Greek Workers (GSEE) and the Civil Servants' Confederation (ADEY), who together represent almost half of the total Greek workforce, called a one-day general strike in protest against the government's economic policies and continued to disrupt work in solidarity with the demonstrators. Elsewhere in Europe, as well as the US and Australia, a flurry of public demonstrations were held in support of the Greek protesters.

As with other uprisings and riots in the Paris banlieues in 2005 and 2007 and in London in 2012, the dramatic death of an individual may have been the trigger for the demonstrations to start, but the causes were rooted in a much deeper and more difficult history. In responding to the protests in Greece, Prime Minister Kostas Karamanlis acknowledged that 'long-unresolved problems, such as the lack of meritocracy, corruption in everyday life and a sense of social injustice disappoint young people' (Kriakidou and Flynn, 2008). Karamanlis said income-tax cuts would go ahead. But he warned against high expectations, saying Greece would have to spend 12 billion euros – about 5 per cent of GDP – just to service its debt: 'Our top priority is to support those hurt the most...[but] this debt is a huge burden that reduces the government's flexibility at this critical time' (ibid). The unrest was set to continue and brought about, first, the resignation of the right-wing government and then its defeat, in November 2009. This gave a huge majority to Papandreou's socialists, who supported the neoliberal solutions to the financial crisis that led to the onslaught of austerity measures.

These austerity measures cut deep into the social fabric of Greek society, with 26 per cent of the population unemployed in 2015, including 50 per cent of young people. The poverty experienced so angered the population that it enabled a collective left populism, which saw the Syriza party's electoral percentage increase from under 5 per cent in 2009 to 27 per cent in June 2012. By 2015 Syriza was in government in an extremely odd coalition with the populist right-wing Independent Greeks party. With 36.3 per cent of the vote, Syriza fell two seats short of the majority required to govern alone. However, despite their ideological differences, the two parties shared a desire to end the cuts mandated by the European Commission, the International Monetary Fund and the European Central Bank that were imposed as a means of 'bailing out' a debt-riddled Athens. After eventually accepting tough austerity measures insisted on by the IMF and the European Union for Greece's third international bailout, twenty-five MPs broke away from Syriza and formed the Popular Unity party, which triggered a snap general election in September 2015. In a low turnout, Syriza held on to office with 35.5 per cent of the vote and renewed its coalition with the Independent Greeks.

Syriza is an acronym that stands for 'coalition of the radical left'. It was founded in 2004 as a federation of smaller organizations, including Maoists, left social democrats, greens, feminists, gay and social rights networks, and Trotskyites, but became a single party after a conference in July 2013. The largest of these groups was Synaspismos, whose leader, Alexis Tsipras, went on to lead Syriza. Tsipras came from a generation whose political past developed through the anti-globalization movement, the massive demonstration against the World Trade Organization in Genoa and the World and European Social Forums (Wainwright, 2015). These experiences were formative to their politics, which spurned a faithfulness to a particular ideology, preferring instead to emphasize an embrace of pluralism and open and collaborative working. This was a generation who had lived through the collapse of the Berlin Wall and the fall of the Soviet Union and wanted to replace worn-out left political scripts to develop alternatives to capitalism that were deemed appropriate to the contemporary context and were as yet unknown.

The context in which Syriza was able to come to power in Greece was complex. It followed a deep social crisis and a history of elite corruption that made people angry and yearn for political change. From the first protests in 2008, Greece witnessed a growing solidarity between trade unions, left parties and social movements. As a consequence, the people involved in the rebellion were very diverse yet found a collective identity in their desire to break with the established political order. Nonetheless, Syriza did not emerge painlessly. Bringing together twelve left political organizations into a single political party was fraught with difficulties, with the smaller groups concerned about being drowned out and the more powerful groups dominating. Like many left organizations, Syriza has its own left element – the Left Platform – that is more Eurosceptic than the leadership. How Syriza works through these differences will be a testimony to its ability to recast politics – an ambition that has already been severely tested (the Left Platform formed the core of the twenty-five MPs who resigned). One key facet of its approach was to set the aspirations of this newly formed coalition to be far more than a party, to have a broader political reach than just 'the left', and to build a united social front – thus linking the politics of being to being political. From the time the party was formed, Syriza activists were not only campaigning on the streets and through neighbourhood assemblies, they were also running 'solidarity kitchens' and bazaars, working in medical social centres, protecting immigrants from attacks against the fascist group Golden Dawn[10] (which won 7 per cent of the votes in both of the 2015 elections), supporting actions against the electricity supply being cut off, providing legal help in courts to cut mortgage payments, and developing new relations with trade unions. They were offline and in the communities dealing with social need. They understood from the outset that, for social transformation to come about, it could not simply be imposed by government: 'I believe you need state political power but what is also decisive is what you are doing in the movements/society before seizing power. Eighty per cent of social change cannot come through government' (Andreas Karitzis, a political co-ordinator within Syriza, cited in Wainwright, 2015). In other words, Syriza began by operating more as a movement than as a political party, and, paradoxically, this enabled its politics to be pushed to the fore. Activists were concerned first and foremost not with recruiting new members to their party, pushing a particular line or taking control but with building a sense of shared principles with practical solutions. Thus, in the demonstration in Syntagma Square, an agreement was reached that, instead of party flags, there would be flags of different nations, including from the Arab Spring countries. In this way, Syriza was seen to break with the sectionalized left politics of old and to build new trust and a sense of possibility that the Troika-imposed measures could be dissolved. It tapped into the politics of being and fed this through into being political. This endeared the party to the young and to the working class in particular, who were encouraged to join in the solidarity networks run on a self-organized democratic basis.

> People are facing problems of survival.... We cannot solve these issues
> but we can be part of socializing them. These solidarity initiatives can
> be a basis for fighting for the welfare state. For example, medical staff
> involved in the social medical centres also fight within the hospitals
> for resources and free treatment. The idea is to change people's idea
> of what they can do – develop, with them, a sense of their capacity
> for power. (Ibid.)

Syriza understood what it meant to build a movement for social
change rather than simply to get a party elected to power. The movement needed to have popular backing and broad-based participation
and therefore to present a real alternative with positive solutions. To
these ends it wanted as much Greek government debt as possible,
mainly held by German and French banks, to be written off. It also
prioritized an end to the humanitarian crisis through measures such
as reconnecting energy supplies cut off as a result of non-payment of
bills and subsidized food for the unemployed. To reform the country's
economy it wanted to promote workers co-operatives and the nation-
alization of banks and privatized utilities and to invest in public
infrastructure. And it wanted to take on Greece's political establishment by restructuring the state to squeeze out corruption, breaking
up media monopolies, cracking down on tax avoidance, and revers-
ing the militarization of the police. The party also stated it wanted
better conditions for marginalized groups, to protect migrant communities and to support same-sex marriage.

This programme of work is in a document that was drawn up by
Syriza members and supporters in 2012 – an inclusive system that
they wished to replicate within the systems of governance by calling
general assemblies of the various civil servants in each ministry to
encourage innovation and discourage hierarchies that enable corruption to thrive. In 2014, while Syriza was still in opposition, this was
turned into the Thessaloniki programmme, as a national reconstruction plan for government. As a manifesto it was heavily criticized
from both left and right. Syriza was well aware of the perils of becoming a party just like any other that is distorted by power and disconnected from its roots and wanted to remain open to members to bring
forward new ideas and shape its direction. When its economic programme was initially published, public assemblies were organized to
discuss the party proposals. An umbrella group, Solidarity4All, was
also created to link the different groups in sympathy with Syriza and
facilitate the exchange of information and knowledge (Prentoulis,
2015).

Regardless of the difficulties it ran into when it found itself compromised by the new loan agreement as part of the third bailout

package (the Economic Adjustment Programme), Syriza represented movement-inspired politics that quite deliberately recognized and connected to the politics of being combined with a programme of political action that was clearly thought through. It was also a politics massively constrained by the austerity demands of the European Union, the International Monetary Fund and the European Central Bank, which wanted to balance budgets through cuts in public spending. The management of the economic crisis by supranational bodies may have alerted global civil society to respond and transnational protest to take place, but left parties seeking to form opposition within state boundaries were weakened by the translocation of power to the tyranny of the Troika. The economy has become the business of banks – a technical matter outside of politics. Unlike many social democratic parties across Europe, Syriza attempted refusal of this stance. But the powers of the Troika were not so easily brought to heel.

Syriza presented a political risk that could give confidence to anti-creditor coalitions such as Podemos in Spain. The European Union responded with alarm to the attempts by Syriza to renegotiate the economic terms cast by the banks. As further funds were withheld and the Greek banks faced bankruptcy, the Syriza-led government found itself facing a possible exit from the eurozone. The Greek prime minister, Alexis Tsipras, held a referendum, and the Greek people voted overwhelmingly against austerity measures. But the democratic vote of the nation was ignored, and the creditors insisted on more austerity as well as a host of national policies that would immediately bring about further privatization and anti-trade union legislation, in the full knowledge that austerity politics does not bring economic recovery (Krugman, 2015) and that more debt would follow. As Koenig (2015: 1) wrote:

> [T]he Greek people, the citizens of a sovereign country...have had the audacity to democratically elect a socialist government. Now they have to suffer. They do not conform to the self-imposed rules of the neoliberal empire of unrestricted globalized privatization of public services and public properties from which the elite is maximizing profits – for themselves, of course. It is outright theft of public property.

The vicious cycle of debt–austerity–privatization was further endorsed by the Greek mainstream media, which continued to spin a narrative that Greece was at fault, that it had overspent and gone broke. The generous banks lent the country money and the corrupt Greek government mismanaged it (Efimeros, 2015). Most of the mass media platforms in Greece defended the banks. Perhaps this is not surprising when it is understood that the one measure the Troika allowed to be postponed was the 20 per cent tax on television advertising. They also overlooked the fact that television companies had not paid their taxes and had been given licenses to broadcast for free. The mainstream media wanted the Troika to win, otherwise the large media corporations would lose profits. So the story that was not told was that the banks pushed Greece into unsustainable debt while insisting that revenue-generating public assets were sold off to global corporations and oligarchs. But Syriza had long since nurtured a social media presence that enabled it to disseminate its message. Twitter became an important source of counter-narrative, with #ThisIsACoup being the second top trending hashtag in worldwide and the top trending hashtag in Germany the Monday that the final bailout deal was struck. But, while social networks could express solidarity and outrage, while the counter-narratives online could offer some hope, they were never going to be any kind of match for the stranglehold of the Troika.

Mattoni and Vogiatzoglou (2014) point to how oppositional politics in Greece has shifted from a focus on actions of protest to the provision of services, as well as a return to mutualism, as a form of resistance to the economic crisis. The attempt at a radical repoliticization in Greece has, then, recognized the need to redemocratize the economy and resocialize politics through reconnecting politics to the public and away from the corrupting influence of elite power (which, some have since argued, it ultimately fell foul of). Furthermore, the initial package of reforms sought to crack down on corruption and tax evasion and enable a return to greater public expenditure. In so doing, there was success in drawing attention to all that is political in the management of the economy. Syriza's election victory and political struggle also encouraged other radical anti-austerity parties, including Spain's Podemos, whose leader, Pablo Iglesias, told a rally in Valencia: 'Hope is coming, fear is fleeing. Syriza, Podemos, we will win' (Smith, 2015). However, this political enthusiasm was short-lived.

The Case of Podemos

The financial crash in 2008 hit Spain hard. Unlike the situation in Greece, the Spanish government's borrowing was under control (more so than in Germany). On Spain's joining the euro in 1999, interest rates fell and credit flowed first into Spanish banks and then into housing, creating a massive property boom and a construction bubble financed by cheap loans to builders and home-buyers. House prices rose rapidly from 2004 to 2008, then fell when the bubble burst. The construction industry crumbled; over-indebted home-owners faced financial misery, and the banks had mounting bad mortgage debts. So, even though the Spanish government had relatively low debt, it had to borrow heavily to deal with the effects of the property collapse. Taxes were raised in 2011, a freeze was imposed on public-sector pay, and austerity measures were put in place. Unemployment soared to 25 per cent and inequality rocketed, with Oxfam (2014) reporting that the twenty richest people in Spain had an income equal to the total income of the poorest 14 million Spaniards. Politicians were felt to be acting at the behest of bankers.

The birth of the Indignados/15M social movement emerged from this crisis. It began with a Facebook group that brought together affinity groups such as XNet and Anonymous under the name of 'Democracia Real Ya!' (Real Democracy Now!). On 15 May 2011 they mobilized many thousands of citizens to demonstrate in the streets across Spain, and the following day people occupied Catalunya Square in Barcelona; they stayed for several months to debate issues that were being ignored in the local elections. This triggered similar occupations in over a hundred Spanish cities, which then spread to over 800 cities around the world (Castells, 2015). The movement, which became known as 15M or the Indignados, had no formal leadership and was initially largely ignored by the mainstream media. It used the internet to spread the word, and people duly came to the squares to participate. But the internet would have made no difference at all had the moment not been right, had the injustices of a failing democracy not been felt, had poverty not been visible, had unemployment not been a common experience, and had political corruption not been rife. 15M ran campaigns against cuts and spawned many protest movements (known as tides) against evictions and home repossessions, the privatization of health care, cuts in education, wage cuts, and attacks on working conditions, among many others.

15M laid four years of foundations for the development of Podemos, which enabled the indignation of protest to turn into explicit policies for political change (the name of the its first manifesto was *Mover ficha: convertir la indignacion en cambio politico* ('Making a move: turning indignation into political change'). Podemos is a party against austerity measures with a commitment to a participatory popular politics (similar to Syriza). Within a year of its formation in January

2014, Podemos (which translates as 'We can'), had become a left-wing party with more than 200,000 members and almost 1,000 circles (horizontally organized local meetings) and frequently topped opinion polls. In May 2014, five months after it was formed, it gained five MEPs in the European elections (equivalent to 8 per cent of the Spanish vote), with an astonishing 1.25 million votes. For a period, then, Podemos posed a serious challenge to the two-party duopoly that has dominated the Spanish political scene in post-Franco years – the Spanish Socialist Workers' Party (PSOE) and the conservative People's Party (PP). Although these parties sound different in name, they had become increasingly similar and had colluded over a change to the Spanish constitution to take away Spanish workers' rights in order to appease the IMF and meet the Troika's austerity measures. Podemos promised something different. It called for:

> a fair distribution of wealth and labour among all, the radical democ-ratisation of all instances of public life, the defence of public services and social rights, and the end of the impunity and corruption that have turned the European dream of liberty, equality and fraternity into the nightmare of an unjust, cynical and oligarchic society. (Maura, 2014)

A large part of what makes Podemos different is where it has come from. It was a product not of the establishment but, rather, of a social movement. Eduardo Maura, a professor of philosophy at Complutense University of Madrid and an international representative of Podemos, notes that:

> The social movements changed perceptions, they enabled people to reconceptualise supposedly individual problems as common ones that demand collective, political responses. Podemos's ability to stand in the European elections was very much dependent on the social power accumulated by the social movements. (Quoted in Dolan, 2015)

In the same interview, Maura talks about the need to keep the movements separate from the party in order to ensure both that the movement remains autonomous and self-regulating and that the party is made more accountable and has a broader appeal to a wider range of people who may not identify as activists or even consider themselves to be on the left. This sense of reaching out to as wide a constituency as possible, of appealing to the unengaged and the non-political, is shared with the early vision of Syriza and is linked to the notion of 'popular unity' (Maura, quoted in Parker et al., 2014) put forward by Podemos. Popular unity refers to a recognition of the need to create a new common sense to counter the dominant discourses of neoliberalism. In order to gain popularity, Podemos has discarded name tags of left and right in favour of a discourse of democracy and 'the people' that speaks to the felt experiences of austerity – disenfranchisement, resentment of the establishment and material deprivation. In doing so, it has managed to gain the support of many traditionally conservative voters, with about a sixth of its supporters (as of January 2015) coming from the People's Party. This is a located politics that has understood the need to appreciate the politics of being in the context of being political. Maura notes:

> I feel the need for change more powerfully than before, in a way that really touches me. This is somehow generational. The way that I and others like me are engaged right now has to do with Podemos. I like the project very much, and I feel part of a work in progress much more than I feel like a member of a party. This has to do with something that cannot be readily translated into the British context. I cannot tell you why. It is something I myself do not understand. This is much more important than many aspects of my personal life. I actually feel it and I am not ashamed, because I understood as well that the political field is not solely constituted by rational actors. I might be an academic, but I am not a completely rational actor in the political field. I also feel all sorts of things that I know are helping me develop this project. That is why I understand, perhaps better than in other countries, the hate and the anger at the establishment. I understand it well and I try to build upon that, rather than tell people that they are anti-political or that they don't know Marx. Emotions are very important in politics, and I feel those emotions right now. I didn't feel them five years ago, though I was already an activist then. (Maura, ibid.)

Podemos took notice of the horizontality and diversity of the radical politics of 15M and the Indignados movement. Like Syriza, it recognized that a politics of everyday life can be more fruitful than the left's traditional focus on production and labour (where production and labour are now so fragmented and insecure that they are difficult to organize around). As Harvey (in Watson, 2015) notes, this is politics organized around the spaces where we live rather than the spaces where we work. Podemos focuses on people's needs and relates improved public services to enhanced democratization in an attempt to forge a link between the particular and the universal. In this manner it moved beyond the focus on horizontality and diversity at all costs to recognize the requirement to cohere around a common political goal that can spread solidarity while still being open to debate and difference.

This resonates with Laclau and Mouffe's theorization of political strategy (discussed in chapter 4) around the need to build chains of equivalence that draw together political demands with the actual feelings of the people: 'I need housing, you need a job: we need democracy!' (Parker et al., 2014). A focus on democracy is also necessarily open-ended and so avoids all of the trappings of an absolutist politics. In order to sustain any sense of a functioning democracy, it must be an open, iterative and dynamic process that is constantly challenged by all those it encompasses and will change in response. A focus on democracy embodies open-ended politics that are conducive to fragmented and multiple identities. But it is also modelled ultimately on the state and national government, so it will always return to representative liberal democracy as its natural manifestation.

As a party of the digital age, Podemos has also adopted what it calls a 'hacker logic'. To create a Podemos circle in a local area or on a particular topic requires nothing more than a Facebook account, an email address and a meeting – there is no membership fee. The principle is to encourage maximum participation from members, who then share in the shaping of the development of the party and hold it to account. The party relies heavily on the internet to increase levels of participation and accountability through a Citizen's Assembly, although the principles are not so very different from the establishment of any organization with aspirations of democratic practice. It used the social networking site Reddit for much of the process but also developed apps for voting and establishing agendas. Draft papers were submitted online relating to specific areas of organization, including ethics (Podemos refuses any funding from financial institutions and representatives are subject to strict limitations on privileges and salaries) and politics; these were then debated, redrafted and reduced. Thereafter there was a period where resolutions were invited on particular topics (as distinct from strategic or manifesto concerns) which were then voted on. Drafts were discussed at a face-to-face conference attended by 7,000 people and were voted on the following week online. The selection of party candidates to represent Podemos involved live streaming of debates and elections operating on a one-person, one-vote system. This process ensured that the most committed activists and those with a vague interest, those who had precious little time to spare and those without the resources to travel, could all take part.

Podemos is, however, already and inevitably facing criticism from activists that it has become a party of the elite and disconnected from its roots, so replicating the problems of all established parties of old. It is accused of being reformist and of the establishment; of being bourgeois and fake by entering into a state-centred political space that will ultimately reproduce the politics of old. 15M is part of Xnet, a group of activists working for democracy and against corruption that has succeeded in taking more than a hundred politicians and bankers to court on corruption charges. Largely crowd-funded and aided by citizen collaboration and leaks, it has exposed fraud and financial scams. It is also critical of Podemos, seeing it as very distinct from 15M and as part of a 'very old left perspective that is Gramsci centred' and still operates within a traditional political model that is closed to genuine citizen participation (interview with key activist). Its use of the attributes of the internet, it is said, serves merely to conceal a centralized and egotistical politics. And it is true that those with substantial cultural capital (notably male economists and academics) have risen to senior positions within the party.

But, along with Syriza, Podemos is also attempting to make visible the power of the Troika, disrupt the discourse of austerity and to work out what an alternative politics might be. In doing so, it is trying to create a politics that is progressively radical but sidesteps the 'isms' (e.g., socialism, communism) that signify a politics felt by many to be outmoded and unsuited to contemporary times. Criticisms *should* abound from social movement activists because, if they did not, then Podemos could not sustain a politics of democracy. Disagreement alongside support is what Podemos is hoping for. Meanwhile, the mainstream media supported by big business paints Podemos as an economic liability and its political representatives as crazed revolutionaries. This, along with other constraints on communication, such as a new 'gag law' brought in to delegitimize public protest in front of Parliament and other government buildings, including making 'unauthorized use' of images of law-enforcement authorities or police punishable by fines of up to €30,000, mean the odds are stacked against building and sustaining an oppositional party.

What do we learn from these two case studies? The first point is that, while the internet can mobilize and involve a lot of people quickly, it does not craft a politics. Although Podemos makes good use of digital media, digital media did not create Podemos. The politics of Podemos arose from a two-party system that had failed the electorate and a programme of austerity that had caused considerable hardship. Without this critical contextual anchorage, a focus on horizontality and diversity runs the risk of being translated into either a liberal tolerance of difference, which in fact prevents substantive questions from being asked, or an anarchic, autonomous and ultimately individualistic politics that prevents substantive change from happening.

If we then move to consider these two case studies through the concepts and practices of being political and the politics of being, we find that both Podemos and Syriza have pushed the need to repoliticize the economy as the means to regain traction for a radical politics to survive. Without some control over the economy, a radical politics has no space to breathe or function. What Podemos and Syriza also reveal is that politics is about doing, and when we do politics together we create solidarity – this does not mean that we all think of politics in the same way. A contemporary solidarity is forged on the recognition of difference and the constant assertion of that difference through contention, but it is solidarity nonetheless. Resocializing the political enables this solidarity to be seen and felt. In a context where corruption has sullied trust, where mainstream media are seen as being de-democratizing because they are part of the elite and part of the problem, to be credible and therefore trusted means you have to be not only visible and transparent in your practices but accountable and inclusive. You also have to be able to show that there is another way of doing politics, and this requires reclaiming the economy.

Repoliticizing The Economy

Both Syriza and Podemos are testimony to the fact that Southern Europe has borne the brunt of the neoliberal response to the eurozone crisis and bears the scars of a brutal programme of debt reduction that has seen unemployment rocket and inequality deepen (Piketty, 2014). The result has been to throttle growth and, with it, economic recovery. The US, where the reduction of the public deficit was approached in a less vicious manner, has seen a fall in unemployment. Piketty's analysis shows us that it is impossible to reduce a high public debt with no inflation and zero growth, and that, in the past, it was often through inflation, debt remission or exceptional measures that an end was brought to a public debt crisis:

> This is the case for Germany and France, who emerged after the second world war with a 200 per cent debt-to-GDP ratio, twice that of Spain today and higher than Greece's. Then, all of a sudden, by 1950 there was no more public debt. What happened? We didn't pay them back. We got rid of the debt through inflation and the cancellation of the newest debts, particularly in Germany. This was a good decision, which allowed us to start over in the 1950s and '60s, to invest in growth, public infrastructure, education.
>   If, on the other hand, we had had to pay back such high debts, with GDP growth of 1 or 2 or 3 per cent a year, we would still be paying

it back. So it seems crazy – like an attack of collective amnesia – to see the same countries today, Germany and France, explaining to southern European countries they have to repay everything, right down to the last penny, with zero inflation. (Piketty and Iglesias, 2015)

In Spain and Italy, the interest paid each year is higher than the budget for their entire university systems. Italy spends 5 to 6 per cent of GDP repaying the interest on public debt and just 1 per cent of GDP on their university system. Yet debt restructuring remains outside of the political realm. The reasons for this are historical and hark back to previous economic difficulties in the 1970s, which saw high inflation and unemployment across Europe. The response then was to develop a currency without a state so that it could be independent and fight inflation. Thus the euro was created, and those in the eurozone handed over monetary sovereignty to an institution over which they now have little control – the European Central Bank.

In the US, economics has become so distanced from the politics of the state and governments have become so enthralled by corporate power that Nichols and McChesney (2013) call it a 'Dollarocracy' – the rule of money rather than the rule of the people – where those with the most dollars get the most votes and own the board. Their analysis traces how corporations and the wealthy spend billions of dollars on lobbying, public relations and donations to political campaigns that influence economic decisions that returns to them in trillions of dollars of revenue. Of course, many areas of government that deal with basic social services do not have the power of corporate industries to cajole and lobby on their behalf and so end up getting trampled on. Public education, public spaces, public transport, social security, Medicare, libraries, electricity and water systems all suffer as a consequence.

Lessig (2011) also argues that the corruption in Congress in the US is built into the political system, which depends on corporate money: a member of Congress needs to spend a considerable amount of time raising funds for re-election. Many ex-members, in return, become lobbyists for the very companies from which they took money in return for political favours. Much like Margaret Thatcher turning a blind eye to monopolies legislation in order to gain favour with Rupert Murdoch, cable and telephone companies in the US obtain government licences that turn them into near monopolies, essentially to privatize the internet (Foster and McChesney, 2011). Davis notes that, in the UK, the Conservative Party receives over 50 per cent of its funds from the financial sector. The revolving door between the corporate and political worlds keeps on spinning:

...when it comes to accounting, taxation and economic policy. It is the same big four accountancy firms that dominate when it comes to both auditing companies and offering these same organizations accounting services; and the same big four that advise governments and tax inspectors on accountancy regulations. It is the same investment bank managers who get senior positions in government treasuries and regulatory institutions, before returning to those same investment banks. And the same esteemed economists who write authoritative reports used in decision-making but which are paid for by vested interests (Ferguson, 2012; Shaxson, 2012; Murphy, 2013). In effect, the production of financial and economic information, that is used to inform decision-making on behalf of the public, is itself riddled with conflicts of interest. This allows tax avoidance by big business and the super-rich on a massive scale. It also produces regressive taxation systems that facilitate the continuing transfer of capital from the poorest to the richest 1 per cent. (Davis, 2015: 5)

Davis goes on to quote the finding of the Bureau of Investigative Journalism (2012) that the UK financial sector spent approximately £92.8 million lobbying the UK government. Similarly, systemic corruption reaches its zenith in the US with the influence of the largest banks over the workings of the federal government. In 2009 the financial sector had seventy former members of Congress lobbying on its behalf. Deregulation became the name of the game, allowing banks to speculate recklessly and operate illegally, and when the global economy collapsed they received bailouts of billions of dollars with precious little legal consequences for behaviour that would in turn ruin the lives of millions. The triumph of neoliberalism has been to extract the economy from the political domain and turn the established political domain into a massage parlour for corporations – whether this is through the outsourcing of public services, which threatens to strangle the NHS in the UK, or the privatization of schools and prisons in the US – private companies take public money and make private profit from it just as they are taxed less and less.

If the structure of the economy is off-limits for political debate, then repoliticizing the economy means returning wealth distribution to the centre of politics.

Resocializing The Political

What the above examples seek to illustrate is that both Podemos and Syriza recognized the importance of the social in the political – the need to come together in a spirit of mutuality and solidarity while respecting differences to deal with the basic problems people are facing on a daily basis: housing, electricity supply, access to welfare, lack of food. In the face of ever-declining respect for politicians and the growing irrelevance of elections, as parties increasingly vie for policies that are all too similar and fail to fulfil electoral promises, politics needs to reconnect with the fundamental requirement of the fair distribution of resources. Going into social spaces and special settings and ensuring basic social needs were met very simply put politics back in touch with the populace. Hence being political stopped being about voting once every few years or signing a few online petitions; it became about doing and being. This should not be confused with the voluntary actions of the charitable sector, which has long since worked to pick up the pieces where the welfare state has failed or been withdrawn. This is a social provision with a directly political purpose, and importantly it reconnects the political with social class and the social realm. This is a politics of democracy that sits closer to what Jacques Rancière (1999) has described as a permanently expansive movement than democracy as an institution or a regime.

It is also, however, part of civil society – understood generally as the non-institutionalized networks of associative activity outside the state – only here the link back to the state via the will to govern is explicit. Civil society is welcomed by many radical democrats as the site of a new 'postliberal' democratic politics, where new social movements and other self-organized groups spearhead a revival of active citizens in a participatory politics. Instead of focusing politics narrowly on the state or within the institutions of economic production alone – sites that were often presupposed to symbolize the ultimate *unity* of social and political identity – civil society purportedly embraces the ongoing self-construction of democracy and the diversity of identities and struggles within it. Civil society invites an expansion of the political and the displacement of instrumental reason by notions of active participation and deliberation that are indeterminate and undecidable. So we have, on the one hand, a defunct political democracy and, on the other, an expansive and diverse civil society. Both Podemos and Syriza attempted to bridge the divide between political society and civil society not just by means of a participatory membership but also by virtue of the actual politics espoused. It is for this reason that both parties prefer to deflect labels of left or right.

A common, liberal image of civil society is of self-limiting, voluntaristic activities, all containable within the rule of the parliamentary state. Indeed, liberal political thought has made a virtue of the idea of a well-ordered civil society built upon tolerant and independent individuals of moral character. However, civil society is often a response to the failures of the state and the sense of the inadequacy of political institutions; as such, it is a fragmented, uneven field of overlapping social identities and competing discourses.

Organizations, groups and individuals operating in civil society often mobilize intensely held fantasies of social order invested with a profound energy that projects contrasting visions of civil life. To preconceive of these varied demands as contained, or containable, within an already unified civil space is rather to miss the way they are constituted through contention, which opens them to new, potentially subversive, sometimes even violent efforts to redefine the boundaries of social space. For Mouffe (2000, 2005), contemporary democratic theory has a persistent tendency to invoke models of democratic community in which differences are harmonized and conflict is reduced to uncontentious matters of interpretation within a wider context of consensus. Such a view – expressed in 'deliberative' theories of democracy (see Dryzek, 2000) – evacuates the political dimension of its conflictuality. That is, it tries to remove the ever-present possibility of antagonism and conflict from political debate. Instead, pluralism is conceived of as a situation in which differences co-exist without antagonism.

For both Mouffe and Rancière, it is conflict rather than consensus that defines the political character of a democratic ethos. And it is conflict rather than consensus that characterizes both the practice and the experience of radical oppositional politics online. Without conflict, division, agonism, and so on – markers of difference and otherness – democracy loses its function as a practice of regulating difference and collapses into an oppressive homogeneity. By smoothing over differential identities, by appealing to consensus, mainstream liberal democratic theory often narrows down citizenship to those who already agree its parameters – what Badiou (2008) calls parliamentarianism. In underscoring the presence of disagreement and conflict, it is possible to promote a democratic ethos that constantly looks to the margins of the public realm to recognize the impossibility of spatial closure, or immunization, of the democratic community from difference. Democracy, in other words, is a condition generated not from the protective enclosure of agreement but, rather, from the very possibilities of conflict brought by our common exposure. Solidarity, then, emerges from contention.

Human beings are social animals – this is as true of our political lives as it is of any other part of our existence. The social is collaborative as well as competitive, just as the political is collective as well as contentious. In our social domains we take note of people whom we trust. We know from consecutive surveys that trust in politicians is at an all-time low (Edelman, 2015; or see the General Social Survey for the years 1972 to 2014) and that those we trust the most are those in our own networks. Syriza made a virtue of this. Marquand notes that:

> [P]eople are not only happier, but also work better, in more construc-
> tive ways, if they feel that their views are fully taken into account. It
> follows that co-operative, collaborative ways of organizing work are
> likely to be more constructive, more productive and indeed more
> innovative than authoritarian top-down systems. It also follows that
> people, as citizens, prefer to have their views properly discussed. Where
> there is insufficient consultation, protest is the natural response.
> (Marquand, 2012)

Syriza may well be mistaken if it thinks it can win the hearts and minds of the Greek population solely by reconnecting to the social. If it continues to fail to deliver on its ambitious political pledges on anti-austerity, then it is unlikely that the public will continue their support for the party. This is not a controllable sphere. But by appreciating the social as the building blocks of the political, by recognizing the bond between *being political and the politics of being*, both Podemos and Syriza were able (albeit only fleetingly) to breathe new life into the prospects for a radical politics to emerge.

Conclusion

Gramsci (1971) employs the concept of the 'bloc'. A bloc is not hard like a stone but instead represents a whole that can be both integrated and disintegrated. It can have contradictions at its very heart, and it appears forcefully at a moment and disappears when it has completed its task. It is a social bloc that originates from conflicts in the material fields (economic poverty, destruction of cultural identity) before crossing over the first threshold into civil society and then moving to the second threshold of political society. So often we consider the social and the dynamics of civil society and then, in a different space and often in a different discipline entirely, consider the political, but rarely are the two ever regarded in tandem and as part of a dynamic totality. In my own field of media and communications, we may point to identity politics, to the shift away from political parties to protest movements; we may describe the way political activists connect and relate to each other in their mediated realms; we may spot the con-tradictions and map a range of responses; but seldom do we critique the politics itself or what gaining political power might actually mean. Yet it is impossible to discuss radical politics in relation to our mediated worlds (or in relation to anything) without discussing this second threshold of political society. Without this we are left hanging with political absences and political emptiness.

A critical exploration of being political and the politics of being requires an approach that can take account of structural questions of power and inequality while also accounting for aesthetics and performance and the affective dimensions of politics. Such a holistic and critically contextual perspective is rare, often leading to a misunderstanding of the nature and impact of the internet on the political contours of contemporary life and, consequently, a misunderstanding of the nature of 'the political' and the complexity of power therein. We must endeavour always to bring together a discussion of structure and agency, political economy, cultural studies, and social and political theory to counter this tendency, strengthen our understanding of contemporary radical progressive politics, and contribute towards our understanding of how potential social and political imaginaries of the future might emerge.

In this frame, this chapter has discussed how a rethinking of political economic approaches and their relationship to those that emphasize the constructive ability of individuals, the importance of subjectivities, and the relevance of identity in a broader and deeper contextual frame enriches our understanding of mediation and its relationship to our social and cultural practices. Politics and the opportunity to be political are beholden to public knowledge. Our systems of public knowledge and information are increasingly dominated by the interests of global corporations. Our representative democratic systems also rely on the adequacy of processes, institutions and organizations of knowledge production and meaning-making of which media and communications are a vital part. We need to understand how the legitimacy of material and social inequality is justified and has been increasingly naturalized. That is why we must look to media concentration, and that is where we often find concentration that has become too powerful for democracy to tolerate.

If we are to generate bold new ideas for radical progressive politics, then we need to pay heed to the aspirations at the core of contemporary global movements. Politics needs to shift from something that is done to us to something that we do ourselves, together. Resocializing the political can get things started, but it is not nearly enough to finish the job. Underpinning and interlacing the resocialization of the political with the repoliticization of the economy enables a radical democratic politics to set about diminishing inequality and radicalizing democracy.

7

Conclusion: Putting Politics Back in the Picture?

The argument I wish to underline in this book is that, if we are talking about the likes of political mobilization, protest, resistance or organization, starting our analyses with technology too frequently ends our analyses with technology, and we lose sight of social and political critique along the way. Putting all our hopes in technology as our political saviour will never deliver social and political change of the magnitude required to deal with the global problems of inequality, poverty and ecological crisis. The costs, then, of interpreting the world through the prism of technology are enormous. Far from answering the key questions of our time – How can we have a sustainable planet? How can we eradicate poverty and inequality? How we can we live together better and more peacefully? – we remain stuck asking the questions that are confined to network niceties.

I have argued throughout this book that it is not enough simply to celebrate resistance through the conduit of the internet and the veneration of the potential of some of its technological capabilities. As new communication technologies enable disparate protest groups to forge transnational alliances and affinities, we may be faced with a new politics marked by the characteristics of speed and space, horizontality and diversity, and connectivity and participation that demands new ways of thinking about the *means of and the meaning of being political*. As chapter 2 argues, the internet may well have ushered in a new form of political activism, but its consequences may not be the ones that were intended or that can necessarily deliver the democratic gains that were hoped for. Networks are not *inherently* liberatory; the internet does not contain the essence of openness that will lead us directly to democracy.

Technologies are drenched from conception, to realization, to practice, in the economic and political context of which they are part. Technologies are never neutral. They are enmeshed with the systems of power within which they exist. As Feenberg (1995, 2002) argues, technology and capitalism have developed together. Similarly, the practices of social media *may* be liberating for the individual user but not necessarily democratizing for society. The hyper-commercialism that configures social media platforms enhances rather than disrupts the contours of global capitalism and encourages individual and connective responses rather than social and collective politics. In the digital age, the internet is an important component in our understanding of the contemporary representation and articulation of contestatory political identities and forms of political mobilization. But it is only one component among many. Allowing ourselves to focus unduly on the technology removes our attention from where the problems really lie.

Radical politics is of course about more than communication and more than participation in communication; it is about more than protest – it is about social, political and economic transformation. As Morozov (2015: 1) points out, the radical critique of technology

> can only be as strong as the emancipatory political vision to which it is attached. No vision, no critique. Lacking any idea of how sensors, algorithms, and databanks could be deployed to serve a non-neoliberal agenda, radical technology critics face an unenviable choice: they can either stick with the empirical project of documenting various sides of American decay (e.g., revealing the power of telecom lobbyists or the data addiction of the NSA) or they can show how the rosy rhetoric of Silicon Valley does not match up with reality (thus continuing to debunk the New Economy bubble). Much of this is helpful, but the practice quickly encounters diminishing returns. After all, the decay is well known, and Silicon Valley's bullshit empire is impervious to critique.... While radical thought about technology is certainly possible, the true radicals are better off theorizing – and spearheading – other, more consequential struggles, and jotting down some reflections on technology along the way.

Morozov goes on to say how the language of technology has itself been depoliticizing, making the downright nasty sound like something really rather nice – turning the harshness of precariousness into the fluffy notion of a 'sharing economy' or the worries of scarcity into savvy and smiley 'smartness'. The collective noun 'social media' does something similar. Suggestive of amity, familiarity, fellowship and togetherness, social media offer a warm, human glow. As social media form the new normal, using them for political ends can only be a good thing. But there are very many qualitatively different dimensions of the social. If we view the social as of society and living together well, then understanding the ways in which social media contribute to a radical progressive politics (or not), rather than simply to the mobilization of resistance, becomes paramount. As Khiabany (2016) notes, the Green Revolution in Iran did not deliver substantial social change, but it was really rather good for Twitter's business.

Similarly, applying what are assumed (often with little evidence) to be inherent values of the internet, such as participation, openness and diversity, onto society, economy and politics because one is used to engage with the other allows Silicon Valley sales speak to demarcate radical politics in particular ways. There are as many different groups as there are types of radical politics online. Not all concur with a politics aligned more to autonomous Marxism and direct democracy, which the characteristics of the internet are said to inspire.

Rather than look to technology as holding the answer, at the most basic level this book urges researchers in the field to put radical politics back in the picture. In order to do this well, I have argued that social, political and economic context is key, that organizational factors are vital, and understanding individual motivations equally so. All impinge directly on our understandings of what equality is or could be, on how liberty can be claimed and practised and how solidarity is experienced. Putting politics back in the picture means, then, describing the room the picture is in (the context) as well what was involved in its creation (the history); it means appreciating the frame in which the picture is hung (the organization) as well as the condition of the canvas and the hue of the paint (the philosophy and nature of the politics practised).

Power

If we return to the question posed at the beginning of this book – What are the circumstances in which politics are rendered open to contestation and revision today? – we can, at the very least, reply that technology is not the best place to start looking for the answer. A better place to start is with power. We need to understand who holds power, how it is wielded and in what forms it exists, whether visibly or invisibly, to understand how those who have it influence the decisions that structure and organize the distribution of resources, including the distribution of knowledge resources, throughout societies. We need to explain and evaluate power and its relationship to the political in order to do critique. Legacy media – newspapers, television and radio – are adapting to the digital age. The vast multimedia transnational corporations of which they are part have not disappeared, and in many instances they have got bigger. Few corporations are more powerful than the transnational media corporations epitomized by the Murdoch empire. Media ownership has become more and more concentrated as policies of deregulation and privatization continue to work in favour of private enterprise. At the time of writing, in the UK, the BBC is facing its biggest challenge in a generation as it battles for its life and purpose as part of its periodic charter review. Rupert Murdoch's antagonism to the BBC (particularly BBC online), based on its extensive popularity, which he claims monopolizes the media market, has been allowed to frame the terms of the consultation (DCMS, 2015). This latter is so preoccupied with the assumed negative impact of the BBC on the commercial media market that it ignores the considerable evidence of the corporation's enormous contribution to the UK's creative industries and to society more generally. This is just one example of how contemporary digital media are shot through with neoliberal politics.

But the BBC is not immune from ideological shifts in society more generally. Wendy Brown describes eloquently how liberal democracy has been hollowed out and filled in with neoliberal values that place economic concerns above all others:

> [T]he neoliberal triumph of *homo oeconomicus* as the exhaustive figure of the human is undermining democratic practices and a democratic imaginary by vanquishing the subject that governs itself through moral autonomy and governs others through popular sovereignty. The argument is that economic values have not simply supersaturated the political or become predominant over the political. Rather, a neoliberal iteration of *homo oeconomicus* is extinguishing the agent, the idiom, and the domains through which democracy – any variety of democracy – materializes. (2015: 79; emphasis in the original)

The reiteration of this political degradation is felt far and wide. As corporations and transnational financial agencies command the global economy, so national governments are left trying to manage their 'debts' through austerity policies and controlling and disciplining dissent as a consequence of vastly increasing inequalities. As the poor no longer see any point in voting for political parties whose economic policies increasingly exclude them and from which they stand to gain nothing, so those very political parties which chase popularity on a cycle of elections respond most favourably to older, wealthier voters. As political parties rely on mainstream news coverage to capture and persuade potential voters, so these mainstream news channels, often owned and controlled by mega-corporations, reflect the interests of corporate capitalism. So all the mainstream political parties are nudged (and sometimes shoved) ever more to the right.

Leys and Player (2011), writing about the BBC's coverage of the National Health Service (NHS) in the UK in the wake of the 2012 Health and Social Care Act, which has brought in massive privatization to health services in the UK, reveals how the corporation, by defining its commitment to political impartiality in terms of standing mid-way between the views of the major political parties, now stands near the middle of a neoliberal consensus. Thus, views that run counter to a market logic, and would have been a mainstream *critical* standpoint twenty years ago, gradually come to be seen as eccentric, marginal and unrealistic. And so we are left with a frighteningly singular, frighteningly depoliticized version of what neoliberal culture is that is ever more naturalized, unchangeable and inevitable – the NHS is a huge inefficient beast that requires market pressures of a privatized industry in order to function effectively.

Brown (2015: 108) goes on to argue that, in neoliberalism, *homo oeconomicus* has displaced *homo politicus* through the insistence that there are only rational market actors in every sphere of human existence, such that the 'citizen-subject converts from a political to an economic being and that the state is remade from one founded in juridical sovereignty to one modeled on a firm.' The neoliberal response to contemporary problems is framed by markets – more markets, better markets; by finance – more financialization, better securitization; and by technologies – new technologies, better monetization of those technologies. It is not genuinely collaborative; it does not involve deliberative and contested decision-making and democratic implementation through legislative procedures and public policy-making; it does not properly plan for the future; it offers no one but elites control over the conditions of their existence.

As neoliberalism subjects all aspects of life to economization, the consequences are seen neither just in the limiting of functions of state and citizen nor in the ever-expanding ways in which freedom is defined in economic terms instead of through common investment in public life and public goods; rather, the consequences are felt in the ways in which the exercise of freedom in social and political life is radically reduced and weakened (one example here would be how this happens for many through inequality). When it comes to economic transformation, we need to recognize that banks, financial agencies and corporations seek increasingly to dictate the terms of our economies and the national policies that underpin them. This political disjuncture, the way in which the global flow of capital has been severed from politics, puts enormous constraints on the possibilities of being political to effect progressive social change across the board. As this removes democratic sovereignty from nation-states and they are left to deal with the fallout from a politics of austerity, so they become increasingly draconian in their response to acts of civil disobedience that fiercely, and often violently, constrain the possibilities for progressive democratic politics to take hold.

Neoliberal governance may take place in the name of freedom – in relation to our mediated worlds, this includes the free press and communicative freedom in online pluralistic spaces – but at the same time it disintegrates the very basis of freedom in sovereignty for states and subjects:

> States are subordinated to the market, govern for the market, and gain or lose legitimacy according to the market's vicissitudes; states are also caught in the parting ways of capital's drive for accumulation and the imperative of national economic growth. Subjects, liberated from the pursuit of their own enhancement of human capital, emancipated from all concerns with and regulation by the social, the political, the common, or the collective, are inserted into the norms and imperatives of market conduct and integrated into the purposes of the firm, industry, region, nation or postnational constellation to which their survival is tethered. (Brown, 2015: 108)

Ultimately, then, unless these fundamental issues relating to the grounding of freedom are tackled, radical politics (in the terms described in chapter 1) does not exist. According to Castoriadis (1980), the essential political issue debated by society is the balance between liberty and equality, which he sees as the defining difference between socialism (used here as an example of radical politics) and capitalism. Put simply, capitalism values liberty through the free market, and socialism values equality through the redistribution of resources. Castoriadis argues that society makes the two concepts exclusionary when in fact they are complementary, and crucially so for a just and democratic society to exist. The first question of liberty is the equality of all in the participation of power. This is part of what Brown (2015) infers when she explains how capitalism presents the inherent contradiction of the two concepts because it assumes that total equality and liberty are impossible together. This creates a problematic society because the exploitation of the poor by the rich is legitimized as the only possible system. If considered from a different viewpoint, democracy is impossible unless everyone is empowered to change the social and political system of which they are part. Democracy is then impossible without equality. Castoriadis goes on to argue that, as democratic society is constantly open and always contains the real possibility of questioning the law and its foundations, the problem of a singular policy translation of multiple different viewpoints (wherein every person has control over their own existence) dissipates – since errors can be corrected along the way. Castoriadis's argument remains relevant today. The problem lies not just in implementing new laws but in being able to change them:

> To abolish heteronomy does not mean to abolish the difference between instituting society and instituted society – which would be impossible anyway – but to abolish the enslavement of the first by the second. The collectivity will give itself rules, knowing that it gives them to itself, that they are or will always become inadequate, that it can change them. (1980: 105)

Even the best laws become outdated, so the solution is not the perfection of the ultimate societal structure. The objective is to create an open system, one that everyone is able to challenge and change.

Powerlessness

The above discussion brings to the fore that, in order to better understand politics and extend the possibilities for progressive social change, we need to interrogate the relationship between politics and power and test power against equality. We need also to understand what powerlessness feels like. As technology and capitalism have developed together in the name of freedom, so capitalism and democracy are at odds as the power of individuals over their own lives is ever depleted. McChesney points out that capitalism and democracy vie for opposite conclusions – one creates massive inequality and the other is premised upon political equality:

> Political equality is undermined by economic inequality; in situations of extreme economic inequality it is effectively impossible. The main contradiction of capitalist democracy (making it for the most part an

oxymoron) lies in the limited role played by what was classically called the *demos* or the poorer classes, as compared to the well-to-do. Capitalist democracy therefore becomes more democratic to the extent that it is less capitalist (dominated by wealth) and to the extent to which popular forces – those without substantial property – are able to organize successfully to win great victories, like the right to unionize, progressive taxation, health care, universal education, old-age pensions, and environmental and consumer protections. (McChesney, 2012: 1)

Analyses by Bartels (2008), Gilens (2005) and Hacker and Pierson (2010), discussed in chapter 3, all reveal how, in the US, the interests and opinions of the poor bear little or no influence over the decisions made by Congress unless they align with the interests of the corporate lobby or of the wealthy. Bartels (2008) notes how politicians on the whole will take precisely the opposite position of that adopted by the poorest third of their constituents. In chapter 6 I have outlined how Crouch (2004) terms our current condition as one of 'post-democracy'. When sections of the public no longer think that change is possible, then democracy has failed. Where governments no longer carry out manifesto pledges, then democracy has failed. When elite interests prevail and the political system no longer works for the mass of ordinary people, then democracy has failed. When people feel that they are dispensable, that their lives no longer matter and they do not need to be listened to, then democracy has failed.

The general pessimism outlined above falls back on the structuring forces of neoliberalism and the lack of any real political alternative emerging. But, while subjects will always be subjected to dominant power, individual and collective identities can and do emerge from resistance over time. A radical politics does not just emerge from thin air or even from international networks in the ether; it emerges from particular histories and the contradictions between how we are told the world works best and our experiences of it. In many places across Europe and the US we may be told (by politicians and mainstream media alike) that the only way out of our economic crisis is through a politics of austerity, despite the fact that the analysis on which a politics of austerity is based has been largely discredited by the vast majority of economists (Krugman, 2015).[1] Still, the more austerity we have, the less economic growth we experience, and so the mismatch grows between what the politicians (and often the mainstream news outlets) tell us and what our experiences show us.

As chapter 4 notes, the emergence of subjects of resistance is usually accompanied by a huge sense of injustice, of a wrong that must be righted. Protest happens first and foremost as a response to symptoms – a heartfelt response to problems of the prevailing social system. It is wrong that my family should go hungry; it is wrong that I have no means to decent shelter; it is wrong that the state should destroy a public park; it is wrong that I am discriminated against, etc. This does not usually arrive with a formally worked-out plan of how justice can be claimed and applied universally. The next step is often to determine why this particular condition of impoverishment has come about. So, it is not just wrong that my family should live in poverty and go hungry. It is wrong *because* of austerity measures that are nothing to do with me and will not make any difference in the long term. It is wrong *because* long-standing institutions of social democracy have been decimated, leaving the vulnerable unprotected. This process of knowledge production is the basis from which a radical politics can emerge.

A *protest* politics alone rarely presents an immediate challenge to the social order because it has no alternative proposition to make other than remedial solutions. But it is only through particular acts of resisting particular configurations of power that the seeds of an alternative normative position can be sown, that the realization that 'another world is possible' can come into being which then requires the engagement of a broader public. There are many attempts to create such spaces protected from colonization by capital, and much digital content provides the means not only to legitimate but to challenge, resist and counter the hegemony of a neoliberal political-economic order. These constitute alternative bids for political meaning and value, but most are still at the very early stages of articulating what this might mean: What type of planetary political and economic system(s) could engender liberty, equality and ecological sustainability and not be susceptible to domination by 'massive administrative apparatuses, complex markets and the historically powerful peoples and parts of the globe?' (Brown, 2015: 220). How can a common social order be inclusive of regional, cultural and religious differences? How would politics be administered in a radical political system? Who would make decisions? And how about the means of production, distribution and redistribution of resources and consumption?

If the politics of resistance that circulates online and on the streets is the beginnings of a new radical politics, what does it look like? Chapter 2 describes a politics that came into view in 1999 with the Battle of Seattle and was marked by the characteristics of the internet of horizontality and diversity, connectivity and participation. This was a politics that began to make good use of digital media, and it was also a politics of non-representation, a politics of affect and antagonism. It foregrounded a multiplicity of experiences that were often hybrid, contradictory and contingent. But it did so *not* because the architecture of the internet fashioned it in its image but because of disillusionment with mainstream politics, which has become captured by capital (and this includes the mainstream media), and a profound distrust in electoral democracy. Networks of resistance revealed through the likes of the anti-globalization movement and Occupy displayed a politics that is messy, angry and passionate. The politics of transnational new social movements facilitated by new technology reveals the extent of this multitude of difference – a network of networks, a movement of movements, irreducible to single truths, actively resistant of grand narratives, embracing of non-representative politics. Networks do not claim to be democratic institutions; they do not apportion membership or citizenship; they do not conform to legislative models of governance or representative models of election. And it is partly these characteristics that make them attractive – they are both different from conventional state-bound politics and embrace difference. As Douzinas (2013, 2015) argues, what the left needs is not a new model party or an all-encompassing brilliant theory. It needs to learn from the popular resistances that broke out without leaders, parties or common ideology and to build on the energy, imagination and novel institutions created. The historical opportunity has been created not by party or theory or technology but by ordinary people.

Chapter 3 makes the point that, as media and communications scholars, we cannot understand the contemporary politics of resistance by recourse to old conceptions of liberal democracy and the public sphere – by a constant reliance upon and return to the notion of being political in a liberal democratic frame. The liberal democratic frame has been so evacuated of meaning, and public sphere theorists have been too quick to elide pluralism with communicative freedom, which is then correlated with political participation, that these approaches threaten to do neoliberalism's job for it by imbuing the individual with the power to and by denying the broader influence of forces that have power over (both the individual and the state).

Advocating political pluralism is one thing – we can all imagine the glorious freedom of everybody in all their manifold differences expressing their political desires. But pluralism as endless multiplicity that cascades into ever-increasing circles of relativism can also evade the political. Everyone can speak, anyone can blog, everyone is a producer – what wonderful plurality, what joyous freedoms – when all the time the power endowed through such plurality and freedom may be, in Wendy Brown's terms, hollow and fleeting. Forms of mediation too frequently masquerade as liberal democracy through donning some of its easily recognizable accoutrements – the technicolour dreamcoat of pluralism, the fancy pants of freedom – but hide a body politic beneath that has morphed into something rather different: neoliberal democracy (Fenton and Titley, 2015). Conceiving of radical politics and networks of resistance in this way reveals the limits of liberal democracy and how we conceive of it in a digital age.

In a situation where political party membership is falling yet political activity is increasing, we need to recognize that representative democracy alone is unlikely to bring about transformative shifts. Those groups, organizations and social movements that use digital media for a host of activities have challenged liberal democracy's shortcomings. One example that brings this into sharp relief is the Occupy movement.

Occupy and the Limits of Liberal Democracy

In 2011 a new social movement was born in response to the economic crisis, the bankers' bailouts and claims of corrupt political and economic systems that benefit a few people to the detriment of the many. The Occupy movement began on 17 September of that year in Liberty Square in Manhattan's financial district, where people assembled and then stayed, putting up tents and promising to occupy the space until a process was created to address the problems they identified and solutions were generated appropriate to everyone. By January 2012 it had spread like wildfire across the US. Pulling together data from Facebook, news coverage, lists produced by Chase-Dunn and Curran-Strange and the main websites in use at the time, Castells (2015) maps the location of Occupy-related activity in over 1,000 American cities and towns in all fifty states and Puerto Rico. Occupy also claimed to have generated activities in 1,500 cities globally. The activities were as varied as they were widespread. They involved demonstrations, regular meetings, teach-ins and encampments, with media centres, medical tents, kitchens, childcare, libraries and even community banks. The movement stated that it was inspired by popular uprisings in Egypt and Tunisia and aimed to 'fight back against the richest 1% of people that are writing the rules of an unfair global economy that is foreclosing on our future' (www.occupywallst.org/about/).

Occupy Wall Street was born into a digital age and embodied digital practice. Calls to demonstrate and join the camps went out on Twitter, Facebook and blogs. YouTube and Tumblr were used not only to share videos and pictures of the protest activities but also to tell the stories of those whose lives had been ravaged by debt.

Understanding how the means of communication was used to good effect is important in appreciating how mobilization happens, but it does not tell us why the movement existed and what it was trying to achieve. To do this we must look more closely at its politics. What was so striking about the Occupy movement is that it was a peaceful, collective attempt to deal with failed democracies through coming together in protest camps in public places to publicize disaffection and debate the way forward. This was a desperate search for new political forms of democracy that could be taken out into communities and into society more generally. Developing new forms of democracy is inevitably a painful and difficult task but one that was at the heart of Occupy's practice and wholly embraced through the daily assemblies. It was a practice based on a deep-seated distrust of the political process entrenched in the liberal democratic model that was felt to have turned away from them and towards powerful elites in society. The occupations were organized using a non-binding consensus-based collective decision-making process known as a 'People's Assembly' or 'General Assembly'. People gathered to deliberate and take decisions based upon a collective agreement or consensus. There was no leader or governing body as it operated with the aim of equality of voice. Individual political autonomy was central to the practice of the assembly, where the aim was that many singularities of viewpoints could come together in a consensus that was at once expressive of the differences it embodied.

The Occupy London website described the commitment to the consensus process as 'a living demonstration that each one of us is important. It's a counter to systems that tell us some people count while others don't. In consensus, everyone matters. But for consensus to work, we must also be flexible, willing to let go.... Unity is not unanimity – within consensus there is room for disagreement, for objections, reservations, for people to stand aside and not participate' (http://occupyLSX.org/?page_id=1999).

Occupy London has the following statement on its website (http://occupyLSX.org/?page_id=575), which was collectively agreed by over 500 people on the steps of St Paul's on 26 October 2011. It emphasizes that 'like all forms of direct democracy the statement will always be a work in progress':

1   The current system is unsustainable. It is undemocratic and unjust. We need alternatives; this is where we work towards them.
2   We are of all ethnicities, backgrounds, genders, generations, sexualities, dis/abilities and faiths. We stand together with occupations all over the world.

3   We refuse to pay for the banks' crisis.
4   We do not accept the cuts as either necessary or inevitable. We demand an end to global tax injustice and our democracy representing corporations instead of the people.
5   We want regulators to be genuinely independent of the industries they regulate.
6   We support the strike on the 30th November and the student action on the 9th November, and actions to defend our health services, welfare, education and employment, and to stop wars and arms dealing.
7   We want structural change towards authentic global equality. The world's resources must go towards caring for people and the planet, not the military, corporate profits or the rich.
8   The present economic system pollutes land, sea and air, is causing massive loss of natural species and environments, and is accelerating humanity towards irreversible climate change. We call for a positive, sustainable economic system that benefits present and future generations.[2]
9   We stand in solidarity with the global oppressed and we call for an end to the actions of our government and others in causing this oppression.
10 This is what democracy looks like. Come and join us!

Occupy London also states that it is working towards an international, global collaboration and that it 'will unite the occupy movements across the world in their struggle for an alternative that is focused on and originates from people and their environment' (http://occupyLSX.org/?page_id=2851).

Because the movement was premised on diversity and inclusivity and its politics rejected the political establishment, it was impossible for it to go beyond the list of demands above and campaign for specific outcomes. Any one outcome might be unacceptable to another and be likely to be appropriated into the political mainstream. The Occupy movement was criticized by the traditional left for refusing to make demands that could lead to some short-term achievable goals which would energize and fuel hope in the movement. Returning to the discussion of what is 'political' in chapter 1, it is fair to say that much of what happened in Occupy would likely not fulfil Gramsci's (1991) criteria for 'being political'. In its celebration of 'struggle for the sake of struggle' and 'the act for the act's sake' (Smucker, 2014), Occupy, rather, resembles Gramsci's descriptions of marginalism and utopianism: 'The attribute "utopian" does not apply to political will in general, but to specific wills which are incapable of relating means to end and hence are not even wills, but idle whims, dreams, longings etc.' (1991: 175). Gramsci criticizes activism based on utopianism because it possesses no pragmatic plan for how to realize the vision and can never therefore implement its dream. But we can look at Occupy in a different way, as part of the politics of being (chapters 5 and 6), which contained a palpable feeling of the political – the felt politics of anger at the injustice of the moment and the felt politics of hope that things could be otherwise. Occupy's main achievement went beyond a demands-based politics to the linking of inequality and the demise of democracy. Its politics supported the analysis by Wilkinson and Pickett, which provided systematic supporting evidence for their claim that 'the health of our democracies, our societies and their people is truly dependent on equality' (2009: 298). Occupy showed empirically how political and social failings are indelibly connected. Notably, Thomas Piketty (2013) and Danny Dorling (2014) have reinforced this critique. Each analysis reveals how increasing inequalities in societies lead to vastly impoverished democracies. Bensaid argues that, for democracy to survive, it must:

> keep pushing further, permanently transgress its instituted forms, unsettle the horizon of the universal, test equality against liberty. Because democracy incessantly smudges the uncertain divide between the political and the social and stoutly challenges the assaults of private property and the infringements of the state on the public space and goods. It must ultimately attempt to extend, permanently and in every domain, access to equality and citizenship. (Bensaid, 2011: 43)

Some (e.g., Castells, 2015: 197) went so far as to say that the Occupy movement shattered the American dream hinged on equality of opportunities on the basis of personal effort, with 61 per cent of the US population believing that the country's economic system now 'unfairly favors the wealthy'. In other words, it brought the issue of social class back into people's consciousness. Although Occupy did not have a worked-out programme for how to achieve any of its demands, those demands did direct attention onto the material consequences of inequality and the damages this wrought on democracy. This was no mean achievement.

Counter-Power

However, for a politics to be radical it must also seek progressive social and political change. To do so, a radical politics must claim power. But of course power cannot simply be produced from thin air, particularly when it has already been given to the financial institutions, corporations and debt agencies. For power to be used for democratic gain it must be wrested from those who have too much and reinvested in those who have too little, But the question remains – how exactly? How do we pull together new sources of collective power and build a radical politics that can turn into feasible political systems?

The resurgence of left politics in Europe, with the rise of the Syriza party in Greece and Podemos in Spain, the referendum in the UK for Scottish independence, which hinged much of its popularity on increased democracy for Scotland, and most recently the success of a left candidate – Jeremy Corbyn – in the Labour Party leadership contest in the UK, means that these issues are beginning to be tackled. All are motivated by a politics that is anti-austerity and by a failure of social democratic parties to mount any sort of coherent opposition to neoliberal agendas. In the case of Podemos and Syriza, which have emerged more directly from social movements (see chapter 6), there has also been a decision that a radical politics must be more than protest and social mobilization and must address the issue of political power. If radical change is required, then this will be achieved only through winning government office. This involves acceptance that no decision can ever be perfect and will always represent a decision made up to a certain moment in time but one that is ever open to challenge. Power becomes real at the point at which it is institutionalized. For a critical and realistic politics, institutions are both necessary and necessarily imperfect, such that they can be transformed or destroyed. This is what is meant by the notion that democracy is perpetually unfinished (Dussel, 2008). To be always open to change, counter-power must always remain in force beneath institutions and actions. The political party, then, requires the social movement to hold it to account even to get close to approximating democracy. This is what I have referred to in chapter 6 as the need to 'resocialize the political'. Politics has become so disconnected from and distrusted by the majority of people that it needs desperately to reconnect with the social. A process of resocializing involves mutual recognition and information, dialogue, and shared radical praxis, as these movements slowly and progressively advance a hegemony that includes all demands but may prioritize some. This is what Dussel (2008) calls a 'critical consensus', which could lead to a 'critical democracy' based on the real participation of the oppressed, of the disenfranchised as equals in a new political order. A critical democracy, by its very purpose, will call constantly into question the existing levels of achieved democratization, but, crucially, it will also translate this into an institutional reality. Political transformation is as much about institutional creation as it is about taking power. It will therefore always appear as reformist to the anarchist and as foolishly dangerous to the conservative.

What we learn from a consideration of the actual politics of radically progressive groups rather than from a focus solely on the forms of mediation is that, for most, democracy and equality are at their core (although these concepts may be manifest in very diverse ways). We see an insistence that the institutional configuration of a critical democracy must ensure that political actors are accountable to all. It must entail broad participation, the defence of the economic interests of the weakest, a renewed administrative effectiveness grounded in a new social pact and in new constitutions that give rise to new structures within a transformed state. For critical democracy to work, its institutional translation must not end in institutional power for itself; rather, it must create the means whereby the potential for everyone to be political is realized. Everyone includes the disenfranchised and the poor, but it also includes the middle classes and the wealthier – democracy cannot work for some and not for others. A critical democracy is inclusive at its core.

Resocializing the political can get things started, but it is not nearly enough to finish the job. Underpinning and interlacing the resocialization of the political with the repoliticization of the economy enables us to begin the difficult process of imagining a progressive politics that can set about diminishing inequality and radicalizing democracy. A radical politics, then, must be more than resistance: it must develop an alternative politics that can advance freedom, equality, collectivism and ecological sustainability while avoiding corporate, financial and market domination. This will not happen spontaneously but will require organization that must itself always strive for critical democracy in its own practice – for the symmetrical participation of all those involved. We saw the beginnings of this with Occupy and the extension of these beginnings with Podemos and Syriza, which have learnt not only about the power of popular mobilization, and harnessed the support for an alternative social order, but also about the difficulties of leading a heterogeneous movement in the face of viciously hostile mainstream media. The experience of the Syriza party in Greece and its attempt to govern by representing the political choices of its citizens has also taught us about the extra-political power of the banks and financial agencies, and that financial power is politically and socially unaccountable. It is on these social and political realities that a radical politics of the future will emerge, though it may not be visible yet.

Look Left: Rediscovering The Political Commons

At the end of what is probably his best-known book, *Culture and Society*, Raymond Williams concludes:

> There are ideas, and ways of thinking, with the seeds of life in them, and there are others, perhaps deep in our minds, with the seeds of a general death. Our measure of success in recognizing these kinds, and in naming them making possible their common recognition, may be literally the measure of our future. (1961: 324)

We need to recognize the ideas with the seeds of life in them and name them. It was Raymond Williams who pointed out that a key contribution of the Labour movement was in its creation of social institutions (unions, co-operatives, the Workers' Educational Association, and mutual support arrangements, such as the forerunners of the NHS in Welsh mining communities) that prefigured a different and more just society. In this he was on the same wavelength as Antonio Gramsci (1991), who, in talking about 'prefigurative struggle', suggested that the process of fighting for social and economic justice creates the embryonic forms of the alternative society that the socialist movement was trying to create. The radical politics of the last quarter of a century have had to deal with the 'end of socialism' and the global dominance of corporate capitalism. But it is in these radical politics that we find ideas based on more equality and better democracy with the seeds of life in them. This may be a radical politics that is residual much of the time and emergent at best, but it is there. These seeds of ideas for a renewed radical politics come from understanding the relationship of social life to political consciousness. We do not find this politics in the technology. We find it in the philosophies and practices of political organizations and activists – practices that have put basic social needs first – jobs, food, warmth, housing, education and health – seeking to show that in a democratic society these needs can be met and then actively trying to meet them.

The difference between contemporary social movement-based politics and party politics in current (neo)liberal democracies is that the former do not need to be in political office to start the process of meeting social need, and so the hunger for political power, the vote chasing at any cost, dissipates. Resocializing the political means just that – political parties that emerge from social movements consist of people who are part of the communities that are dealing with the problems they face, through establishing community banks and soup kitchens, tackling corruption, resisting evictions – it is politics with a social practice and one that is without orthodoxy because it is premised on a constant hum of conversation and action that brings experimentation and adaptation so very different from the top-down politics of old. Operationally, this creates the need both to formulate mechanisms of genuine citizen participation and to control the spaces we inhabit that can interface with institutional politics – you cannot have mutuality and horizontality without entitlements and regulation. The ordinary politics of daily life must combine with the extraordinary politics of institutional change, and this will require new forms of state relations that prioritize the value of the public over profit, patience over productivity, and collaboration over competitiveness. An anti-poverty politics must also tackle the accumulation and concentration of global wealth (Harvey, 2014). This is no easy task but, when democracy has mutated and been debased, reconstituting it demands a collective remobilization of the citizenry. It will require a far more open politics with multiple points of access, which builds on the notion of the assemblies that emerged through the Occupy movement – a politics that is willing to relinquish the conceitedness of unitary party competitiveness to work with all those who share a passion for a more equitable and just society, who desire to live together better. The digital media of radical politics (or the internet more specifically) may be part of this conversation: it can help facilitate the process, shed light on the workings of power, help build the solidarity that comes through shared passions and struggles, help many to experience the politics of being (see chapter 6) – crowdsource the politics even. However, focusing on technology as a means to transform democracy will at best be illusory and, at worst, will play into the hands of the economic oligarchy of corporate and financial elites, all too happy exploit the data trail we leave behind for corporate gain and then use their wealth to buy off democratic politics. And while the politics on offer online hides behind the thin veil of the 'social' in social media, it also deflects attention away from human association – the dense sociality that comes from democratically self-governing groups, collectives and organizations; the kind of sociality that puts lived content back into politics; the kind of sociality where democracy becomes something that is done by us rather than something that is done to us.

The challenge to the field of media and communication studies is to actively put politics back in the picture; to reinvigorate critical research that is explanatory, practical and normative. Critical analysis tackles political transformation and the role of the media therein by addressing and analysing the actual politics (both conceptually and pragmatically), as well as the nature and forms of its mediation. To be politically emboldened will also necessitate looking up and down as well as looking left and right in order to assess the context, root out the problems of prevailing systems, and suggest where progressive alternatives may be found. To begin to understand how society could be more equal, fair and democratic, how we could reclaim media, power and politics for progressive ends, we must insist upon an integrated, contextual analysis that places the technological alongside and in relation to its social, economic, cultural and political histories. Only then can we begin to advance an emancipatory project that aims at deepening and radicalizing the democratic horizon. To do otherwise is not to deal with politics at all. To bypass what radical politics is and might become is to ditch explanatory value, to limit our political imaginations, to let capital off the hook, to be accepting of inequality. But, worst of all, it is to focus only on the 'ideas and ways of thinking...with the seeds of a general death in them' (Williams, 1961) – and what is the point of that? If we wish to research arenas of the political, then we must open our arms and our minds a little wider to embrace and analyse the actual politics, such that we can start both to deal with the political problems and to consider what the conditions of possibility for radical political solutions might be. Let's get to it.

Notes

Chapter 1 Introduction

1 *The X Factor* is a popular reality television competition to find new singers that draws its contestants from public auditions. The winner receives a recording contract. The programmes are produced by Simon Cowell, who also acts as a judge on the show, and his company Syco TV. The show has been criticized for creating a 'sterile pop monopoly' of corporatized music (*The Guardian*, 21 December 2009), with the winner taking the Christmas number 1 slot in the charts for four consecutive years. In December 2009, Jon and Tracy Morter set up a Facebook group to advocate voting for a track by the rap metal band Rage Against the Machine and so succeeded in preventing a song by the latest *X Factor* winner, Joe McElderry, from following suit (see chapter 4).

2 As part of the negotiations to remain in the eurozone, the Greek prime minister was told that he needed to move towards replacing the Greek government because it did not suit the views of the bankers.

3 There are, of course, scholars who do take a critical perspective and deal with a raft of political concerns when considering the media in its many forms and its relationship with new social movements, political mobilization and protest, as well as those that focus on alternative and community media. One excellent example is the collection of articles in Dencik and Leistert's *Critical Perspectives on Social Media Protest* (2015), while another is Barassi's *Activism on the Web: Everyday Struggles against Digital Capitalism* (2015). Few authors, however, address politics as both a philosophical and an organizational dimension and thus its consequences for the prospects of political transformation.

Chapter 2 Digital Activism

1 Marchart (2007) uses the term 'post-foundational' to refer to a range of quite different theoretical traditions. Here the term is used more narrowly to refer to a particular autonomist/horizontalist tradition that is hostile to the notions of universalism and representation in preference to a 'networked' micro-politics.

Chapter 3 Digital Media, Radical Politics and Counter-Public Spheres

1 For a range of key essays in this area, see William Dutton (ed.) (2013) *Politics and the Internet: Critical Concepts in Political Science* (London: Routledge).

2 For a critique of this view, see chapter 1 in Curran, Fenton and Freedman, 2012 and 2016.

3 For a further elaboration of this argument, see Fenton and Titley (2015). I am indebted to Gavan Titley for his significant contribution to my thoughts on these issues and the debate in this chapter.

4 At the time of writing, analysis for the 2015 election result was not available. What we do know is that the voter turnout across the UK went up by 1 per cent, to 66.1 per cent of the population, although this was greatly influenced by the mobilization of the Scottish vote following a referendum for Scottish independence.

5 This is particularly evident at the World Social Forum (WSF) and European Social Forum (ESF).

Chapter 4 Passion and Politics

1 It is important to appreciate, however, that notions of individualism and agency in liberal thought have changed over time according to socio-historical context.

2 See Blackman and Cromby (2007) for an excellent overview of theories of affect.

Chapter 5 Radical Politics and Organizational Form in Theory and Practice

1 Autonomy and participatory democracy as political ideology were part of the social struggles of the 1960s and 1970s (particularly in Italy and Germany) (see Katsiaficas, 2006).

2 I owe this phrase to one of my many conversations with Milly Williamson ruminating on 'whither politics?'

Chapter 6   On Being Political and the Politics of Being

1   This is a crude summary of a variety of work that is far more nuanced and sophisticated than is given credit for here. But the point remains the same – research that recognizes resistance usually stops at the point of identification and falls short of a consideration of the potential for political project(s).

2   The political public sphere refers to the distinction made by Habermas (1989) between the literary/cultural public sphere and the political public sphere – the public sphere of the political realm.

3   This is a crude description that oversimplifies a range of political economic approaches. In particular, Golding and Murdock (2000) point to the differences between those who do critical political economic analysis and those who engage in classical political economic analysis. The argument in this chapter is directed largely at the latter.

4   In the UK, the Media Reform Coalition (MRC) focuses its campaigning around issues of media plurality and the concentration of media ownership, while Hacked Off, which came about as a result of the phone hacking scandal, campaigns for free and accountable media, largely through the need to bolster independent self-regulation of the press. The author declares an interest in being a founding member of the MRC and vice-chair of the board of directors of Hacked Off. Similar groups exist globally – Free Press in the US is one of the largest organizations fighting for a free and open internet, against excessive media consolidation, to protect press freedom, and to ensure plurality. Also in the US, the Media and Democracy Coalition is a collaboration of twenty-five local and national organizations committed to promoting open and equal access to a democratic media system that serves the public interest.

5   Twenty cabinet ministers met senior Murdoch executives 130 times in the first fourteen months of the government's term of office. See the full list on the Number 10 website: http://webarchive.nationalarchives.gov .uk/20130109092234/http://www.cabinetoffice.gov.uk/content/ ministers-transparency-publications.

6   Transcript of morning hearing, 14 June 2012, pp. 82–3, www.leveson-inquiry.org.uk/wp-content/uploads/2012/06/Transcript-of-Morning-Hearing-14-June-2012.pdf.

7   The PCC has since been replaced by the Independent Press Standards Organization (IPSO), which has been heavily criticized for being neither independent of the industry nor effective (Media Standards Trust, 2013).

8   Rupert Murdoch and family, www.forbes.com/profile/rupert-murdoch/.

9   This has not been experienced equally across all states. For example, the political agency of the German state in the economy has been shown to have rather more power than the Greek state. But nonetheless the point remains – state and capital are far from independent of each other.

10 Golden Dawn was formed in the early 1990s as a marginal semi-legal fascist organization. Its appeal was revived in recent times by recourse to a xenophobic, anti-immigrant response to the social ills caused by austerity measures.

Chapter 7 Conclusion

1 On the same day that the Centre for Macroeconomics in the UK announced that the vast majority of British economists disagreed that austerity is good for growth, the national daily newspaper *The Telegraph* published on its front page a letter from 100 business leaders stating the opposite.
2 Article 8 was added to the statement following a proposal being passed by the Occupy London General Assembly on 19 November 2011.

References

Adorno, T., and Horkheimer, M. (1973) *Dialectic of Enlightenment*. London: Allen Lane.

Alexander, J. C. (2011) *Performative Revolution in Egypt*. London: Bloomsbury.

Allan, D. (2014) Twitter announces most followed accounts in the UK: One Direction dominates, www.itproportal.com/2014/12/10/twitter-announces -followed-accounts-uk-one-direction-dominates/.

Amin, A., and Thrift, N. (2013) *Arts of the Political*. Durham, NC: Duke University Press.

Andrejevic, M. (2004) The web cam subculture and the digital enclosure, in N. Couldry and A. McCarthy (eds), *MediaSpace: Place, Scale and Culture in a Media Age*. London: Routledge, pp. 193–209.

Andrejevic, M. (2013) *Infoglut: How Too Much Information Is Changing the Way We Think and Know*. London: Routledge.

Andrews, P. (1989) Inside Microsoft – a 'velvet sweatshop' or a high-tech heaven?, *Seattle Times*, 23 April, www.seattletimes.com/business/archive -inside-microsoft-a-velvet-sweatshop-or-a-high-tech-heaven/.

Atton, C. (2007) A brief history: the web and interactive media, in K. Coyer, T. Dowmunt and A. Fountain (eds), *The Alternative Media Handbook*. London: Routledge, pp. 59–65.

Badiou, A. (2005) *Metapolitics*, trans. J. Baker. New York: Verso.

Badiou, A. (2007) *The Century*. Cambridge: Polity.

Badiou, A. (2008) The communist hypothesis, *New Left Review* 49, January–February, http://newleftreview.org/II/49/alain-badiou-the-communist -hypothesis.

Badiou, A. (2010) *The Meaning of Sarkozy*. London: Verso.

Badiou, A. (2012) *The Rebirth of History: Times of Riots and Uprisings*. London: Verso.

Badiou, A. (2013) Our contemporary impotence, *Radical Philosophy*, September–October: 43.

Barassi, V. (2010) Mediated resistance: alternative media, imagination, and political action in Britain, PhD thesis, University of London.

Barassi, V. (2015a) Social media, immediacy and the time for democracy: critical reflections on social media as 'temporalizing practices', in L. Dencik and O. Leistert (eds), *Critical Perspectives on Social Media Protest: Between Control and Emancipation*. London: Rowman & Littlefield.

Barassi, V. (2015b) *Activism on the Web: Everyday Struggles against Digital Capitalism*. London: Routledge.

Barnett, C. (2003) *Culture and Democracy: Media, Space and Representation*. Edinburgh: Edinburgh University Press.

Barnett, C. (2010) Publics and markets: what's wrong with neoliberalism?, in S. J. Smith, R. Pain, S. A. Marston and J. P. Jones III (eds), *The Sage Handbook of Social Geography*. London: Sage, pp. 269–96.

Barnett, C. (2011) Theory and events, *Geoforum* 42(3): 263–5.

Bartels, L. M. (2008) *Unequal Democracy*. New York: Russell Sage Foundation.

Bauman, Z. (1999) *In Search of Politics*. Cambridge: Polity.

Bauman, Z. (2000) *Liquid Modernity*. Cambridge: Polity.

Bauman, Z., and Bordini, C. (2014) *State of Crisis*. Cambridge: Polity.

Bayat, A. (2010) *Life as Politics: How Ordinary People Change the Middle East*. Stanford, CA: Stanford University Press.

Bayat, A. (2011) Egypt and the post-Islamist Middle East, *openDemocracy*, 8 February, https://www.opendemocracy.net/asef-bayat/egypt-and-post-islamist-middle-east.

Benkler, Y. (2006) *The Wealth of Networks: How Social Production Transforms Markets and Freedom*. New Haven, CT: Yale University Press.

Bennett, L., and Segerberg, A. (2013) *The Logic of Connective Action: Digital Media and the Personalization of Contentious Politics*. Cambridge: Cambridge University Press.

Bennett, L., Segerberg, A., and Walker, S. (2014) Organization in the crowd: peer production in large-scale networked protests, *Information, Communication & Society* 17(2): 232–60.

Bennett, W. L. (2005) Social movements beyond borders: understanding two eras of transnational activism, in D. della Porta and S. Tarrow (eds), *Transnational Protest and Global Activism*. Lanham, MD: Rowman & Littlefield, pp. 203–27.

Bensaid, D. (2011) Permanent scandal, in G. Agamben, A. Badiou, D. Bensaid, W. Brown, J.-L. Nancy, J. Rancière, K. Ross and S. Žižek, *Democracy in What State?* New York: Columbia University Press, pp. 16–44.

Benson, R. (2014) Challenging the 'new descriptivism', https://qualpolicomm.wordpress.com/2014/06/05/challenging-the-new-descriptivism-rod-bensons-talk-from-qualpolcomm-preconference/.

Berlant, L. (2010a) Affect & the politics of austerity, *Variant* 39/40, www
.variant.org.uk/39_40texts/berlant39_40.html.

Berlant, L. (2010b) Cruel optimism, in M. Gregg and G. J. Seigworth (eds),
The Affect Reader. Durham, NC: Duke University Press.

Berry, M. (2013) The *Today* programme and the banking crisis, *Journalism*
14(2): 253–70.

Bhabha, H. (1994) *The Location of Culture*. London: Routledge.

Birdwell, J., and Bani, M. (2014) *Introducing Generation Citizen*. London:
Demos.

Blackman, L. (2012) *Immaterial Bodies: Affect, Embodiment, Mediation*.
London: Sage.

Blackman, L., and Cromby, J. (eds) (2007) *Affect and Feeling: Special Issue,
Critical Psychology* 21, London: Lawrence & Wishart.

Blackman, L., Cromby, J., Hook, D., Papadopoulos, D., and Walkerdine, V.
(2008) Creating subjectivities, *Subjectivity* 22: 1–27.

Blank, G., and Groselj, D. (2015) A Weberian approach to understanding
internet use, Paper presented at the Media, Communication and Cultural
Studies Association Conference, Northumbria University, January.

Bloch, E. (1988) *The Utopian Function of Art and Literature: Selected
Essays*, trans. J. Zipes and F. Meck. Cambridge, MA: MIT Press.

Bloch, E. ([1959] 1996) *The Principle of Hope*, 3 vols, trans. N. Plaice,
S. Plaice and P. Knight. Cambridge, MA: MIT Press.

Blyth, M. (2013) *Austerity: The History of a Dangerous Idea*. Oxford:
Oxford University Press.

Bohman, J. (2004) Expanding dialogue: the internet, the public sphere and
the prospects for transnational democracy, in N. Crossley and J. M.
Roberts (eds), *After Habermas: New Perspectives on the Public Sphere*.
Oxford: Blackwell, pp. 131–56.

Boltanski, L., and Chiappello, E. (2005) *The New Spirit of Capitalism*, trans.
G. Elliott. London: Verso.

Bookchin, M. (2015) *The Next Revolution: Popular Assemblies and the
Promise of Direct Democracy*. London: Verso.

Bosteels, B. (2011) *Badiou and Politics*. Durham, NC: Duke University Press.

Braidotti, R. (1991) The subject in feminism, *Hypatia* 6(2): 155–72.

Brodock, K., Joyce, M., and Zaeck, T. (2009) *Digital Activism Survey
Report*, DigiActive, http://akgul.bilkent.edu.tr/DigitalActivisim-Survey
Report2009.pdf [*sic*].

Brown, W. (2005) Neoliberalism and the end of liberal democracy, in Brown,
Edgework: Critical Essays on Knowledge and Politics. Princeton, NJ:
Princeton University Press.

Brown, W. (2011) We are all democrats now …, in G. Agamben, A. Badiou,
D. Bensaid, W. Brown, J.-L. Nancy, J. Rancière, K. Ross and S. Žižek,
Democracy in What State? New York: Columbia University Press.

Brown, W. (2015) *Undoing the Demos: Neoliberalism's Stealth Revolution*.
New York: Zone Books.

Butler, J. (1990) *Gender Trouble: Feminism and the Subversion of Identity*.
London: Routledge.

Calabrese, A., and Fenton, N. (2015) A symposium on media, communication and the limits of liberalism, *European Journal of Communication* 30(4): 1–4.

Calingaert, D. (2012) Challenges for international policy, in L. Diamond and M. F. Plattner (eds), *Liberation Technology: Social Media and the Struggle for Democracy*. Baltimore: Johns Hopkins University Press, pp. 157–74.

Cammaerts, B. (2008) Critiques on the participatory potentials of Web 2.0, *Communication, Culture and Critique* 1(4): 358–77.

Carnegie Trust UK (2010) *Enabling Dissent*. London: Carnegie Trust UK.

Carpentier, N. (2011) *Media and Participation: A Site of Ideological-Democratic Struggle*. London: Intellect.

Castells, M. (1996) *The Rise of the Network Society*, Vol. 1: The Information Age: Economy, Society and Culture. Oxford: Blackwell.

Castells, M. (1997) *The Power of Identity*. Oxford: Blackwell.

Castells, M. (2009) *Communication Power*. Oxford: Oxford University Press.

Castells, M. (2015) *Networks of Outrage and Hope: Social Movements in the Internet Age*. 2nd edn, Cambridge: Polity.

Castoriadis, C. (1980) Socialism and autonomous society, *Telos*, no. 43: 91–105.

Castoriadis, C. (1991) *Philosophy, Politics, Autonomy: Essays in Political Philosophy*. New York: Oxford University Press.

Cathcart, B. (2012) *Everybody's Hacked Off: Why We Don't Have the Press We Deserve and What to Do about It*. London: Penguin.

Caygill, H. (2013) *On Resistance: A Philosophy of Defiance*. London: Bloomsbury.

CCMR (Co-ordinating Committee for Media Reform) (2011) *The Media and the Public Interest*, preliminary briefing paper, 4 November, www .mediareform.org.uk/.

Celikates, R., and Jansen, Y. (2013) Reclaiming democracy: an interview with Wendy Brown on Occupy, sovereignty and secularism, *Critical Legal Thinking*, 30 January, http://criticallegalthinking.com/2013/01/ 30/reclaiming-democracy-an-interview-with-wendy-brown-on-occupy -sovereignty-and-secularism/.

Cleaver, H. (1999) Computer-linked social movements and the global threat to capitalism, www.eco.utexas.edu/faculty/Cleaver/polnet.html.

Clough, P. (2008) The affective turn: political economy and the biomediated body, *Theory, Culture and Society*, 25(1): 1–24.

Coleman, S. (2012) It's time for the public to reclaim to the public interest, *Television & New Media*, 13 January: 7–11.

Cornfield, M. (2004) Presidential campaign ads online, Pew Internet and American Life Project, 3 October, www.pewinternet.org/2004/10/03/ presidential-campaign-ads-online/.

Coretti, L. (2014) The Purple Movement: social media activism in Berlusconi's Italy, PhD thesis, University of Westminster.

Costanza-Chock, S. (2012) Mic check! Media cultures and the Occupy movement, *Social Movement Studies* 11(3–4): 375–85.

Cottle, S. (ed.) (2003) *News, Public Relations and Power*. London: Sage.

Couldry, N. (2010) *Why Voice Matters: Culture and Politics after Neoliberalism*. London: Sage.

Couldry, N., Phillips, A., and Freedman, D. (2010) An ethical deficit: accountability, norms and the material conditions of contemporary journalism, in N. Fenton (ed.), *New Media, Old News: Journalism and Democracy in the Digital Age*. London: Sage, pp. 51–69.

Credit Suisse (2014) *Global Wealth Report*, http://economics.uwo.ca/people/davies_docs/credit-suisse-global-wealth-report-2014.pdf.

Crouch, C. (2004) *Post-Democracy*. Cambridge: Polity.

Crouch, C. (2011) *The Strange Non-Death of Neoliberalism*. Cambridge: Polity.

Curran, J. (2002) *Media and Power*. London: Routledge.

Curran, J. (2016) The internet of dreams: reinterpreting the internet, in Curran, *Misunderstanding the Internet*. 2nd edn, London: Routledge.

Curran, J., and Seaton, J. (2003) *Power without Responsibility*. 6th edn, London: Routledge.

Curran, J., Coen, S., Aalberg, T., Hatashi, K., Jones, P., Splendore, S., Papathanassopoulos, S., Rowe, D., and Tiffen, R. (2013) Internet revolution revisited: a comparative study of online news, *Media, Culture & Society* 35(7): 880–97.

Curran, J., Fenton, N., and Freedman, D. (2012) *Misunderstanding the Internet*. London: Routledge.

Curran, J., Fenton, N., and Freedman, D. (2016) *Misunderstanding the Internet*. 2nd edn, London: Routledge.

Dahlberg, L., and Siapera, E. (eds) (2007) *Radical Democracy and the Internet: Interrogating Theory and Practice*. London: Palgrave Macmillan.

Dahlgren, P. (2009) *Media and Political Engagement: Citizens, Communication, Democracy*. Cambridge: Cambridge University Press.

Davies, N. (2008) *Flat Earth News*. London: Chatto & Windus.

Davis, A. (2002) *Public Relations Democracy*. Manchester: Manchester University Press.

Davis, A. (2005) Media effects and the active elite audience: a study of media in financial markets, *European Journal of Communications* 20(3): 303–26.

Davis, A. (2010) *Political Communication and Social Theory*. London: Routledge.

Davis, A. (2015) *The Economics of Public Knowledge*, Goldsmiths, University of London, PERC Papers Series no. 1, www.gold.ac.uk/media/magrated/media/goldsmiths/departments/academicdepartments/politics/pdf/PERC-1-Davis-Public-Knowledge-1.pdf.

Day, R. J. F. (2005) *Gramsci is Dead: Anarchist Currents in the Newest Social Movements*. London: Pluto Press.

DCMS (Department for Culture, Media & Sport) (2015) *BBC Charter Review Public Consultation*. London: DCMS.

Dean, J. (2009) *Democracy and Other Neoliberal Fantasies: Communicative Capitalism and Left Politics*. Durham, NC: Duke University Press.

Dean, J. (2014) Enclosing the subject, *Political Theory*, 2 December, http://ptx.sagepub.com/content/early/2014/12/01/0090591714560377.abstract.

Dean, J., Anderson, J. W., and Lovink, G. (2006) *Reformatting Politics: Information Technology and Global Civil Society*. London: Routledge.

Dean, M. (2011) *Democracy under Attack: How the Media Distort Policy and Politics*. London: Policy Press.

Deibert, R. (2012) International mechanisms of cyberspace control, in L. Diamond and M. F. Plattner (eds), *Liberation Technology: Social Media and the Struggle for Democracy*. Baltimore: Johns Hopkins University Press, pp. 33–46.

Deibert, R., and Rohozinski, R. (2012) Liberation vs. control: the future of cyberspace, in L. Diamond and M. F. Plattner (eds), *Liberation Technology: Social Media and the Struggle for Democracy*. Baltimore: Johns Hopkins University Press, pp. 18–32.

Deibert, R., Palfrey, J., Rohozinski, R., Zittrain, J., and Haraszti, M. (eds) (2010) *Access Controlled: The Shaping of Power, Rights and Rule in Cyberspace*. Cambridge, MA: MIT Press.

Deleuze, G., and Guattari, F. (1988) *A Thousand Plateaus: Capitalism and Schizophrenia*. London: Athlone Press.

della Porta, D. (2005) Multiple belongings, tolerant identities and the construction of 'another politics': between the European social forum and the local social fora, in D. della Porta and S. Tarrow (eds), *Transnational Protest and Global Activism*. Lanham, MD: Rowman & Littlefield, pp. 175–203.

della Porta, D. (2013) Bridging research on democracy, social movements and communication, in B. Cammaerts, A. Mattoni and P. McCurdy (eds), *Mediation and Protest Movements*. Bristol: Intellect, pp. 23–7.

della Porta, D., and Diani, M. (1999) *Social Movements: An Introduction*. Oxford: Blackwell.

della Porta, D. and Diani, M. (2006) *Social Movements: An Introduction*. 2nd edn, Oxford: Blackwell.

Delli Carpini, M. S., and Williams, B. A. (2001) Let us infotain you: politics in the new media environment, in W. L. Bennett and R. M. Entman (eds), *Mediated Politics: Communication in the Future of Democracy*. Cambridge: Cambridge University Press.

Dencik, L., and Leistert, O. (2015) *Critical Perspectives on Social Media Protest*. London: Rowman & Littlefield.

Derrida, J. (1997) *Of Grammatology*. Baltimore: John Hopkins University Press.

Diamond, L. (2012) Introduction, in L. Diamond and M. F. Plattner (eds), *Liberation Technology: Social Media and the Struggle for Democracy*. Baltimore: Johns Hopkins University Press, pp. ix–xxvii.

Diamond, L., and Plattner, M. F. (eds) (2012) *Liberation Technology: Social Media and the Struggle for Democracy*. Baltimore: Johns Hopkins University Press.

Dolan, A. (2015) Podemos: politics by the people, *Red Pepper*, February, www.redpepper.org.uk/podemos-politics-by-the-people.

Donath, J. (2007) Signals in social supernets, *Journal of Computer-Mediated Communication* 13(1): 231–51.

Dorling, D. (2011) *Injustice: Why Social Inequality Persists*. Bristol: Policy Press.

Dorling, D. (2014) *Inequality and the 1%*. London: Verso.

Douzinas, C. (2013) *Philosophy and Resistance in the Crisis: Greece and the Future of Europe*. Cambridge: Polity.

Douzinas, C. (2015) Notes towards an analytics of resistance, *New Formations* no. 83: 79–98.

Downey, J., and Fenton, N. (2003) Constructing a counter-public sphere, *New Media and Society* 5(2): 185–202.

Downey, J., and Fenton, N. (2007) Global capital, local resistance, *Current Sociology* 55(5): 651–73.

Dryzek, J. (2000) *Deliberative Democracy and Beyond: Liberals, Critics, Contestations*. Oxford: Oxford University Press.

Dussel, E. (2008) *Twenty Theses on Politics*. Durham, NC: Duke University Press.

Dutton, W., and Blank, G., with Groselj, D. (2013) *Cultures of the Internet: The Internet in Britain*. Oxford: Oxford Internet Institute, http://oxis.oii.ox.ac.uk/wp-content/uploads/sites/43/2014/11/OxIS-2013.pdf.

Edelman (2015) *Edelman Trust Barometer 2015: Global Results*. http://www.slideshare.net/EdelmanInsights/2015-edelman-trust-barometer-global-results

Efimeros, C. (2015) 'Mainstream media lie in Greece', *The Press Project*, 9 July, www.thepressproject.gr/details-en.php?aid=79064.

Elkin, M. (2011) Tunisia internet chief gives inside look at cyber uprising, *Wired.co.uk*, 31 January, www.wired.co.uk/news/archive/2011-01/31/tunisia-egypt-internet-restrictions.

Ellis, D., and Tucker, I. (2011) Virtuality and Ernst Bloch: hope and subjectivity, *Subjectivity* 4(4): 434–50.

Elster, J. (ed.) (1998) *Deliberative Democracy*. Cambridge: Cambridge University Press.

Ester, P., and Vinken, H. (2003) Debating civil society: on the fear for civic decline and hope for the internet alternative, *International Sociology* 18(4): 659–80.

European Commission (2014) Youth unemployment, http://ec.europa.eu/social/main.jsp?catId=1036.

Faris, D. (2013) *Dissent and Revolution in a Digital Age: Social Media, Blogging and Activism in Egypt*. London: I. B. Tauris.

Feenberg, A. (1995) Subversive rationalization: technology, power and democracy, in A. Feenberg and A. Hannay (eds), *Technology and the Politics of Knowledge*. Bloomington: Indiana University Press.

Feenberg, A. (2002) *Transforming Technology*. Oxford: Oxford University Press.

Fenton, N. (2000) The problematics of postmodernism for feminist media studies, *Media, Culture & Society* 22(6): 723–41.

Fenton, N. (2006) Another world is possible, *Global Media and Communication* 2(3): 355–67.

Fenton, N. (2007) Bridging the mythical divide: political economy and cultural studies approaches to the media, in E. Devereux (ed.), *Issues and Key Debates in Media Studies*. London: Sage.

Fenton, N. (2008a) Mediating hope: new media, politics and resistance, *International Journal of Cultural Studies* 11(2): 230–48.

Fenton, N. (2008b) Mediating solidarity, *Global Media and Communication* 4(1): 37–57.

Fenton, N. (ed.) (2010) *New Media, Old News: Journalism and Democracy in the Digital Age*. London: Sage.

Fenton, N. (2011) Multiplicity, autonomy and the mediated politics of new social movements, in L. Dahlberg and S. Phelan (eds), *Discourse Theory and Media Politics*. London: Palgrave.

Fenton, N. (2012a) The internet and radical politics, in J. Curran, N. Fenton and D. Freedman, *Misunderstanding the Internet*. London: Routledge.

Fenton, N. (2012b) The internet and social networking, in J. Curran, N. Fenton and D. Freedman, *Misunderstanding the Internet*. London: Routledge.

Fenton, N. (2013) Cosmopolitanism as conformity and contestation: the mainstream press and radical politics, *Journalism Studies* 14(2): 172–86.

Fenton, N. (2016) The internet of me (and my friends), in J. Curran, N. Fenton and D. Freedman, *Misunderstanding the Internet*. 2nd edn, London: Routledge.

Fenton, N., and Barassi, V. (2011) Alternative media and social networking sites: the politics of individuation and political participation, *Communication Review* 14(3): 179–96.

Fenton, N., and Downey, J. (2003) Counter public spheres and global modernity, *Javnost – The Public* 10(1): 15–32.

Fenton, N., and Titley, G. (2015) Mourning and longing: media studies learning to let go of liberal democracy, *European Journal of Communication* 30(4): 1–16.

Ferguson, C. (2012) *Inside Job: The Financiers Who Pulled Off the Heist of the Century*, Oxford: Oneworld.

File, T., and Ryan, C. (2014) *Computer and Internet Use in the United States: 2013*, US Census Bureau, www.census.gov/content/dam/Census/library/publications/2014/acs/acs-28.pdf.

Fishkin, J. S. (2011) *When the People Speak*. Oxford: Oxford University Press.

Forster, M. (2011) *Divided We Stand: Why Inequality Keeps Rising*. Paris: OECD.

Foster, J. B., and McChesney, R. W. (2011) The internet's unholy marriage to capitalism, *Monthly Review* 62(10): 1–30.

Foucault, M. (2004) *Society Must Be Defended*. London: Penguin.

Franklin, B. (1997) *Newzak and News Media*. London: Edward Arnold.

Franklin, B. (2005) McJournalism: the local press and the McDonaldization thesis, in S. Allan (ed.), *Journalism: Critical Issues*. Maidenhead: Open University Press.

Fraser, N. (1995) From redistribution to recognition? Dilemmas of justice in a 'post-socialist' age, *New Left Review* 1/212, July–August.

Freedman, D. (2014) *The Contradictions of Media Power*. London: Bloomsbury.

Freedman, D., and Bailey, M. (eds) (2011) *The Assault on Universities: A Manifesto for Resistance*. London: Pluto Press.

Freedom House (2011) *Freedom on the Net*, https://freedomhouse.org/report/freedom-net/freedom-net-2011.

Garland, J., and Terry, C. (2015) *The 2015 General Election: A Voting System in Crisis*. London: Electoral Reform Society.

Garnham, N. (1992) The media and the public sphere, in C. Calhoun (ed.), *Habermas and the Public Sphere*. Cambridge, MA: MIT Press.

Gerbaudo, P. (2012) *Tweets and the Streets: Social Media and Contemporary Activism*. London: Pluto Press.

Ghannam, J. (2011) *Social Media in the Arab World: Leading up to the Uprisings of 2011*. Washington, DC: Center for International Media Assistance, www.cima.ned.org/wp-content/uploads/2015/02/CIMA-Arab _Social_Media-Report-10-25-11.pdf.

Gilbert, J. (2008) *Anticapitalism and Culture: Radical Theory and Popular Politics*. Oxford: Berg.

Gilbert, J. (2014) *Common Ground: Democracy and Collectivity in the Age of Individualism*. London: Pluto Press.

Gilens, M. (2005) Inequality and democratic responsiveness, *Public Opinion Quarterly* 69(5): 778–96.

Giroux, H. A. (2004) When hope is subversive, *Tikkun* 19(6): 38–9.

Gledhill, J. (1994) *Power and its Disguises: Anthropological Perspectives on Politics*. London: Pluto Press.

Golding, P., and Middleton, S. (1982) *Images of Welfare: Press and Public Attitudes to Poverty*. London: Robertson.

Golding, P., and Murdock, G. (2000) Culture, communications and political economy, in J. Curran and M. Gurevitch (eds), *Mass Media and Society*. 3rd edn, London: Edward Arnold, pp. 70–92.

Graeber, D. (2002) The new anarchists, *New Left Review*, 13, January–February, www.newleftreview.org/A2368.

Gramsci, A. (1971) *Selections from the Prison Notebooks*, ed. and trans. Q. Hoare and G. Nowell-Smith. London: Lawrence & Wishart.

Gramsci, A. (1991) *Prison Notebooks*, ed. Joseph A. Buttigieg. New York: Columbia University Press.

Habermas, J. (1989) *The Structural Transformation of the Public Sphere: An Inquiry into a Category of Bourgeois Society*. Cambridge: Polity.

Habermas, J. (1992) Further reflections on the public sphere, in C. Calhoun (ed.), *Habermas and the Public Sphere*. Cambridge, MA: MIT Press, pp. 421–61.

Habermas, J. (1996) *Between Facts and Norms: Contributions to a Discourse Theory of Law and Democracy*. Cambridge: Polity.

Habermas, J. (1998) *Inclusion of the Other: Studies in Political Theory*. Cambridge: Polity.

Habermas, J. (2006) Political communication in media society – does democracy still enjoy an epistemic dimension? The impact of normative theory on empirical research, Paper presented to the ICA annual conference, Dresden.

Hacker, J. S., and Pierson, P. (2010) *Winner-Take-All Politics*. New York: Simon & Schuster.

Haight, M., Quan-Haase, A., and Corbett, B. A. (2014) Revisiting the digitial divide in Canada: the impact of demographic factors on access to the internet, level of online activity, and social networking usage, *Information, Communication and Society* 17(4): 503–19.

Hands, J. (2011) *@ is for Activism: Dissent, Resistance and Rebellion in a Digital Culture*. London: Pluto Press.

Hansard Society (2013) *Audit of Political Engagement: The 2013 Report*. London: Hansard Society, www.hansardsociety.org.uk/audit-of-political -engagement-10/.

Hardt, M., and Negri, A. (2000) *Empire*. Cambridge MA: Harvard University Press.

Hardt, M., and Negri, A. (2004) *Multitude*. New York: Penguin.

Hardt, M., and Negri, A. (2009) *Commonwealth*. Cambridge MA: Belknap Press.

Harvey, D. (2014) Foreword, in M. Sitrin and D. Azzellini, *They Can't Represent Us: Reinventing Democracy from Greece to Occupy*. London: Verso.

Heil, B., and Piskorski, M. (2009) New Twitter research: men follow men and nobody tweets, https://hbr.org/2009/06/new-twitter-research-men-follo.

Held, D. (1999) *Global Transformations: Politics, Economics and Culture*. Cambridge: Polity.

Hill, K., and Hughes, J. (1998) *Cyberpolitics: Citizen Activism in the Age of the Internet*. Oxford: Rowman & Littlefield.

Hindman, M. (2008) *The Myth of Digital Democracy*. Princeton, NJ: Princeton University Press.

Hintz, A. (2015) Social media censorship, privatized regulation and new restrictions to protest and dissent, in L. Dencik and O. Leistert (eds), *Critical Perspectives on Social Media Protest: Between Control and Emancipation*. London: Rowman & Littlefield.

Hirschkind, C. (2009) *The Ethical Soundscape: Cassette Sermons and Islamic Counterpublics*. New York: Columbia University Press.

Hirst, P. Q. (1976) Althusser and the theory of ideology, *Economy and Society* 5(4): 385–412.

Holloway, J. (2002) *Change the World without Taking Power: The Meaning of Revolution Today*. London: Pluto Press.

Holt, R. (2004) *Dialogue on the Internet: Language, Civic Identity, and Computer-Mediated Communication*. Westport, CT: Praeger.

Horkheimer, M. (1972) *Traditional and Critical Theory*. New York: Herder & Herder.

Horkheimer, M. (1982) *Critical Theory*. New York: Seabury Press.

House of Lords (2008) *Communications – First Report, Session 2007–08*. London: The Stationery Office, www.publications.parliament.uk/pa/ld200708/ldselect/ldcomuni/122/12202.htm#evidence.

Howard, P. N., and Hussain, M. M. (2012) Egypt and Tunisia: the role of digital media, in L. Diamond and M. F. Plattner (eds), *Liberation Technology: Social Media and the Struggle for Democracy*. Baltimore: Johns Hopkins University Press, pp. 110–23.

Hughes, C. (2011) Salivary identities: the matter of affect, *Subjectivity* 4(4): 413–33.

International Labour Organization (2014) *Global Employment Trends 2014*. Geneva: ILO.

Internet World Stats (2015a) Internet users in the world by regions, www.internetworldstats.com/stats.htm.

Internet World Stats (2015b) Internet world users by language, www.internetworldstats.com/stats7.htm.

Ipsos MORI (2013) Perceptions are not reality: the top 10 we get wrong, https://www.ipsos-mori.com/researchpublications/researcharchive/3188/Perceptions-are-not-reality-the-top-10-we-get-wrong.aspx.

Ipsos MORI (2014) Perceptions are not reality: things the world gets wrong, https://www.ipsos-mori.com/researchpublications/researcharchive/3466/Perceptions-are-not-reality-Things-the-world-gets-wrong.aspx.

Jenkins, H. (2015) Affective publics and social media: an interview with Zizi Papacharissi, *Confessions of an Aca-Fan: The Official weblog of Henry Jenkins*, henryjenkins.org/2015/01/affective-publics-and-social-media-an-interview-with-zizi-papacharissi-part-two.html.

Jones, O. (2014) *The Establishment: And How They Get Away with It*. London: Allen Lane.

Juris, J. (2008) *Networking Futures*. Durham, NC: Duke University Press.

Kahn, R., and Kellner, D. (2004) New media and internet activism: from the 'battle of Seattle' to blogging, *New Media & Society* 6(1): 87–95.

Kahn, R., and Kellner, D. (2007) Globalisation, technopolitics and radical democracy, in L. Dahlberg and E. Siapera (eds), *Radical Democracy and the Internet: Interrogating Theory and Practice*. London: Palgrave Macmillan.

Katsiaficas, G. N. (2006) *The Subversion of Politics: European Autonomous Social Movements and the Decolonization of Everyday Life*. Updated edn, Oakland, CA: AK Press.

Kaun, A. (2015) 'This space belongs to us!': Protest spaces in times of accelerating capitalism, in L. Dencik and O. Leistert (eds), *Critical Perspectives on Social Media Protest: Between Control and Emancipation*. London: Rowman & Littlefield.

Keane, J. (1991) *The Media and Democracy*. Cambridge: Polity.

Keck, M. E., and Sikkink, K. (1998) *Activists beyond Borders: Advocacy Networks in International Politics*. Ithaca, NY: Cornell University Press.

Keen, R. (2015) *Membership of UK Political Parties*, Briefing Paper no. SN/05/5125. London: House of Commons Library.

Kellner, D. (1990) Critical theory and the crisis of social theory, *Sociological Perspectives* 33(1): 11–33.

Khiabany, G. (2010) Media power, people power and politics of media in Iran, Paper presented to the IAMCR conference, Braga, Portugal.

Khiabany, G. (2016) The importance of 'social' in social media: some lessons from Iran, in A. Bruns, G. Enli, E. Skogerbø, A. O. Larsson and C. Christensen (eds), *The Routledge Companion to Social Media and Politics*. New York: Routledge.

Klein, N. (2000) *No Logo*. New York: Flamingo.

Klein, N. (2002) Farewell to the 'end of history': organisation and vision in anti-corporate movements, *Socialist Register* 38: 1–14.

Koenig, P. (2015) Greece – risk of false-flagging Greece into submission and chaos? *Global Research*, 3 July, www.globalresearch.ca/greece-risk-of-false-flagging-greece-into-submission-and-chaos/5460323.

Kowal, D. (2002) Digitizing and globalizing indigenous voices: the Zapatista movement, in G. Elmer (ed.), *Critical Perspectives on the Internet*. Lanham, MD: Rowman & Littlefield, pp. 105–29.

Kriakidou, D., and Flynn, M. (2008) Riots rock Greece amid election calls, *Reuters UK*, 9 December.

Kriesberg, L. (1997) Social movements and global transformation, in J. Smith, C. Chatfield and R. Pagnucco (eds), *Transnational Social Movements and Global Politics: Solidarity beyond the State*. Syracuse, NY: Syracuse University Press, pp. 3–17.

Krugman, P. (2015) The austerity delusion, *The Guardian*, 29 April, www.theguardian.com/business/ng-interactive/2015/apr/29/the-austerity-delusion.

Laclau, E. (2004) *The Making of Political Identities*. London: Verso.

Laclau, E., and Mouffe, C. (1985) *Hegemony and Socialist Strategy: Towards a Radical Democratic Politics*. London: Verso.

Lanning, T., and Rudiger, K. (2012) *Youth Unemployment in Europe: Lessons for the UK*. London: IPPR.

Lee-Wright, P., Phillips, A., and Witschge, T. (2011) *Changing Journalism*. London: Routledge.

Leistert, O. (2015) The revolution will not be liked: on the systemic constraints of corporate social media platforms for protests, in L. Dencik and O. Leistert (eds), *Critical Perspectives on Social Media and Protest: Between Control and Emancipation*. London: Rowman & Littlefield.

Lekakis, E. (2013) *Coffee Activism and the Politics of Fair Trade and Ethical Consumption in the Global North: Political Consumerism and Cultural Citizenship*. Basingstoke: Palgrave.

Lessig, L. (2011) *Republic, Lost: How Money Corrupts Congress and a Plan to Stop It*. New York: Twelve Books.

Leveson, Lord Justice (2012) *An Inquiry into the Culture, Practices and Ethics of the Press*, 4 vols. London: The Stationery Office, http://webarchive

.nationalarchives.gov.uk/20140122145147/http:/www.levesoninquiry.org .uk/about/the-report/.

Levitas, R. (1998) Educated hope: Ernst Bloch on abstract and concrete utopia, in J. Daniel and T. Moylan (eds), *Not Yet: Reconsidering Ernst Bloch*. London: Verso, pp. 65–79.

Levy, D., and Nielsen, R. (eds) (2010) *The Changing Business of Journalism and its Implications for Democracy*. Oxford: Reuters Institute for the Study of Journalism.

Lewis, J., Williams, A., and Franklin, B. (2008) A compromised fourth estate? UK news journalism, public relations and news sources, *Journalism Studies* 9(1): 1–20.

Leys, C., and Player, S. (2011) *The Plot Against the NHS*. London: Merlin Press.

Lin, Y.-R., Keegan, B., Margolin, D., and Lazer, D. (2014) Rising tides or rising stars? Dynamics of shared attention on Twitter during media events, *PLoS ONE* 9(5), http://journals.plos.org/plosone/article?id=10 .1371/journal.pone.0094093.

Littler, J., and Gilbert, J. (2009) Radicalism: strategies, ecologies, roots, in J. Pugh (ed.), *What is Radical Politics Today?* London: Palgrave Macmillan, pp. 127–36.

Livingstone, S., and Bovill, M. (2002) *Young People, New Media: Research Report*, http://eprints.lse.ac.uk/21177/1/Young_people_new_media_%28 LSERO%29.pdf.

Livingstone, S., Bober, M., and Helsper, E. (2005) *Internet Literacy among Children and Young People: Findings from the UK Children Go Online Project*, http://eprints.lse.ac.uk/archive/00000397.

Loader, B. (ed.) (2007) *Young Citizens in the Digital Age: Political Engagement, Young People and New Media*. London: Routledge.

Lodge, G., and Gottfried, G. (2011) *Worst of Both Worlds: Why First Past the Post No Longer Works*. London: IPPR.

Lodge, G., Gottfried, G., and Birch, S. (2013) *The Political Inclusion of Young Citizens*. London: IPPR, http://eprints.lse.ac.uk/56306/1/Democratic -Audit_Lodge-Gottfried-and-Birch_The-Political-Inclusion-of-Young -Citizens.pdf.

Louw, E. (2005) *The Media and the Political Process*. London: Sage.

Lunt, P., and Livingstone, S. (2013) Media studies' fascination with the concept of the public sphere: critical reflections and emerging debates, *Media Culture & Society* 35(1): 87–96.

Lyotard, J. (1984) *The Postmodern Condition: A Report on Knowledge*. Minneapolis: University of Minnesota Press.

McCarthy, J. D. (1997) The globalization of social movement theory, in J. Smith, C. Chatfield and R. Pagnucco (eds), *Transnational Social Movements and Global Politics: Solidarity beyond the State*. Syracuse, NY: Syracuse University Press, pp. 243–60.

McChesney, R. (2012) This isn't what democracy looks like, *Monthly Review* 64(6), http://monthlyreview.org/2012/11/01/this-isnt-what-democracy -looks-like/.

McChesney, R. (2014) *Digital Disconnect: How Capitalism is Turning the Internet Against Democracy*. New York: New Press.

McChesney, R., and Nichols, J. (2010) *The Death and Life of American Journalism: The Media Revolution that Will Begin the World Again*. Philadelphia: Nation Books.

Mackinnon, R. (2012) China's 'networked authoritarianism', in L. Diamond and M. F. Plattner (eds), *Liberation Technology: Social Media and the Struggle for Democracy*. Baltimore: Johns Hopkins University Press, pp. 78–94.

McKinsey & Company (2014) *Education to Employment: Getting Europe's Youth into Work*, www.mckinsey.com/insights/social_sector/converting_education_to_employment_in_europe.

Mair, P. (2006) Ruling the void? The hollowing of Western democracy, *New Left Review* 42, November–December: 25–51.

Marchart, O. (2007) *Post-Foundational Political Thought: Political Difference in Nancy, Lefort, Badiou, and Laclau*. Edinburgh: Edinburgh University Press.

Marcos, Subcomandante Insurgente (2001) *Our Word Is Our Weapon: Selected Writings of Subcomandante Insurgente Marcos*. New York: Seven Stories Press.

Marquand, J. (2012) Economics as a public art, *openDemocracy*, 15 February, https://www.opendemocracy.net/ourkingdom/judith-marquand/economics-as-public-art.

Marshall, J. (2009) *Membership of UK Political Parties, Standard Note* SN/SG/5125. London: House of Commons Library.

Mason, P. (2012) *Why It's Kicking Off Everywhere: The New Global Revolutions*. London: Verso.

Massumi, B. (2002) *Parables for the Virtual: Movement, Affect, Sensation*. Durham, NC: Duke University Press.

Mattoni, A., and Vogiatzoglou, M. (2014) Italy and Greece, before and after the crisis: between mobilization and resistance against precarity, *Quaderni* 84 (spring): 57–71, https://quaderni.revues.org/805?lang=en.

Maura, E. (2014) Europe needs to change – and using grassroots democracy is how we do it, *The Guardian*, 13 October, www.theguardian.com/commentisfree/2014/oct/13/europe-new-politics-grassroots-resistance-podemos-syriza.

Media Reform Coalition (2015) *Who Owns the UK Media?* London: MRC.

Media Standards Trust (2013) *IPSO – An Assessment*. London: Media Standards Trust.

Meier, P. (2012) Ushahidi as a liberation technology, in L. Diamond and M. F. Plattner (eds), *Liberation Technology: Social Media and the Struggle for Democracy*. Baltimore: Johns Hopkins University Press, pp. 95–109.

Miessen, M. (2007) Articulated power relations – Markus Miessen in conversation with Chantal Mouffe, https://www.hitpages.com/doc/6600432994484224/1#pageTop.

Miladi, N. (2011) Tunisia: a media led revolution? *Aljazeera*, 17 January, http://english.aljazeera.net/indepth/opinion/2011/01/2011116142317498 666.html.

Milan, S. (2015) Mobilizing in time of social media: from a politics of identity to a politics of visibility, in L. Dencik and O. Leistert (eds), *Critical Perspectives on Social Media and Protest: Between Control and Emancipation*. London: Rowman & Littlefield.

Miller, D. (2010) How neoliberalism got where it is: elite planning, corporate lobbying and the release of the free market, in K. Birch and V. Mykhnenko (eds), *The Rise and Fall of Neoliberalism: The Collapse of an Economic Order?* London: Zed Books.

Miller, D. (2014) Media power and class power: overplaying ideology, in S. Coban (ed.), *Media and Left*. Leiden: Brill, pp. 44–67.

Miller, V. (2008) New media, networking, and phatic culture, *Convergence* 14(4): 387–400.

Morozov, E. (2011) *The Net Delusion: How Not to Liberate the World*. London: Allen Lane.

Morozov, E. (2012) Whither internet control?, in L. Diamond and M. F. Plattner (eds), *Liberation Technology: Social Media and the Struggle for Democracy*. Baltimore: Johns Hopkins University Press, pp. 47–62.

Morozov, E. (2015) The taming of tech criticism, *The Baffler* no. 27, www .thebaffler.com/salvos/taming-tech-criticism.

Mouffe, C. (2000) *The Democratic Paradox*. London: Verso.

Mouffe, C. (2005) *The Return of the Political*. London: Verso.

Murphy, R. (2013) *Over Here and Undertaxed: Multinationals, Tax Avoidance and You*. London: Vintage Digital.

Murray, R. (2004) The new political economy of public life, *Soundings* 27: 19–32.

Nash, K. (ed.) (2000) *Contemporary Political Sociology*. Oxford: Blackwell.

Negt, O., and Kluge, A. (1972) *Public Sphere and Experience: Towards an Analysis of the Bourgeois and Proletarian Public Sphere*. Minneapolis: University of Minnesota Press.

Nelson, B. (2011) Politics of the senses: Karl Marx and empirical subjectivity, *Subjectivity* 4: 395–412.

Nichols, J., and McChesney, R. (2013) *Dollarocracy: How the Money-and-Media Election Complex Is Destroying America*. New York: Nation Books.

Nielsen (2012) State of the media: the social media report 2012, www .nielsen.com/us/en/insights/news/2012/social-media-report-2012-social -media-comes-of-age.html.

Norris, P. (2001) *Digital Divide: Civic Engagement, Information Poverty and the Internet Worldwide*. Cambridge: Cambridge University Press.

Norris, P. (2002) *Democratic Phoenix: Reinventing Political Activism*. Cambridge: Cambridge University Press.

Norval, A. (2007) *Aversive Democracy*. Cambridge: Cambridge University Press.

NUJ (2006) *National Union of Journalists Surveys of Members*. London: National Union of Journalists.

OECD (2014) Income inequality and poverty, www.oecd.org/social/inequality-and-poverty.htm.

Ofcom (2007) *Communications Market Special Report: Ethnic Minority Groups and Communications Services*. London: Ofcom, http://stakeholders.ofcom.org.uk/binaries/research/cmr/ethnic_grps.pdf.

Ofcom (2010) *Digital Participation: 2010 Metrics Bulletin*. London: Ofcom, http://stakeholders.ofcom.org.uk/binaries/research/media-literacy/digi-participation/2010-metrics/metrics-bulletin-2010.pdf.

Ortiz, I., and Cummins, M. (2013) The age of austerity: a review of expenditures and adjustment measures in 181 countries, Initiative for Policy Dialogue, http://policydialogue.org/publications/working_papers/age_of_austerity/.

Oswell, D. (2006) *Culture and Society*. London: Sage.

Oxfam (2014) *Working for the Few: Political Capture and Economic Inequality*. Oxford: Oxfam.

Oxfam (2015) Wealth: having it all and wanting more, Oxfam Issue Briefing, January, https://www.oxfam.org/sites/www.oxfam.org/files/file_attachments/ib-wealth-having-all-wanting-more-190115-en.pdf.

Papacharissi, Z. (2010a) *A Networked Self: Identity, Community and Culture on Social Network Sites*. New York: Routledge.

Papacharissi, Z. (2010b) *A Private Sphere: Democracy in a Digital Age*. Cambridge: Polity.

Papacharissi, Z. (2015) *Affective Publics: Sentiment, Technology and Politics*. Oxford: Oxford University Press.

Park, A. (2004) *British Social Attitudes: The 21st Report*. London: Sage.

Park, A., Bryson, C., Clery, E., Curtice, J., and Phillips, M. (eds) (2013) *British Social Attitudes: the 30th Report*. London, National Centre for Social Research.

Parker, L., and Mountain, D., with Manousakis, N. (2014) ¿Más allá de la izquierda y la derecha? (Beyond left and right?): an interview with Eduardo Maura of Podemos, *Platypus Review* 72, December–January, http://platypus1917.org/2014/12/01/mas-alla-de-la-izquierda-y-la-derecha/.

Patterson, T. (2010) Media abundance and democracy, *Media, Journalismo e Democracia* 9(2): 13–31.

Pew Research Center (2012) *State of the News Media 2012*, www.pewresearch.org/2012/03/19/state-of-the-news-media-2012/.

Pew Research Center (2015) *Internet Seen as Positive Influence on Education but Negative Influence on Morality in Emerging and Developing Nations*, www.pewglobal.org/files/2015/03/Pew-Research-Center-Technology-Report-FINAL-March-19-20151.pdf.

Phillips, A. (2014) *Journalism in Context*. London: Routledge.

Piketty, T. (2013) Should we make the richest pay to meet fiscal adjustment needs?, in S. Princen and G. Mourre (eds), *The role of Tax Policy in Times of Fiscal Consolidation*. Brussels: European Commission, pp. 99–102.

Piketty, T. (2014) *Capital in the Twenty-First Century*. Cambridge MA: Harvard University Press.

Piketty, T., and Iglesias, P. (2015) Reforming Europe: Thomas Piketty meets Pablo Iglesias, *openDemocracy*, 20 February, https://www.opendemocracy .net/can-europe-make-it/thomas-piketty-pablo-iglesias/reforming-europe -thomas-piketty-meets-pablo-iglesia.

Prentoulis, M. (2015) From protest to power: the transformation of Syriza, *Red Pepper*, January, www.redpepper.org.uk/by/marina-prentoulis/.

Prichard, A. (2010) Bringing anarchy in, *Centre for the Study of Democracy Bulletin* 17(1/2): 22–5.

Rancière, J. (1999) *Disagreement: Politics and Philosophy*, trans. J. Rose. Minneapolis: University of Minnesota Press.

Rancière, J. (2011a) *La Haine de la democratie*. Paris: La Fabrique.

Rancière, J. (2011b) On the theory of ideology: Althusser's politics, appendix to *Althusser's Lesson*, trans. E. Battista. London: Continuum.

Redden, J. (2011) The mediation of poverty: the news, new media and politics, PhD thesis, Goldsmiths, University of London.

Ribeiro, G. L. (1998) Cybercultural politics: political activism at a distance in a transnational world, in S. E. Alvarez, E. Dagnino and A. Escobar (eds), *Cultures of Politics, Politics of Cultures: Re-Visioning Latin American Social Movements*. Boulder, CO: Westview Press, pp. 325–52.

Roberts, J. M. (2014) *New Media and Public Activism: Neoliberalism, the State and Radical Protest in the Public Sphere*. Bristol: Policy Press.

Salter, L. (2003) Democracy, new social movements and the internet: a Habermasian analysis, in M. McCaughey and M. D. Ayers (eds), *Cyberactivism: Online Activism in Theory and Practice*. London: Routledge, pp. 117–45.

Sassen, S. (2014) *Expulsions: Brutality and Complexity in the Global Economy*. Cambridge MA: Belknap Press.

Schäfer, A., and Streeck, W. (eds) (2013) *Politics in the Age of Austerity*. Cambridge: Polity.

Scott, J. W. (ed.) (1996) *Feminism and History*. Oxford: Oxford University Press.

Sen, A. (1999) *Commodities and Capabilities*. New York: Oxford University Press.

Sennett, R. (1974) *The Fall of Public Man*. New York: Random House.

Sennett, R. (2008) *The Craftsman*. London: Penguin.

Shane, P. (ed.) (2004) *Democracy Online: The Prospect for Political Renewal through the Internet*. London: Routledge.

Shaxson, N. (2012) *Treasure Islands: Tax Havens and the Men Who Stole the World*. London: Vintage.

Skeggs, B. (2014) Values beyond value: is anything beyond the logic of capital?, *British Journal of Sociology* 65(1): 1–20.

Skelton, D. (2011) Government of the technocrats, by the technocrats, for the technocrats, *New Statesman*, 16 November, www.newstatesman.com/ blogs/the-staggers/2011/11/european-greece-technocrats.

Sloam, J. (2013) Voice and equality: young people's politics in the European Union, *West European Politics* 36(4): 836–58.

Sloam, J. (2014) New voice, less equal: the civic and political engagement of young people in the United States and Europe, *Comparative Political Studies* 47(5): 663–88.

Smith, H. (2015) Greece's new anti-austerity government set on collision course with Brussels, *The Guardian*, 26 January, www.theguardian.com/world/2015/jan/26/greece-anti-austerity-government-alexis-tsipras.

Smucker, J. M. (2014) Can prefigurative politics replace political strategy?, *Berkeley Journal of Sociology*, 7 October, http://berkeleyjournal.org/2014/10/can-prefigurative-politics-replace-political-strategy/.

Spivak, G. (1992) French feminism revisited: ethics and politics, in J. Butler and J. Scott (eds), *Feminists Theorize the Political*. London: Routledge, pp. 54–85.

Starn, O., Degregori, C. I., and Kirk, R. (2005) *The Peru Reader: History, Culture, Politics*. Durham, NC: Duke University Press.

Stengers, I. (2010) *Cosmopolitics*. Minneapolis: University of Minnesota Press.

Stiglitz, J. E. (2015) *The Great Divide*. London: Penguin.

Streeck, W. (2011) The crises of democratic capitalism, *New Left Review* 71, September–October.

Streeck, W. (2012) Markets and peoples, *New Left Review* 73, January–February.

Streeck, W. (2014) How will capitalism end?, *New Left Review* 87, May–June: 35–64.

Sunstein, C. (2001) Republic.com. Princeton, NJ: Princeton University Press.

Tapscott, D., and Williams, A. (2008) *Wikinomics: How Mass Collaboration Changes Everything*. London: Atlantic Books.

Tarrow, S. (1994) *Power in Movement*. Cambridge: Cambridge University Press.

Tarrow, S., and della Porta, D. (2005) Globalization, complex internationalism and transnational contention, in D. della Porta and S. Tarrow (eds), *Transnational Protest and Global Activism*. Lanham, MD: Rowman & Littlefield, pp. 227–47.

Taylor, C. (1994) The politics of recognition, in A. Gutmann (ed.), *Multiculturalism: Examining the Politics of Recognition*. Princeton, NJ: Princeton University Press, pp. 25–73.

Taylor, L. (2006) Deeply disillusioned but not without hope, *Times Higher Educational Supplement*, 3 March.

Terranova, T. (2004) *Network Culture: Politics for the Information Age*. London: Pluto Press.

Thomassen, L. (2007) Beyond representation, *Parliamentary Affairs* 60(1): 111–26.

Thompson, E. P. (2014) *E. P. Thompson and the Making of the New Left: Essays and Polemics*, ed. C. Winslow. London: Lawrence & Wishart.

Thrift, N. (2007) *Non-Representational Theory: Space, Politics, Affect*. London: Routledge.

Tormey, S. (2005) From utopian worlds to utopian spaces: reflections on the contemporary radical imaginary and the social forum process, *ephemera* 5(2): 394–408.

Tormey, S. (2006) *Anti-Capitalism: A Beginner's Guide*. Oxford: Oneworld.

Tormey, S., and Townshend, J. (2006) *Key Thinkers from Critical Theory to Post-Marxism*. London: Sage.

Traugott, M. (1995) Recurrent patterns of collective action, in M. Traugott (ed.), *Repertoires and Cycles of Collective Action*. Durham, NC: Duke University Press, pp. 1–15.

TUC (Trades Union Congress) (2015) *TUC Directory 2015*. London: TUC.

Tufekci, Z. (2014) Social movements and governments in the digital age: evaluating a complex landscape, *Journal of International Affairs* 68(1): 1–18.

Tunstall, J. (1996) *Newspaper Power: The National Press in Britain*. Oxford: Oxford University Press.

Tyler, I. (2013) *Revolting Subjects: Social Abjection and Resistance in Neoliberal Britain*. London: Zed Books.

Van Deth, J. W. (2011) The impact of the economic crisis in Europe: 'I'm doing fine', in M. Rosema, B. Denters and K. Aarts (eds), *How Democracy Works*. Utrecht: Pallas, pp. 223–39.

Venn, C. (2009) Identity, diasporas and subjective change: the role of affect, the relation to the other and the aesthetic, *Subjectivity* 26(1): 3–28.

Virno, P. (2004) *A Grammar of the Multitude: For an Analysis of Contemporary Forms of Life*. Cambridge, MA: Semiotext(e).

Wacquant, L. (2008) *Urban Outcasts: A Comparative Sociology of Advanced Marginality*. Cambridge: Polity.

Wacquant, L. (2009) *Punishing the Poor: The Neoliberal Government of Social Insecurity*. Durham, NC: Duke University Press.

Wainwright, H. (2015) Greece: Syriza shines a light, *Red Pepper*, January, www.redpepper.org.uk/greece-syriza-shines-a-light/.

Warrell, H. (2011) Police chief testifies on Met public relations staffing, *Financial Times*, 20 July, www.ft.com/cms/s/0/ef6997cc-b1e5-11e0-a06c-00144feabdc0.html#axzz40WDkhNNH.

Warschauer, M. (2003) *Technology and Social Inclusion: Rethinking the Digital Divide*. Cambridge, MA: MIT Press.

Watson, M. (2015) David Harvey: on Syriza and Podemos, *Verso Blog*, 19 March, www.versobooks.com/blogs/1920-david-harvey-on-syriza-and-podemos.

Wayne, M., Petley, J., Murray, C., and Henderson, L. (2010) *Television News, Politics and Young People: Generation Disconnected?* London: Palgrave Macmillan.

Whyte, J. (2013) Michel Foucault on revolution, neoliberalism and rights, in B. Golder (ed.), *Re-Reading Foucault: On Law, Power and Rights*. Abingdon: Routledge, pp. 208–28.

Wilkinson, H., and Mulgan, G. (1995) *Freedom's Children*. London: Demos.

Wilkinson, R. G., and Pickett, K. (2009) *The Spirit Level: Why More Equal Societies Almost Always Do Better*. London: Allen Lane.

Williams, R. (1961) *The Long Revolution*. London: Chatto & Windus.
Williams, R. (1982) Democracy and parliament, *Marxism Today*, June: 14–21.
Wrong, D. (1994) *The Problem of Order*. New York: Free Press.
Yahyanejad, M., and Gheytanchi, E. (2012) Social media, dissent and Iran's green movement, in L. Diamond and M. F. Plattner (eds), *Liberation Technology: Social Media and the Struggle for Democracy*. Baltimore: Johns Hopkins University Press, pp. 139–56.
Yla-Anttila, T. (2006) The World Social Forum and the globalization of social movements and public spheres, *ephemera* 5(2): 423–42.
Zald, M. N., and McCarthy, J. D. (eds) (1987) *Social Movements in an Organizational Society*. New Brunswick, NJ: Transaction Books.
Žižek, S. (1997) *The Plague of Fantasies*. London: Verso.
Žižek, S. (2011) For Egypt, this is the miracle of Tahrir Square, *The Guardian*, 10 February, www.theguardian.com/global/2011/feb/10/egypt-miracle -tahrir-square.
Žižek, S. (2012) *The Year of Dreaming Dangerously*. London: Verso.
Žižek, S. (2013) Trouble in paradise, *London Review of Books*, 18 July: 11–12.
Žižek, S., and Daly, G. (2004) *Conversations with Žižek*. Cambridge: Polity.

Index

mutated and debased 178
nature of 55
need for 152
new forms of 172
offering a vital impulse to 60
overthrown or stymied 3
participation and 78
people interested in 46
plural 39
politics of 153, 157
possibility for 122
preservation of 'formal' aspects of
  142
pretence of 16
protection from the footloose logic
  of the market 19
protests as exercises in 123
radical(izing) 39, 82, 160, 176
representing corporations instead
  of people 173
resistance crucial to actual practice
  of 123
social 169
techno-scientific form of 120
thoroughly mediated 115
true 122
understanding of 42, 59, 77, 123
undone 1
usurping 9
vastly impoverished 23, 66, 174
see also conceptions of democracy;
  deliberative democracy; direct
  democracy; liberal democracy;
  parliamentary democracy;
  participatory democracy;
  post-democracy notion;
  representative democracy
democratic politics 48, 86, 91, 98,
  129
challenges posed to 23
emergence of 114
postliberal 157
progressive 166

radical 160
sustainable 13
using wealth to buy off 178
demonstrations *see* protests/
  demonstrations
Denmark *see* Danish People's Party
deregulation 10, 20, 54, 123, 142,
  156, 164
financial capitalism 1
market 15, 140
media 3
newspaper industry 136–8
Derrida, J. 37, 87, 98
Descartes, René 83
Diamond, L. 18, 26, 29, 40, 47, 71
Diani, M. 76, 125, 126
dictatorships 1
difference 83, 145, 151, 172
articulation of 114
capitalism and socialism 166
co-existing without antagonism
  158
commitment to the value of 76
commonality and 105
conceptual 130
constant struggle to maximize 39
continual acknowledgement of 75,
  109
cultural 169
dealing with 6
digital media and radical politics
  105
dissonance and 11
diversity and 56, 82, 97, 109
embrace of 11, 21, 37, 56, 75,
  86
fetishized 22, 129
group, in radical politics 6
harmonized 158
horizontality and 132
identity and 39, 79
ideological 144
inclusive politics of 82